# THE BRITISH CHRISTIAN WOMEN'S MOVEMENT

This book presents a timely study of a neglected British Christian women's movement. Jenny Daggers charts the inception of the movement in the exciting times of the post-sixties decades, amid new currents generated in the British denominational churches, and the wider current of Women's Liberation. Focusing on Christian women's concern with the position of women in the church, this book identifies a core Christian women's theology which affirms a (rehabilitated) 'new Eve in Christ', and so contrasts with a concurrent paradigm shift taking shape in North American feminist theology. Daggers argues that this divergence is primarily due to the effect of the prolonged Church of England women's ordination debate upon the ethos of the British Christian women's movement.

## ASHGATE NEW CRITICAL THINKING IN RELIGION, THEOLOGY & BIBLICAL STUDIES

The *Ashgate New Critical Thinking in Religion, Theology & Biblical Studies* series brings high quality research monograph publishing back into focus for authors, international libraries, and student, academic and research readers. Headed by an international editorial advisory board of acclaimed scholars spanning the breadth of religious studies, theology and biblical studies, this open-ended monograph series presents cutting-edge research from both established and new authors in the field. With specialist focus yet clear contextual presentation of contemporary research, books in the series take research into important new directions and open the field to new critical debate within the discipline, in areas of related study, and in key areas for contemporary society.



*Other Titles in the Series:*

John Hick's Pluralist Philosophy of World Religions
*Paul Rhodes Eddy*
Feminist Biblical Interpretation in Theological Context
*J'annine Jobling*

# The British Christian Women's Movement

## A rehabilitation of Eve

JENNY DAGGERS
*Liverpool Hope University College, UK*

Routledge
Taylor & Francis Group
LONDON AND NEW YORK

First published 2002 by Ashgate Publishing

Reissued 2018 by Routledge
2 Park Square, Milton Park, Abingdon, Oxon OX14 4RN
711 Third Avenue, New York, NY 10017, USA

*Routledge is an imprint of the Taylor & Francis Group, an informa business*



A Library of Congress record exists under LC control number: 2002071144

ISBN 13: 978-1-138-71714-5 (hbk)
ISBN 13: 978-1-138-71712-1 (pbk)
ISBN 13: 978-1-315-19651-0 (ebk)

# Contents

# Glossary of Abbreviations

| | |
|---|---|
| AGOW | Anglican Group for the Ordination of Women |
| AIL | Association for Inclusive Language |
| ARM | Alliance of Radical Methodists |
| BCC | British Council of Churches |
| BCC WG CWMC | BCC Working Group: Community of Women and Men in the Church |
| BU | The Baptist Union of Great Britain and Ireland |
| CEDGWC | Cambridge Ecumenical Discussion Group on Women and the Church |
| CF | Christian Feminist |
| CLS | Catholic Lesbian Sisterhood |
| CLWS | Church League for Women's Suffrage |
| COS | Church of Scotland |
| COSPEC | Christian Organisations for Social Political and Economic Change |
| CPG | Christian Parity Group |
| CR | Consciousness-raising |
| CWIRES | Christian Women's Information and Resources [formerly Christian Women's Information and Resource Service – CWIRS] |
| CWMC | Community of Women and Men in the Church |

| | |
|---|---|
| CWN | Catholic Women's Network |
| CWRC | Christian Women's Information and Resource Centre [Dulwich, London] |
| CWSS | Catholic Women's Suffrage Society |
| EFCWO | European Forum of Christian Women's Organisations |
| EFECW | Ecumenical Forum of European Christian Women |
| EFT | Ecumenical Feminist Trust |
| ESWTR | European Society of Women in Theological Research |
| FTP | Feminist Theology Project |
| GCM | Gay Christian Movement |
| GCM WG | Gay Christian Movement Women's Group |
| LC | Laity Commission |
| LCFs | London Christian Feminists |
| LGCM | Lesbian and Gay Christian Movement |
| MOW | Movement for the Ordination of Women |
| MRRN | Matriarchy Research and Reclaim Network |
| MSG | Matriarchy Study Group |
| NAFC | Newman Association Family Committee |
| NBCW | National Board of Catholic Women |
| NPC | National Pastoral Congress |
| OCWG | Oxford Christian Women's Group(s) |
| ONE | One for Christian Renewal |
| OWTG | Oxford Women's Theology Group [name adopted by Catholic Oxford Feminists in their submissions to the National Pastoral Congress] |
| OWTS | Oxford Women's Theology Seminar |

| | |
|---|---|
| PWTG | Plymouth Women's Theology Group |
| QWG | Quaker Women's Group |
| RCFs | Roman Catholic Feminists |
| SCM | Student Christian Movement |
| SCM WP | Student Christian Movement of Britain and Ireland Women's Project |
| SHC | St Hilda Community |
| SJIA | St Joan's International Alliance |
| SMWC | Society for the Ministry of Women in the Church |
| UWG | Unitarian Women's Group |
| UWPFT | Unitarian Working Party on Feminist Theology |
| WCC | World Council of Churches |
| WCC CWMC | World Council of Churches Community of Women and Men in the Church Programme |
| WIT | Women in Theology |
| WSCF WP | World Student Christian Federation Women's Project |
| YM | Yearly Meeting [of the Society of Friends] |

**List of Abbreviated Titles of CWIRES Serials**

| | |
|---|---|
| *Arachne* | A Magazine of Wimmins Spirituality: A Journal of Matriarchal Studies |
| *CC* | Catholic Citizen: Journal of St Joan's International Alliance |
| *CF NL* | Christian Feminist Newsletter |
| *Chrysalis* | Movement for the Ordination of Women Journal |
| *CLS NL* | Catholic Lesbian Sisterhood Newsletter |

| | |
|---|---|
| *CPG NL* | Christian Parity Group Newsletter |
| *CWN NL* | Catholic Women's Network Newsletter |
| *EFECW NL* | Ecumenical Forum of European Christian Women Mailings |
| *ESWTR NL* | European Society of Women in Theological Research Newsletter |
| *GCM NL* | Gay Christian Movement Journal |
| *GCMW NL* | Gay Christian Movement Women's Newsletter |
| *GPV NL* | Greenham Peace Vigil Newsletter |
| *LGCM NL* | Lesbian and Gay Christian Movement Journal |
| *LGCMW NL* | Lesbian and Gay Christian Movement Women's Newsletter |
| *MOW NL* | Movement for the Ordination of Women Newsletter |
| *MWG NL* | Men, Women and God Mailing |
| *PWTG NL* | Plymouth Women's Theology Group Newsletter |
| *QWG NL* | Quaker Women's Group Newsletter |
| *RCF NL* | Roman Catholic Feminist Newsletter |
| *SCMWP NL* | SCM of Britain and Ireland Women's Project Newsletter |
| *Signum* | Documentation Service for Religious |
| *SMWC NL* | Society for the Ministry of Women and Men in the Church Newsletter |
| *UWG NL* | Unitarian Women's Group Newsletter |
| *WIT* | Women in Theology Mailing |
| *WS* | Women Speaking |
| *WSCFEWP NL* | World Student Christian Federation European Women's Project Newsletter |

# Preface

The origins of this book lie in another century, another place, which seems increasingly strange in the context of the new challenges of the third millennium. Yet those same challenges are a stark reminder that we forget our history at our peril: the past has a way of creeping up on us, disturbing our current preoccupations with its unfinished business. The book offers an assessment of a movement among Christian women in Britain, during the 1970s and 1980s, a movement which, as we will discover, was fuelled by a number of currents in post-1960s British culture. My hope is that this record, or rather reading, of a vibrant movement, active over two eventful decades, will make visible the concerns of the Christian women involved, amidst our present preoccupations and projects.

Although the book concerns the 1970s and 1980s, it is a product of the 1990s. Looking back to the inception of the doctoral research project on which the book is based, I remember with pleasure my MA in Social and Pastoral Theology (with Feminist Studies) at the University of Manchester, and the commitment and passions of both staff and students involved. The then Centre for Feminist Studies in Theology, later incorporated within the ongoing Centre for Religion, Culture and Gender, provided a stimulating research environment. Overall, postgraduate study at Manchester enabled me to redirect my earlier attempts to make sense of Christian religion in the post-1960s context, in the direction of a deep and serious engagement with issues of gender and religion.

I also remember with affection the Saturday dayschools in Feminist Theology, which ran over a period of three years in the evocative location of the Pankhurst Centre in Nelson Street, Manchester. In an upper room, above the parlour where Emmeline Pankhurst and friends had once launched the Women's Social and Political Union, a gathered community of interested women (and sometimes men) grappled together with issues ranging from the postmodern 'shadow of spirit' to art and feminist theology. A number of engaging keynote speakers facilitated our efforts, while those gathered experienced the familiar extremes of elation and frustration engendered during such meetings.

I am indebted to many people for their various forms of support over the years of researching and writing. The late A.O. Dyson, Samuel Ferguson Professor of Social and Pastoral Theology, gave much encouragement in the early stages. His successor to the chair, Elaine Graham, had the vision to see the importance of the archive on which the book is based, to secure it, and to conceive of my research project. She also committed valuable time to guiding my work. The postgraduate Wiley seminar offered both fun and a significant rhetorical space, while teaching at the University of North Wales, Bangor, and contributing to the development of a Masters level Gender Studies Dimension, at Westminster College Oxford, were valuable formative experiences. I am grateful also to those Christian women who agreed to be interviewed, entrusting me with their views and experiences. Josephine Bax, Catherine Norris, Josephine Teagle, Frankie Ward, Asphodel, Heather Walton, Angela West, Judith Jenner, Janet Morley, Mary Condren, Jacqueline Field-Bibb, Jo Garcia, Tony Lacey, Katie Hambrook and Mary Neave were generous with their time, hospitality and insight. I am grateful also to my external and internal PhD examiners, Professors Mary Grey and Grace Jantzen respectively, for their serious engagement with my work. My thanks are also due to Sarah Lloyd and her colleagues at Ashgate Press for their encouragement and advice. However, the responsibility for this final outcome, with any errors or failings, is, of course, entirely my own.

Further acknowledgements are appropriate. The grant of the Audenshaw bursary, donated by the later Mark Gibbs, was an essential factor enabling me to undertake the research. When the bursary expired, my parents, Anna and Peter Tambling, reassumed their onetime practice of financial support, and were unstinting in their encouragement, despite the considerable contrast in our perceptions and practices. Gifts from my aunt, Diana Sellors, and her interest, were also much appreciated. The grant of a Celia Hughes bursary helped me to meet the costs incurred by research interviews. Staff of the John Rylands University Library of Manchester provided me with study space, albeit at first amid the heating pipes in the basement, and bibliographical advice, while IT support staff made available to me a defunct computer, then regularly turned out to coax it back to life.

Friends old and new helped me face the rigours of completing my PhD. Celia and Dave Dixie, and Kathleen Llanwarne, offered practical support and theoretical insight, while Paul Wilding took an interest in the project from its inception, and was creative in devising appropriate earning opportunities. Paul was also generous with his time, and with critical advice and encouragement, drawn from his own long experience of research, writing and supervision. Martin Steward and Jo and Doug Edwards gave invaluable support in rising to the myriad challenges involved in using computer technology.

Occasional meetings of an informal women's drinking circle, in the hostelries of Withington, helped to sustain me, and the same women gave much help in caring for my children, before these learnt how to care for themselves. (Heather Steward, Di Perryman, Candy Stokes, Joanie Yoffe and Carol Elwheshi deserve particular mention.) No less significant are my many friends in the Anglican congregation at Holy Innocents in Fallowfield, Manchester, who also played their part.

I salute my new colleagues at Liverpool Hope, particularly Diana Neal and Sharon Jones, for their humour and companionship, as we envision the present and future shape of teaching and research in 'Gender and Identity'. Working at Hope has been a welcome step beyond my completed research project.

Finally, I thank my family. My husband, Alan, has shouldered a considerable burden as principal breadwinner role during recent years. Tom and Jessica have learnt to enjoy their own contrasting lifestyles while I went about my project, all the while constructing and protecting my own, fragile, identity as researcher and author, in tension with the already evident and robust identities of wife and mother.

Jenny Daggers
Manchester, UK

# Introduction

This book is the first in-depth study of the British Christian women's movement of the 1970s and 1980s. My aims are threefold. I reveal the origins of the movement in four dynamic currents within the post-1960s churches, each lending impetus to a concern with the position of women in the Church. This line of enquiry emphasises the roots of the Christian women's movement within the denominational life of the churches.

Next, I locate the Christian women's movement as a neglected aspect of British 'second-wave' feminism, though it was slightly out of phase with the broader movement. Women's Liberation grew in strength from the late 1960s, through the 1970s, becoming diffused within wider change in social institutions as the 1980s progressed. In contrast, the British Christian women's movement gathered momentum from the late 1970s and continued in strength into the 1990s.

My third aim is to explain the effects of an unfinished agenda of 'first-wave' Church feminism on the ethos of the British Christian women's movement. The thwarted impulse towards women's inclusion in the priesthood in Catholic, Anglican and Methodist denominations, in the early decades of the twentieth century, gathered new momentum in the post-1960 climate in the churches. I argue that the ongoing campaign for women's ordination in the Anglican Church, during the 1970s and 1980s, is the key factor determining the character of the British Christian women's movement. Effectively, a 'second-wave' Christian feminist consciousness fused with the demand that women be fully included in the denominational churches. This fusion is the defining characteristic of the British movement. The Christian women's Eve is symbolic of this ethos, and the British Christian women's project is aptly represented as a 'rehabilitation of Eve': the expression appears as subtitle of this book.

## British Christian Women

In 1978, the women of the incipient movement launched the Christian Women's Information and Resources (CWIRES) project, to facilitate their work. An account of the inception of CWIRES and the contribution made by the project during its life span – 1978 to 1992 – appears in chapter two. The resulting archive – now housed in the John Rylands University Library in Deansgate, Manchester – provides a wealth of information concerning the Christian women's movement.

Although the CWIRES project extended its networking beyond the British Christian groups involved, exchanging material with groups in the US, Europe,

Australia and New Zealand, this study is confined to the British movement. The interpretation of the movement offered here relies on a thorough engagement with the CWIRES material. The book is a revised, and hopefully readable and accessible, version of my doctoral dissertation. To facilitate the flow of the text, references have been reduced to a minimum. However, the bibliography is arranged in two parts, the first listing generally available books and papers, and the second listing CWIRES papers. I hope the inconvenience of having two bibliographies to search for references is justified by the clarity this enables concerning my indebtedness to CWIRES materials. Readers interested in a detailed presentation of the CWIRES evidence, including the relevant CWIRES catalogue references, are recommended to consult my dissertation (Daggers, 2000).

Throughout the book, when I speak of 'Christian women' the term embraces those involved in the movement recorded in CWIRES. Other Christian women, who lived through the decades of the 1970s and 1980s, with very different preoccupations, have equal claim on the term – but they are not the concern of this book.

## Three Phases in the Life of the Movement

Preliminary analysis of the CWIRES material reveals three clear phases in the life of the movement. The first 'pre-CWIRES phase', between 1972 and 1978, covers the years preceding the launch of the CWIRES project, when post-1960s concern with the position of women in the churches became evident. Once CWIRES was in existence, material concerning these early events was donated to the archive, allowing their reconstruction within the book.

'CWIRES phase one', between 1978 and 1983, represents a new phase in the life of the Christian women's movement, in part stimulated by the formation of CWIRES, when a variety of new groups, linked as an informal network, came into being. 'CWIRES phase two', between 1983 and 1990, represents a reconfiguration of the movement by the almost simultaneous launch of respective Catholic and Anglican networks – the Catholic Women's Network and Women in Theology, respectively. The two networks worked together from their inception, and maintained links with continuing groups, so that it is appropriate to speak in terms of a single movement, comprised of a variety of constituent groups. Chapter two gives an overview of these three phases in the life of the movement, giving particular attention to the events of the watershed year, 1978, in which CWIRES was conceived, and in which the preliminary pre-CWIRES phase was superseded.

## Five Influential Currents

Four discernible currents in the churches, in confluence with a fifth wider current – the 'second-wave' of feminism – were decisive in their influence upon the emergence of the 1970s and 1980s British Christian women's movement, with its distinctive concern – the position of women in the church. The four currents are as follows: post-Vatican II Catholic renewal; the World Council of Churches Community of Women and Men in the Church programme; the Anglican women's ordination debate; and radical Christianity, caught up with the spirit of the post-1960s New Left.

The shaping influence of the fifth current is sufficiently strong to justify my claim that the British Christian women's movement merits recognition as an – hitherto unacknowledged – aspect of the British 'second-wave' women's movement. The first of my chosen analytical categories, Christian women's consciousness – the subject of chapter three – allows the debt to the wider 'second-wave' movement to be clarified.

## The Denominational Profile of the Movement

The Christian women's movement was predominantly Catholic and Anglican – but also Quaker and Unitarian. In addition, there was significant Methodist activity, particularly in the late 1970s and early 1980s among women involved in the Alliance of Radical Methodists, and in inclusive language submissions during the preparation of a new Methodist/United Reformed Church hymnbook. Individual women committed to Free Church traditions made substantial contributions to the movement in the latter 1980s, but by working with Anglican women's initiatives, rather than by founding bases within their own traditions. Reasons accounting for this profile are outlined below, in terms of the effects of the inherited legacy of 'first-wave' Church feminism.

A further significant absence requires comment. Reflecting wider ecumenical relations of the time, the movement was confined to the white denominations, with no links being forged with women in the black churches.

### *The Inherited Legacy of 'First-wave' 'Church Feminism'*

Church feminism depended on spiritual womanhood, with its notions of women's moral superiority, as its primary vehicle. This nineteenth century construction of femininity attributed spiritual superiority to women, in contrast to their assumed inferiority to men in other areas of life. 'First-wave' Church feminists were emboldened by their confidence in spiritual womanhood to open the question of women's ordination in the Catholic, Anglican, Methodist and Unitarian churches. This legacy was significant in shaping the distinctive ethos of the British movement, and also explains its denominational profile. Unfinished business concerning women's ordination in the Catholic and Anglican churches, in contrast to the effects of Pauline Webb's successful intervention in the Methodist debate over women's ordination, explains Catholic and Anglican predominance. Despite the presence of post-1960s radical Christianity within Methodism, which encouraged those Methodist women involved towards an openness to 'second-wave' feminism, removal of barriers to Methodist women's ordination cooled their ardour, in comparison with that of their Catholic and Anglican sisters.

The conservative climate within the Free Churches, the acceptance of women for ordination by the mid-1970s, and the absence of any notable 'first-wave' feminist tradition, explains the absent middle of denominational Free Church women's groups within the movement.[1] At the opposite end of the denominational spectrum to the Catholic and Anglican churches, nineteenth century Quaker and Unitarian feminist traditions were reinvigorated under post-1960s conditions. Chapter one examines this inherited legacy in more detail.

*The Anglican Women's Ordination Debate as Lynchpin of the Movement*

However, it was the Anglican women's ordination debate, renewed during the 1960s but unresolved in Britain until the early 1990s, which acted as lynchpin for the wider British Christian women's movement. Solidarity with the Anglican campaign had the effect of toning down more radical voices, for fear of compromising progress on this single issue. The five currents, introduced above, clearly extended far beyond the UK in their impact. But the third of these, the Anglican debate on women's ordination, took a different course in Britain to that charted elsewhere in the Anglican Communion. This difference was to have a significant impact on the shape of the British Christian women's movement. The campaign was also influential upon the shape of wider activity concerning change in the position of women in the church during the late 1970s and 1980s. My second category of analysis, Christian women's activity – the subject of chapter four – focuses on this aspect in the life of the movement.

To claim that this overshadowing Anglican issue acted as lynchpin is not, however, to reduce all Christian women's activity to this single expression. Catholic concerns reflected both post-Vatican II aspirations towards reform and radical critique; Unitarian women looked back to a successful 'first-wave' intervention into the life of their congregation, and the consequent tradition of women's ministry, which was renewed under post-1960s circumstances; Quaker women alone had no denominational issue concerning women's ministry. Unitarians and Quakers, untrammelled by issues of doctrine, forged the strongest links with British Womanspirit networks, where the pre-Christian Goddess was reconstructed.

Christian women in these various traditions saw themselves as part of a wider movement, not simply as denominational groupings. Denominational differences notwithstanding, there was much in common between groups across the movement – and much in common also with the concerns of the wider Women's Liberation Movement.

## Eve and her Rehabilitation

The Eve theme, as my subtitle implies, is given pride of place in my analysis of the movement. The theme arose within the Anglican context, though it assumed a wider importance. My contention is that the Christian women's project, in its consciousness, activity and theology, attempted a 'rehabilitation of Eve' within the institutional churches, in which the aspirations of 'first-wave' Church feminism became infused with 'second-wave' feminist consciousness of women's autonomy, mutuality and sexuality. Eve was the figure of post-1960s Christian woman, her life touched by the Women's Liberation Movement, claiming, within the life of the churches, a deserved and full place for her new subjectivity and identity. The claim extended to that of a deserved and full inclusion of women within the priesthood.

Where 'first-wave' feminists opted for Mary, figure of their chosen vehicle – spiritual womanhood – 'second-wave' Christian feminists chose to identify with Eve. In demanding a rehabilitation of Eve, post-1960s Christian women are determined that women's sexuality be rehabilitated as a positive value, in the face of centuries of Christian vilification and mistrust. To demand the rehabilitation of Eve is to make a decisive break with 'first-wave' strategic reliance upon spiritual womanhood. To opt for Eve is to repudiate spiritual womanhood, even in its modified form, as model of ideal femininity. Yet, as we will see in the opening chapter, the patient commitment to reformist activism within the churches, epitomised by the (Anglican) Movement for the Ordination of Women, demonstrated a reinvigoration of 'first-wave' Church feminism. If Eve symbolised a 'second-wave' consciousness among Christian women, the direction of the demand for her rehabilitation – towards the institutional churches – signalled continuity with earlier Church feminism.[2]

### *Christian Women's Theology*

The Anglican campaign generated the most substantial theological writing to emerge from the movement. Theological arguments claimed a place for women in terms of their unequivocal inclusion in the salvation of Christ, to be reflected in a priesthood representative of both sexes. This traditional theology, demanding a full rehabilitation of Eve, and thus of her contemporary daughters, represents the core of Christian women's theology – the subject of analysis in chapter five.

## The British Christian Women's Movement and 'the Struggle for Justice'

By the late 1980s, via two related moves, North American feminist theology was clearly defined by its focal commitment to the struggle for justice: through the identification of feminist theology as feminist liberation theology; then through Carter Heyward's relational 'passion for justice'. Undoubtedly, many women within the British movement were as deeply concerned with justice issues. CWIRES materials give ample evidence of the involvement of Christian women in peace issues, including the Greenham Common Peace Camp, in campaigns to redress world poverty, and in current 'second-wave' campaigns concerning issues such as abortion, male violence and women's employment rights. A selection of this evidence will be presented during the course of this book. In the British 'second-wave' feminist movement of the 1970s, such concerns were theorised primarily in terms of 'liberation' – but clearly they merit inclusion within 'the struggle for justice'.

However, my contention is that to subsume the consciousness, activity and theology of the British Christian women's movement beneath the defining project of dominant North American feminist theology – the struggle for justice – is to ignore the particularities of the British movement. These found expression in the new Eve symbolic, with the related demand for a rehabilitation of Eve, which was shaped as much by the inherited legacy of an incomplete Church feminist agenda, as by the newly arrived concerns of 'second-wave' feminism. The contrasts between North American feminist theology and British Christian women's concerns are the subject of chapter six.

For the purposes of this introduction, it may be helpful to add the following observations. Many onlookers outside the churches saw women's continuing exclusion from the priesthood, both Catholic and Anglican, as anachronistic: the issue was justice for women, to be achieved by removing exclusive barriers, in line with the principle of equal opportunities established elsewhere in institutional life. For Christian women, seeking change in the position of women in the churches, the situation was more complex. Women in Catholic traditions were more likely to speak of 'justice', given the Vatican II theme of the Church's vocation to work for social justice in the world: talk of justice was church-sponsored. Similarly, commitment to social justice was a well-established principle in the Society of Friends and in the Unitarian denomination.

In contrast, Anglican women, embroiled in the women's ordination debate, were more likely to argue – as 'first-wave' Church feminists had once done – that women's special gifts were needed in church life. To speak of justice for women was to risk dismissal on grounds that the case was argued on (inappropriate) secular grounds, derived from the women's movement, rather than from Christian tradition. The Eve symbolic, and the demand for a rehabilitation of Eve, embodied a *de facto* struggle for justice, but one couched in the acceptable language of traditional theology.

## Eve as Premise, Eve as Promise

If, at first, Eve caught my eye as a recurrent theme within the CWIRES material – Eve as *premise* – as my research progressed, I began to perceive in her an heuristic potential – Eve as *promise*. The question, 'Why Eve?' connects premise and promise.

### *Eve as Premise*

Approaching nineteenth century events, with the CWIRES-induced question, 'Why Eve?', leads to the revelation of a nineteenth century appearance, then vanishing, of Eve, which precedes her eventual reappearance as the 'second-wave' Christian women's Eve. Chapter one places in the spotlight the brief advent of an Owenite Eve, and her subsequent vanishing. The chapter highlights the regained pre-eminence of the Miltonic Eve, which returned an (implied) angelic Mary to her pedestal, in the particular manifestation of Victorian spiritual womanhood. How is

Eve's 'second-wave' reappearance, following her long banishment, to be explained? I have already declared my own reading: that the new Eve symbolic affirms the autonomy, mutuality and – above all – sexuality of 'second-wave' Christian woman. These qualities were briefly celebrated in Owenite feminism, only to be demoted during the long hegemony of spiritual womanhood. The reappearance of Eve signals the end of that ascendancy.

Diana Collins' polemical coining of the phrase, 'the rehabilitation of Eve' (Collins, 1978), is the key with which I solved this puzzle and, as my subtitle indicates, her words are central to my reading of the movement. Writing at a significant historical moment during 1978 – that eventful year, when optimism about the outcome of the Anglican ordination debate, with its pivotal importance for the Christian women's movement, reached its highpoint – Collins declared: 'The time has come for "the rehabilitation of Eve"' (1978:5). The wider resonance of her words with the Christian women's project is the principal subject of this book.

### *Eve as Promise*

Eve's promise is unlocked in two ways: by identifying discrete interpretations of Eve, and by clarifying available strategies for 'rehabilitation'.

*Interpretations of Eve* Eve is a mythical figure, first appearing in the Judaeo-Christian biblical book of Genesis. Christoph Rehmann-Sutter's work, on the social function of the Frankenstein myth, is useful in developing the heuristic potential of interpretations of Eve. Rehmann-Sutter makes the following definition:

> A myth is essentially a tale, deeply rooted in a common tradition, formulating common desires, and most importantly serving as a medium through which we perceive as meaningful key situations of the real world (1996:271).

He finds a remarkably consistent interpretation of 'meaningful key situations' to arise from the Frankenstein myth – one that opposes all genetic modification as 'Frankenstein science'. Similarly, there is a *traditional* interpretation of the Genesis myth, which is also of remarkable persistence. Here, negative guilt for original sin, and thus for the Fall, is attributed to Eve and, in consequence, contemporary women should be confined within domesticity, silence and subordination. The Genesis myth is deeply rooted within Judaeo-Christian tradition, and therefore within Western civilisation of the Christian era. To that extent the myth, including the figure of Eve, still comprises a common tradition. Further, the myth remains in currency in secular culture outside Judaeo-Christianity. Historiographical studies identify the emergence of this traditional Christian reading (Meyers, 1988; Pagels, 1988; Norris, 1998). Significantly, Milton, in *Paradise Lost*, makes a powerful modern Protestant restatement of this reading thus, as Gilbert and Gubar put it, 'summarizing a long misogynistic tradition' (1979:188).

However, both the Christian women's Eve and the Owenite Eve demonstrate the possibility of alternative, positive interpretations of the Genesis myth, which consequently perceive a more expansive potential for contemporary women. Merlin Stone makes the fascinating assessment that 'The [nineteenth century] vindication of the rights of woman was in a sense a vindication of the woman Eve' (1976:246). The implication is that an alternative interpretation of the Genesis myth informed 'first-wave' equal rights feminism. The nineteenth century vanishing of Eve poses a challenge to Stone's view of British – but not North American – 'first-wave' feminism. However, her observation fits with mine regarding the 'second-wave' British Christian women's Eve – though her wording is a little archaic for the post-1960s world.

There is also a third option, which is to have nothing to do with Eve, so refusing to engage with the myth, choosing rather to construct a more expansive potential for women, without a backward glance at the Genesis myth of origins. This is the option taken by 'second-wave' radical feminist critique of the Genesis myth as the foundation myth of patriarchy (Daly, 1973; Stone, 1976). Following this revelation, both Stone and Daly ignore the myth and refuse any alternative interpretation. The effectiveness of this strategy depends on whether the myth then disintegrates, so losing its status as a powerful aspect of common tradition, and its power over perception of the position of contemporary women, or whether it merely reinforces the power of the traditional interpretation.

Distinguishing traditional and alternative interpretations of Eve allows these to be discriminated wherever Eve appears directly in the remainder of the book. Views on the lives of contemporary women may be informed by either traditional or alternative interpretations of Eve – or through the third option of refusing to engage with the Genesis myth. Eve's promise is thus not restricted to direct sightings of Eve. Rather, Christian women's identification with Eve means that attention to strategies of rehabilitation of Eve yields a further heuristic tool, capable of probing not only where Eve is present, but also where she is merely implied, or even absent.

In this book, I use the Christian women's phrase, 'the rehabilitation of Eve', in the Christian women's sense, to focus on necessary changes in the lives of contemporary women. The expression serves to highlight strategies for the rehabilitation of woman even where there is no explicit reference to Eve. Though this usage is somewhat contrived when I discuss strategies at play in the wider British women's movement, where Eve has little resonance, I consider the device is justified by my central concern with the British Christian women's movement.

### *'The Rehabilitation of Eve' as Heuristic Device*

**Rehabilitate** **1a** to restore to a former capacity; reinstate.

**1b** to restore to good repute; reestablish the good name of.

**2b** to restore to a condition of health or useful and constructive capacity (eg after illness or imprisonment).

(*Longman Dictionary of the English Language*, 1984).

Traditional and alternative interpretations of Eve are found to correlate with contrasting strategies for her rehabilitation. Thus the traditional interpretation correlates with a strategy for the rehabilitation of Eve in the sense appearing as 1b above: 'to restore to good repute'. By acquiescing in the traditional, patriarchal formula, woman's ill repute, due to the legacy of Eve, is made good in her domesticity, silence and subordination.

The alternative interpretation correlates with a strategy for the rehabilitation for Eve, either in the sense of 1a, or in the sense of 2b, above. Thus the rehabilitation of Eve may be by her restoration to a former, pre-Lapsarian capacity of sexual equality with Adam. Or it may be by her restoration to a new constructive capacity, after her long period of patriarchal confinement. In the remainder of the book, we will be vigilant in spotting the use of these three strategies for the rehabilitation of Eve: restoration to good repute; restoration to a former capacity; and restoration to a new constructive capacity.

## An Outline of the Book

This Introduction has inducted the reader into the predominant themes, which will be developed throughout the book. Eve as heuristic device provides the main structure for the chapters, which follow. Chapter one investigates the nineteenth century appearance and vanishing of Eve, with particular attention to 'first-wave' Church feminism. Chapter two provides an overview of the movement, to which the reader may wish to refer while following the analysis in subsequent chapters. (Appendix 1 reproduces the original CWIRES information sheet, and Appendix 2 provides tables of the groups comprising the movement, as a further aid to clarity).

Chapters three, four and five deal in turn with Christian women's consciousness, activity and theology, always relying on Eve as heuristic device. (Appendices 3 and 4 reproduce, in whole or in part, significant documents relating to leading Anglican and Catholic groups within the movement. These are intended to familiarise the reader with aspects of the CWIRES evidence, which informs my interpretation of events.) Finally, chapter six locates the British Christian women's 'rehabilitation of Eve' on the wider stage of the feminist theology developing concurrently with the British movement, in North America and elsewhere.

We now turn to our first task, by examining more closely the relationship between Eve and spiritual womanhood in the years preceding the cultural shift of the 1960s. In chapter one we account for the appearance and subsequent vanishing of Eve in the years between 1800 and 1960. Given the significance of the legacy of 'first-wave' Church feminism in shaping the British Christian women's movement of the 1970s and 1980s, particular attention is focussed on the implications of Eve and spiritual womanhood for this legacy.

---

## Notes

[1] The extraordinary *ex-officio* Free Church ministry of Hatty Baker, during the early decades of the twentieth century, is the exception, which proves the rule. As we will see, in chapter one, Baker gained more support from Catholic and Anglican feminists than from her own denomination, commenting on the extreme conservatism of leaders within her own tradition, where her ministry never gained official recognition. Her linking with Church feminists outside her own denomination was repeated in the contribution of feminists such as Janet Wootton, of the Free Congregational Church, and Jan Berry, of the United Reformed Church, to Women in Theology during the 1980s.

[2] I am grateful to Mal Martin, a research student at Liverpool Hope, for her observation that, in contemporary Protestant evangelical congregations, Eve is model for subservient womanhood, encouraging Christian women to atone for sin by fulfilment of their traditional role. Here the 'modified spiritual womanhood', which we will encounter in chapter one, persists: Eve is substituted for Mary as symbolic. As we will see, this substitution is entirely consistent with the Miltonic Eve of *Paradise Lost*: Martin's observation spotlights the perpetuation of Milton's strategy within contemporary Protestant evangelicalism. In contrast, the attempted 'rehabilitation of Eve', by the Christian women's movement of the 1970s and 1980s, newly minted the Eve symbolic as a celebration of women's autonomy, mutuality and sexuality.

# Chapter 1

# Eve and Spiritual Womanhood, 1800-1960

This chapter sets the stage for our exploration of the rehabilitation of Eve in the British Christian women's movement of the 1970s and 1980s. The dynamics of the relationship between Eve and Christian women, in the years between 1800 and 1960, illuminate aspects of post-1960 concern with the position of women in the churches. Here we investigate Owenite and Miltonic antecedents to the Christian women's Eve, in relation to cultural conceptualisations of femininity during the period 1800-1960. In particular, by locating Eve in relation to 'first-wave' feminism, and to the position of women in the churches, we can pinpoint strands, which are continued into the post-1960 period.

In later chapters, these strands are relevant in one of two ways. They may be either reinvigorated, or subject to a decisive challenge. As we will discover, reinvigorated strands were significant in the post-1960 Christian women's movement. Conversely, analysis here illuminates the nature of the decisive challenge to other ongoing strands which, is also important in the life of the post-1960 Christian women's movement.

Returning to our immediate task, here we unravel an explanation for the appearance of Eve in her respective Owenite and Miltonic forms, and for her subsequent vanishing, only to reappear in the post-1960 (Christian) women's movement. As will become clear, while (post-1960) reinvigorated strands are marked by the absence of Eve, decisive challenge to older strands is marked by her reappearance.

There are six distinct aspects to our investigation. We find a significant antecedent for the post-1960s rehabilitation of Eve in the secularising feminist Eve of Owenism. Then we turn to a second antecedent, the Miltonic Eve of *Paradise Lost*. The crucial part played by the Miltonic Eve in Victorian constructions of femininity – epitomised by the 'Angel in the house' – becomes clear. The Miltonic Eve thus contradicted – even erased – the effect of the Owenite rehabilitation of Eve.

During the Victorian and early twentieth century hegemony of spiritual womanhood, Eve vanishes from our sight. The reason for her disappearance is that spiritual womanhood effects a rehabilitation of Eve by her restoration to good repute, in which the connection is severed between morally superior woman, and morally inferior Eve. Through the Victorian female civilising mission, spiritual womanhood exceeded its prior domestic confinement. Significantly, in the consequent expanded scope of women's lives, the boundaries between spiritual womanhood and 'first-wave' feminism became blurred.

In consequence, we discover spiritual womanhood as the chosen vehicle of British 'first-wave' feminism after the 1840s, including early twentieth century 'Church feminism'. Thus spiritual womanhood, rather than any attempted 'vindication of the woman Eve', became the watchword of British 'first-wave' feminism.

Next, we see that spiritual womanhood – with its associated construction of women as asexual – continued to act as vehicle for the sexuality debates which began in the 1860s, so perpetuating assumptions of a restricted, maternal and 'spiritualised' women's sexuality within these debates. Eve's absence endures, though she is implied in the figuration of 'fallen women' – prostitutes – as Magdalenes.

Finally, it is instructive to perceive post-1920 constructions of women's sexuality within marriage as a form of 'modified spiritual womanhood', perpetuating notions of 'spiritualised sexuality', which emerged from the post-1860s sexuality debates, up until the cultural shift of the 1960s. Eve, as vanished and absent, is sustained in this conceptualisation.

Our task here is clearly focused on preparing the way for understanding the Christian women's movement of the 1970s and 1980s. Our chosen concerns are highlighted without attempting to do justice to the complexities of the historical span, 1800-1960. We begin with the pre-Victorian feminist Eve of Owenism, where we discover a significant antecedent of the post-1960s, Christian women's rehabilitation of Eve.

## The Owenite Feminist Eve

The 'Rational Religion' of Owenite socialism (Taylor, 1983:160) promoted the principle of co-operative relations in workplace and home during the 1830s and 1840s. In her study of the movement, Barbara Taylor's choice of title, *Eve and the New Jerusalem*, bears testimony to the significance she attaches to the figure of Eve, for women caught up as leaders and followers within the loosely-organised movement of Owenism. When Taylor states that 'Eve must organise to make the New Jerusalem' (1983:182), she casts Eve as Everywoman within the Owenite movement.

Early nineteenth century Britain was marked by radical political activity, particularly in the cities. Within this ferment, Owenite socialism grew to prominence during the 1820s, becoming a working class movement from the late 1820s until its collapse in 1845 (Taylor, 1983:83).[1] Contemporary observers – both supporters and opponents of Owenism – reported the large numbers of women attending Owenite meetings (Taylor, 1983:57).[2] Taylor analyses the developments of the women's rights tradition – given distinctive voice in 1792 in Mary Wollstonecraft's *Vindication of the Rights of Women* – within Owenism.[3]

Women preachers on socialist platforms, such as Eliza Sharples, Margaret Chappellsmith, Eliza Macauley and Emma Martin, were schooled in the evangelical tradition but forsook Christianity for Owenism (Taylor, 1983:64,129,130-3). As Taylor states, 'Revisions of the story of the Fall were popular' in the secularising discourse of socialist freethought, where the Christian doctrine of original sin was rejected in favour of the dogma of human perfectability (1983:146).[4] A feminist version of this widespread scriptural re-interpretation occurs in Eliza Sharples' address to a Rotunda[5] audience in 1832, which exemplifies Eve as Everywoman within the socialist movement:

> The tyrant God, Necessity, said to subject man: 'Of the tree of knowledge of good and evil thou shalt not eat'. Sweet and fair liberty stepped in...spurned the order...of the tyrant, 'she took of the fruit thereof, and did eat, and gave also to her husband with her, and he did eat.' Do you not, with one voice exclaim, well done woman! LIBERTY FOR EVER! If that was a fall, sirs it was a glorious fall, and such a fall as is now wanted...I will be such an Eve, so bright a picture of Liberty! (Quoted in Taylor, 1983:146).

In Sharples' feminist Eve, an alternative interpretation of the Genesis myth is put to the service of women's emancipation. Sharples' words signify a British nineteenth century 'vindication of the woman Eve'. Sharples' identification of herself with Eve joins the vindication of the rights of women with her vindication of the woman Eve. However, after the decline of Owenism, British 'first-wave' feminism was not primarily concerned with such a vindication of Eve – though this task was to be resumed in the Christian women's movement of the 1970s and 1980s.

There are two further aspects of Owenite socialism, which are relevant to the return of Eve in the 1970s Christian women's movement. First, Owenism challenged the Pauline linkage between feminine virtue and women's social dependency. This challenge was of central importance in the rejection of original sin in favour of the socialist New Jerusalem (Taylor, 1983:148). When Eliza Sharples told her Rotunda audience that 'St Paul forbade women to speak in churches, and they have held their tongues…[but] suppressed speech gathers into a storm' (quoted in Taylor, 1983:128), her words have a resonance beyond her own secularising project. Both Taylor's observation and Sharples' words make visible the parallel between this early nineteenth century British expression of feminist secularising freethought and the culmination of the American nineteenth century 'vindication of the woman Eve': Elizabeth Cady Stanton's *The Women's Bible* (1985 [1895]).

Second, in the envisaged New Jerusalem, which 'Eve' set out to construct, women and men were to live together in co-operation and equality, enjoying free (hetero)sexual relations outside the bonds of marriage (Taylor, 1983:37-48).[6] From the 1830s, the churches mounted a counteroffensive against the secularising Rational Religion, which led to Owenite women preachers facing clergymen and ministers on public platforms. Emma Martin drew crowds of between two and three thousand to such debates, often gaining the better of her clerical opponents (Taylor, 1983:140). However, as Owenism declined, the clerical opposition effectively won the contest. Owenite women preachers were successfully discredited on grounds of sexual impropriety: the crowds, which had once applauded Emma now subjected her, and Margaret Chappellsmith, to clerically-induced attack and verbal abuse as witch, she-devil and whore (Taylor, 1983:152-3). As Taylor observes, Martin's tracts were 'far from being libertine' but her advocacy of 'Nature's chastity'[7] against the 'slave market' of conventional Christian marriage (1983:148), 'automatically placed [her] outside the pale of respectable womanhood' (1983:153).

Thus Eve as 'bright picture of Liberty' was eclipsed in the demise of Owenism in the 1840s. Early in the twentieth century, in her socialist feminist text, *Women and Labour*, Olive Schreiner refigures the Genesis myth, her words resonating with those spoken by Sharples, nearly eighty years before:

> We also have our dream of a Garden: but it lies in the distant future. We dream that women shall eat of the tree of knowledge together with men, and that ...they shall together raise about them ...an Eden created by their own labour and made beautiful by their own fellowship (Schreiner, 1911:282).

Though Schreiner reiterates Sharples' constructive Eve, Eden replaces the Owenite New Jerusalem, and Eve no longer appears by name. Schreiner represents a development within the socialist feminist tradition that stretches forward from Owenism, but which exceeds the limits of our current concern in this book. With this fleeting reference to the secularising socialist project, we return to the 1840s, and to the reassertion of conventional forms of eighteenth century femininity. Here, a contrasting influence comes into play, as the stage is (re)assumed by our second antecedent to the Eve of the Christian women's movement – the Miltonic Eve of *Paradise Lost*.

## 'Milton's Bogey': the Legacy of Paradise Lost

Writing in 1929, Virginia Woolf declared, in *A Room of One's Own*, that literate women must 'look past Milton's bogey' (quoted in Gilbert and Gubar, 1979:187-8). Eve features large in Gilbert and Gubar's explication of Woolf's allusion to Milton. Thus they perceive that for Woolf, as for other women writers, Milton's 'inferior and Satanically inspired Eve' – together with the author himself and his 'favored creature' Adam – 'constitute the misogynistic essence of ... patriarchal poetry' (Gilbert and Gubar, 1979:188). Woolf's cryptic reference demonstrates that – three decades into the twentieth century – the legacy of *Paradise Lost* bore upon her identity as a woman writer. Here, I examine the effects of Milton's powerful restatement of the traditional interpretation of the Genesis myth upon nineteenth century women.

My own interest is less in the particular predicament of the nineteenth century woman writer than in the more general effects of 'Milton's bogey'. In his *Letters to a Young Lady*, published in 1789, the Reverend John Bennett recommended *Paradise Lost* to his addressees as valuable reading, as the poem 'places before them a picture of Eve who reveres her husband before whom she feels herself annihilated and absorbed' (quoted in Gill, 1994:17). Whether or not the young ladies concerned heeded his advice, his recommendation encapsulates the effect of Milton's legacy, which I wish to investigate here.

Nineteenth century women's literature holds some clues. Charlotte Brontë's *Shirley* depicts, in Shirley's imagination, a titanic Eve who 'kneeling face to face ... speaks with God. That Eve is Jehovah's daughter, as Adam was his son' (Brontë, 1974 [1849]:316). Thus Brontë, in literary form, creates an alternative for contemporary women, to Bennett's (desired) annihilating effect of the Milton's Genesis myth. In this respect, Brontë's titanic Eve is closer to the Owenite Eve than to the strategies of many other nineteenth century women writers, in their dealings with the Miltonic Eve.

As one example, George Eliot's *Middlemarch*, through the character of Dorothea Brooke, makes a more typical réprochement with Milton. The epigraph to chapter three, taken from *Paradise Lost* (Eliot, 1962 [1871]:34), gives the clue to Dorothea's implied identification with Eve in her seeking counsel from the archangel, or Casaubon, who may be seen as Milton personified. Dorothea is then placed in similar relation to Casaubon as Milton's three wives and daughters to Milton. By taking on the role of dutiful wife, daughter and pupil – 'an admiring Eve waiting to be instructed' (Gilbert and Gubar, 1979:217) – Dorothea seeks the core of truth in terms of Casaubon's [and Milton's] mastery of classics and theology – as epitomised in *Paradise Lost*. Even Dorothea's passionate philanthropic zeal over new housing for the poor might be called into question, as it does not originate from such classical learning. In short, Eliot portrays in Dorothea the predicament of nineteenth century women, which I seek to highlight.

My concern is with *Paradise Lost* as a powerful expression of post-Reformation Protestant consciousness, in its attempted compensation for the effects of the new absence of Catholic mariology from the cultural construction of femininity. Once again, Gilbert and Gubar's analysis is instructive, in their attention to the disassociation of woman into the figures of 'angel' and 'monster', in Milton's myth of origins. Thus as Milton's Satan dwindles from angel to serpent, so too his Eve 'is gradually reduced from an angelic being to a monstrous and serpentine creature' (Gilbert and Gubar, 1979:196). Crucially for my argument, Gilbert and Gubar observe that this male-generated, Miltonic Eve is both the primary monster – assertive and aggressive as befits a male life of 'significant action' – and the rationale for the angel in her 'contemplative purity' (Gilbert and Gubar, 1979:28).

The angel/monster dichotomy evidently mirrors its Catholic theological equivalent, the Mary/Eve pair. Where in Catholic theology, Mary plays the 'angel' to Eve's 'monster', in the Protestant Miltonic Eve these contradictory qualities are combined within the annihilated Protestant wife, absorbed in adoring and reverent domestic subservience. Given Eve's monstrosity, any self-initiated projects – even philanthropic new housing for the poor – must be treated with suspicion. Woman's angelic potential can be realised in domestic subservience alone.

But Milton's contradictory Eve is too difficult. When Coventry Patmore coined the phrase 'The Angel in the House' for his reflections upon ideal Victorian femininity (Gilbert and Gubar, 1979:22-3,28-9), he reserved the term, 'Daughter of Eve' for the failing angel alone: woman's serpentine cunning is constructively integrated within angelic fulfilment of the needs of husband and children. As long as women look for the rehabilitation of Eve's monstrosity through restoration to angelic good repute, the connection between Eve and woman becomes severed and Eve consequently fades from view. By the time of the social purity debates in the 1860s, the severance between Eve and woman was so strong that even prostitutes – those archetypical fallen angels – were referred to, in New Testament terms, as Magdalenes rather than, in terms of the Genesis myth, as daughters of Eve.

Gilbert and Gubar comment that, as a consequence of women's definition within patriarchal mythology 'as created by, from and for men' (1979:12), women writers who journey towards literary autonomy 'must examine, assimilate, and transcend the extreme images of "angel" and "monster" which male authors have generated for her' (1979:17). Their imperative is instructive concerning the project of the Christian women's movement of the 1970s and 1980s: the post-1970 rehabilitation of Eve can be understood as just such an attempt to transcend the angel/monster extremes.

For this claim to be comprehensible, we need to explain how the monstrous Eve is absorbed within the 'Angel in the House' and thus disappears from view by the middle of the nineteenth century. The key lies in the reassertion of eighteenth century constructions of femininity in terms of spiritual womanhood, following the radical ferment in the early decades of the century. We next turn to this Victorian undertaking, proceeding in three steps. First, we analyse the Victorian reassertion of eighteenth century notions of spiritual womanhood – with the associated eclipse of Eve – and the related expansion of women's spiritual influence beyond the home, arguing that spiritual womanhood provided a vehicle for the interrelated means of this expansion: evangelicalism,[8] philanthropy and feminism.

Second, we establish that spiritual womanhood was therefore the vehicle for early twentieth century 'Church feminism', as well as for antecedent nineteenth century developments in women's position within the churches. Third, we analyse the effects of women's assumed asexuality in the sexuality debates – along with those of the continuing vehicle of spiritual womanhood – culminating in notions of a 'spiritualised sexuality'. This conjunction is significant because it reappears in the Christian women's movement of the 1970s and 1980s.

## Spiritual Womanhood

### *Woman Restored to Good Repute*

The radical ferment of the early nineteenth century was a – relatively brief – interruption of the hegemony of a stable, gendered social order, anchored within the home. From the 1840s, married respectability was re-established as the dominant social norm (Taylor, 1983:262). In the ensuing years, 'spiritual womanhood' as the model of womanly virtue – a recognisable feature of eighteenth century society – assumed its peculiar Victorian form, remaining unchallenged for the remainder of the century. In contrast to the Owenite project of building the New Jerusalem, there was a widespread consensus, across the spectrum of Christian denominations, that the stability of the existing social order was divinely sanctioned, natural and desirable. Women and men assumed distinct gendered roles within this stable social order. As Dorothy Thompson puts it, in the years prior to the mid-nineteenth century, a sentimental middle class ideal, of home and family under the control of a patriarchal male head of household, became the all-pervasive norm (cited in Taylor, 1983:262). Radical and socialist articulation of women's right to independence was lost (Rowbotham, 1973:32-5), whereas a chorus of voices developed the cult of spiritual womanhood.

I use the term 'spiritual womanhood' to refer to the construction of femininity associated with the Victorian domestic ideal. Otherwise referred to as the 'cult of domesticity' associated with Pure Womanhood (Bass, 1979:287) and as the 'cult of true womanhood' (Lassetter, 1994:45-9), my choice of term emphasises the origin of this construction within eighteenth century Christianity.

*Paradise Lost* is one expression of seventeenth century Puritan sentiments, which influenced these later developments. Woman as 'Angel in the House' bore responsibility for the nurture and education of children and for the creation of a calm and serene domestic haven to which men could retreat from the brutalising world of work and politics. Woman's gentle and civilising influence was stressed, reflecting her greater piety, with which she imbued the domestic, female sphere of the home. Across the spectrum of nineteenth century Church of England opinion, the cult of spiritual womanhood was promoted and given theological underpinning (Gill, 1994:80-3). William Wilberforce, in his evangelical manifesto of 1797,[9] asserted woman's greater spiritual capacity and her ability to revive her husband's languid piety via conjugal affection (Gill, 1994:30-1). For Wilberforce, home is a haven of true religion in an unholy world (Gill, 1994:31).

The manifesto was published amid the surge of radical activity which accompanied the French Revolution. Concurrent with this spasmodic activity, from the 1790s until the decline of Owenism in the mid-1840s, evangelical religion promoted the patriarchally-ordered home – the legitimate sphere of spiritual womanhood – as anchor in a turbulent world. Thus Hannah More and other evangelical women promoted spiritual womanhood, with its combination of women's spiritual equality and social and sexual subordination (Gill, 1994:41-2), in the same years that Emma Martin and Eliza Sharples preached their feminist message of women's independence,

Eulogies to spiritual womanhood reverberated throughout the Victorian era. In 1864, the educational reformer, John Ruskin, delivered his lectures, *Sesame and Lilies* (1905), in which he set out his views opposing equal education for women. His lectures are a rich expression of Victorian sentiments regarding femininity and masculinity. According to Ruskin, woman's limited education should equip her solely for her 'sacred place' (1905:137) within the home. Here lies 'Power to heal, to redeem, to guide and to guard' (1905:166) and here she is protected from the 'peril and trial' of the world, in which man is 'the doer, the creator, the discoverer and defender' involved in 'adventure, ...war...and conquest' (Ruskin, 1905:135-6). Woman must be 'enduringly, incorruptibly good; instinctively, infallibly wise ... not for self development but for self renunciation' (Ruskin, 1905:138).

Ruskin advises that women should be sufficiently educated to understand and aid the work of men (1905:149) – though this duty should not extend to the study of theology (1905:146). Thus spiritual womanhood might have a theological underpinning, but – in Ruskin's view – women have no business in evaluating that underpinning for themselves. His exclusion of women from theology – which reflected prevalent views – contrasts with Owenite feminist freethought in its revisions of theology and biblical exegesis.

The Anglo-Catholic novelist, Charlotte Yonge, popularised similar sentiments to those expressed by Ruskin. In June Sturrock's view Yonge 'valorizes domestic values, seeing the home as the arena of moral and religious engagement' (1995:98). When Yonge advocates that women's education should be pursued at home, and aimed at domestic usefulness (Sturrock, 1995:38), she expresses sentiments similar to Ruskin's own. Yonge's novels are cautionary tales, affirming the widespread benefits of women's fulfilling their domestic responsibilities, while warning of the certain ill effects of women's independent initiative.[10]

In sum, spiritual womanhood is evidently a construction of a subordinate and domestic femininity. It is complementary to a dominant patriarchal masculinity, which operates in public life and as supreme authority within the home. In spiritual womanhood, women follow the Miltonic Eve in co-operating in the ancient patriarchal formula for her rehabilitation. By accepting domesticity and subordination to her husband, and keeping silence in the world outside her rightful sphere, angelic woman is restored to good repute. Lacking autonomy, she cannot (mis)lead men, and so cannot repeat the actions of monstrous Eve that led to the Fall.

But – as Ruskin and Yonge would agree – men are in need of moral tutelage. Thus Ruskin speaks of the 'gentle counsel' and 'prayerful command' of woman in guiding men's efforts (1905:132) while Sturrock comments upon how the 'patriarchal male in [Yonge's] novels is frequently shown to be in need of correction, of softening ... of conversion' (1995:107). The shift in balance from monster to angel, which occurs when women are assigned moral responsibility for the conduct of men, provided Victorian women with a means of exit from their domestic confinement, through the creation of a broader female civilising mission to the wider world beyond the home.

While Sarah Stickney Ellis, in her 1838 text *The Women of England*, spoke of women's 'moral power', in the following year this 'power' assumed a different shape when Sarah Lewis published her influential *Women's Mission*, a 'landmark text in the Victorian spiritualization of womanhood' (Inkpin, 1996:37). Within Owenite radicalism, such evangelical notions were transformed into 'a rallying-call of Socialist feminist militancy' (Taylor, 1983:182). Thus Emma Martin preached that free women could carry the principles of a purified moral order (Taylor, 1983:148). The same idea was already present in the female messianism associated with Joanna Southcott and continued in its successor form in Owenite millenarianism: the chiliastic 'Doctrine of Woman' and 'the Woman-Power' promoted by Catherine Barmby within the Communist Church of the 1840s (Taylor, 1983:161-82).

With the demise of Owenism, 'Womanly Duty' and the principles of a purified moral order, associated with the socialist feminist Eve, reverted to their place of origin in respectable spiritual womanhood, which now assumed its peculiar Victorian form. The linking of women with superior moral qualities is the defining characteristic of spiritual womanhood in its capacity as vehicle for the civilising mission – inclusive of the feminist component of the wider mission.[11]

My contention is that 'spiritual womanhood' provided a common vehicle for the inter-linked elements of Christian religion, philanthropy and – (post-Owenite) respectable and middle class – 'first-wave' feminism, from which the female civilising mission was forged. Over the ensuing century, the subversion of domesticity wrought in the female civilising mission greatly enlarged the scope of women's lives in comparison with their confinement at the time of Wilberforce's 'manifesto'.

Taylor's interest in the chiliastic Doctrine of Woman (1983) belongs within a wider body of scholarship, which gave new attention to the position of women in religion during the nineteenth century. Malmgreen collects a representative sample in her *Religion in the Lives of English Women, 1760-1930* (1986), arguing for the 'feminisation of religion', during this period, during which religion became confined to women's sphere (1986:2-3). As women expanded their influence beyond the home, their religiosity gained a wider scope.

The interleaving of evangelicalism and philanthropy in spiritual womanhood, and the broadened scope of women's influence beyond domestic life, are evident in the nineteenth century Church of England. Women were in the majority in the Anglican Church – though leadership remained firmly in the hands of men. In parochial life, women were active in hymn writing (Maison, 1986), Sunday school teaching, parochial philanthropy and evangelism (Gill, 1994; Malmgreen, 1987; Gillespie, 1987; Heeney, 1988). By 1864 John Blunt, in his *Directorium Pastorale*, acknowledged women's substantial parochial philanthropic contribution (Gill, 1994:132).

During the century, the widened scope of women's evangelical and philanthropic efforts was also evident in the work of Raynard biblewomen and nurses, in Caroline Talbot's parochial missions, in the Salvation Army and Church Army and in foreign missions (Heeney, 1988:36-7,56-60; Gill, 1994:173-98). The Anglican High Church revival of religious sisterhoods from 1845 (Casteras, 1986; Vicinus, 1985:46-84; Heeney, 1988:63-4; Gill, 1994:148-63) and the Anglican evangelical establishment of Deaconess orders, such as the Mildmay Mission (Vicinus, 1985:46-84; Heeney, 1988:68-70; Gill, 1994:163-7), provided further opportunities for women.

By the 1860s, the rationale for the female civilising mission was largely uncontentious, while its fruits were acknowledged in Anglican circles and beyond. Spiritual womanhood exercised beyond the home, through Church and broader philanthropic structures, was endorsed, though preferably under male supervision. Clerical control placed restrictions upon Anglican women's autonomy within this widened female mission. There were occurrences of female supervision, as in the early days of both the Raynard movement and the Mildmay Mission, and in the independence of sisterhoods from ecclesiastical control (Vicinus, 1985:73; Heeney, 1988:48,69). However, clerical control of women's Church work – both voluntary and paid – was the norm, and the practice of female supervision often reverted to this pattern over time.[12] As I will show, the tension between female aspirations raised within the context of the female civilising mission, and male assumptions concerning women's position within the Church was to give rise to the 'Church feminism' of the early twentieth century.

Turning to 'first-wave' feminism, Christian affiliations and philanthropy were significant here also. This entwining of feminism with religiosity and philanthropy is evident in the feminist Langham Place Circle and in its publication, *The Englishwoman's Journal* (Rendall, 1987b). Feminist concern with equality before the law, creation of paid employment for women in new female professions, and educational opportunity and access for women to existing professions, particularly medicine, was given shape in campaigns originating within the Langham Place Circle and in wider initiatives, sometimes involving its individual members. The outcome was that institutions for education and employment were created, so enlarging women's opportunities.

Despite evident tensions between advocates and opponents of 'women's rights', feminist arguments – like those in favour of the female civilising mission – were frequently grounded upon the social benefits of widening the domestic scope of women's superior, spiritual qualities, so justifying extended opportunities for women's education and employment.[13]

In short, these various feminist projects were articulated in terms of spiritual womanhood, rather than on grounds of women's rights alone. This point is well illustrated by the text of *The Subjection of Women*, by John Stuart Mill (1870 [1869]), the principal Parliamentary advocate of women's suffrage. Mill writes, 'What is now called the nature of women is an eminently artificial thing – the result of forced repression in some directions, unnatural stimulation in others' (1870:38) and – as both sexes are 'moral and rational beings' (1870:42) – advocates the 'complete intellectual education of women' (1870:154). Mill's argument is for the social and political emancipation of women, through which artificially created sex differences will disappear along with women's exclusion and social disadvantage.

However, Mill also has much to say on women's moral influence. Thus he acknowledges women's longstanding 'softening influence' (1870:156) which, though now 'merged in the general influence of public opinion', is still effective 'in fostering the sentiments and continuing the traditions of spirit and generosity. In these points of character, [women's] standard is higher than that of men' (1870:160-1). Mill reassures his readers that women's 'beneficial influence would be preserved and strengthened under equal laws' (1870:165) and argues that the many women who are 'by nature admirably fitted' for charity are also fit for 'the administrative functions of government' (1870:184).

Thus, even in Mill's classic statement of women's rights, there is a subtext which places value on women's distinctive moral qualities and is concerned to demonstrate that these qualities will not be lost in the emancipation of women.[14] In this sense, spiritual womanhood carried at least some of the weight of his equal rights argument.

By emphasising the importance of spiritual womanhood as vehicle, disparate threads of activity are drawn together as sharing a common motivation. This analysis adopts a different strategy to Offen's 'relational feminism' (1981), which enlarges the term feminism to include questions of spiritual womanhood, and to analysis by Bacchi (1990) and Rendall (1987a) which stress feminist attention to women's difference. The focus on spiritual womanhood embraces those conservative women who are excluded by the term 'feminist'. In the various threads of the female civilising mission, orthodox constructions of femininity in terms of spiritual womanhood were manipulated and subverted to enhance the quality of women's lives, so working – sometimes in harmony and sometimes in tension – with 'equal rights' feminism.

Only with 'second-wave' feminism would the vehicle of spiritual womanhood be decisively abandoned and serious challenge to the cultural construction of femininity in terms of spiritual womanhood be mounted.

Malmgreen (1986:3) cites Mary Maples Dunn's assessment concerning religion in the lives of nineteenth century women: 'To be a good woman was to be a good Christian. But to be a good man was to be a good citizen'. The expansion of the sphere of influence of spiritual womanhood in the female civilising mission complicated the ideology of separate spheres in which contrasting religious femininity and civic masculinity were defined. Thus, by the late nineteenth century, women were experienced in the civic workings of local government, as well as in the new professions of housing management and social work. The early twentieth century saw a renewal of the longstanding campaign to breach the final barrier restricting the scope of the female civilising mission: women's exclusion from national government.

The intertwining of Christianity, philanthropy and feminism in the female civilising mission, with spiritual womanhood as principal vehicle, culminated, and was epitomised, in the channelling of 'first-wave' impetus into the single issue of women's suffrage, and in suffragist religiosity. As Inkpin puts it (1996:abstract), suffragists 'invested the vote with "sacramental" as well as instrumental significance, seeing themselves as part of a "salvific" process, bringing "justice" for all through "women's mission"'. 'Good Christian women' – models of spiritual womanhood – were prominent among those seeking to remove the barrier which prevented women from fulfilling their felt destiny as 'good citizens'. Good Christian women – impelled by the interleaved elements of the female mission infused with spiritual womanhood – also confronted restrictive barriers within the churches. I now turn to the early twentieth century upsurge of 'Church feminism'.

### *'Church Feminism'*

Early twentieth century 'Church feminism' (Heeney, 1988:101-2) arose from the dissonance between Christian churchwomen's sense of their own identity – arising through their participation in the female civilising mission – and Christian women's identity in the eyes of male church leaders. Two moments in Anglican politics exemplify this tension and its outworking.

Introduction of new structures of Church government occasioned the emergence of Church feminism. A broad consensus among women – uniting those for 'equal rights' feminism and those against – assumed a legitimate place for women in Church government (Heeney, 1988:77-115). However, Church authorities disagreed, and the issue dragged on from the turn of the century until the end of the First World War, when qualified participation of women was accepted, in the wake of the granting of limited Parliamentary suffrage.

Stimulated by this issue, and by the renewal of suffragist activity, an explicit feminist presence took shape within the turn of the century Church of England. Maude Royden was a prominent Anglican feminist, as were Louise Creighton, Edith Picton-Turbeville and Ursula Roberts, who were simultaneously involved as suffragists, being founder members of the Church League for Women's Suffrage (CLWS) formed in 1909, and as activists in the movement for Church reform (Heeney, 1988:105,110).

Royden's Church feminism was grounded within notions of spiritual womanhood. In claiming that the woman movement was 'profoundly moral' (Fletcher, 1989:1-2), she struck a chord which joined Anglican churchwomen in harmony, whatever their view of women's rights. The unifying factor was the special claim of spiritual womanhood upon women and their felt vocation to contribute their particular moral influence within the sphere of church government. Royden's advocacy won a degree of support within the movement for church reform, including that of the churchman and academic, Scott-Holland (Fletcher, 1989:102).

The second moment arose with the National Mission of 1917, which – like the issue of church government – generated dissonance between women's expectations and mainstream male views over whether women should preach during the mission. Given the importance of women's nineteenth century contribution to church home and foreign missions, and the continuing identification of women with the notion of 'women's mission', there is an irony in the occasion of this second clash between women's self-perceptions that they should be included, and their *de facto* exclusion.

Royden, as an accomplished adult education lecturer and suffragist speaker who had already developed an unofficial preaching ministry (Fletcher, 1989:152), exemplified women's untapped potential as preachers. During the National Mission, Royden was among those who sought endorsement by Church authorities for women to speak before mixed congregations. The unwillingness of the Church of England to open its pulpits to women – thereby putting aside biblical injunctions concerning women's ecclesial silence and prohibitions against women teaching men – led to Royden accepting a post offered by the Congregationalist City Temple, where she exercised a longstanding ministry (Fletcher, 1989:166,174).

A third moment in Anglican church politics is significant for the Christian women's movement of the 1970s and 1980s, though it did not receive the mainstream sympathy of women aroused by the issues of church government and the National Mission. The question of the Anglican ordination of women was first raised in 1910 (Heeney, 1988:127). However, by 1919, when the League of the Church Militant was formed to campaign for women's ordination, there was a marked polarisation between traditionalist and modernising views (Heeney, 1988:108).[15]

Because of this polarisation, leading reformist churchmen, such as Scott-Holland, Gore and Temple, though sympathetic with the aims of Church feminism, opposed extension of preaching and ordained roles to women, on what Temple described as, 'grounds of general expediency and not of fundamental principle' (cited in Heeney, 1988:128). Many moderates – including Louise Creighton – abandoned the League of the Church Militant for similar reasons, seeking rather to expand women's existing opportunities of working under the supervision of male clergy (Heeney, 1988:126, 128). Thus a pattern was set wherein women's ordination was relegated to a marginal position on liberal churchmen's reformist agenda. This position did not change before the 1980s.

By the end of the First World War, Parliamentary government became the model for women's eventual inclusion in Church of England synodical government. However, the second moment of dissonance over women's preaching role had not been resolved in women's favour, whereas – despite the view prevalent among Anglican deaconesses that they were in Holy Orders (Heeney, 1988:71)[16] – women's ordination was too controversial to be seriously considered.

In contrast, the success of Royden's Congregationalist ministry is testimony to the development of women's ministry within the Free Churches. For a small but significant minority of women, the female civilising mission assumed ministerial form, whether official or unofficial. These include Gertrude von Petzold and Margaret Crooke in the Unitarian denomination, Hatty Baker and Constance Coltman Todd within the Congregationalist Church, and Catherine Booth's development of women's ministry within the Salvation Army.

Hatty Baker, writing in the *Suffragette* in 1913, contrasted respect for the equality of women within the Unitarian denomination with the 'bleak' position elsewhere, describing prejudice against women preachers from Nonconformist ministers, which she encountered when touring as speaker for the Women's Social and Political Union (cited in Inkpin, 1996:353). Thus, despite the existence of these significant women ministers, Inkpin (1996:230) remarks on the patriarchal culture within non-conformity and the limited growth of Church feminism outside the Anglican Church

However, Baker – described by Inkpin as a 'Non-conformist Maude Royden' (1996:221) – inspired many women to envisage a church based on new ideals: following advertisements in the suffragist press, the short-lived Church of the New

Ideal was founded at Wallesley in 1914, (Inkpin, 1996:353). The Church issued an Official Statement of Aims and Methods:

> Women are naturally moral and religious beings, yet when they have essayed recognition of themselves and their needs they have been met with refusal. The Anglican, the Roman Catholic and the NonConformist churches ... refuse women any share in conducting their church services. As a result of this exclusion, the interpretation of the practice of Christianity has suffered...
>
> The Church of the New Ideal fulfils, spiritually and historically, the teaching explicit in Christianity, that there shall be neither male nor female in Christ: a teaching not yet put into practice by the established religious bodies. It is the aim of the new church to make good these deficiencies, by providing an organisation in which women shall have the right of access to any position whatsoever of church activity, and in which the special need and outlook of women will be dealt with. Its chief aim is not dogmatic but practical, devotional rather than theological.
>
> For the present the church will be conducted entirely by women, though its services will be open to both sexes: but after a short period it will enter upon its full work of providing for the religious needs of a complete humanity (cited in Inkpin, 1996:356).

The importance of spiritual womanhood is evident in the opening reference to women's natural moral and religious qualities. The moral purpose inherent in the new ideal – which goes beyond arguments for women's inclusion as a matter of justice – is expressed in the statement that 'interpretation and practice of Christianity has suffered': as women are guardians of superior moral qualities, exclusion of women necessarily excludes these qualities also.

Themes evident in this 1914 statement – critique of women's exclusion from conducting church services, the primacy given to the Galatians 3:28 promise that there shall be neither male nor female in Christ, and liturgical gatherings where women take leading roles – were to recur in the post-1960 Christian women's movement. An agenda formed in the interleaving of the renewed suffragist struggle with the female civilising mission was to be reinvigorated in the Christian women's movement of the 1970s.

Two further church developments outside the Church of England are significant in relation to the Christian women's movement of the 1970s and 1980s. The first is the emergence of Catholic feminism in the formation of the Catholic Women's Suffrage Society in 1911, from which the Saint Joan's International Alliance was to grow (Parnell, N.d.). As exemplified in Margaret Fletcher's Christian Feminism: a Charter of Rights and Duties, published in 1915 (Inkpin, 1996:242-3), spiritual womanhood assumed a distinctive Catholic form of domestic 'Christian feminism' based on exemplary Catholic maternal practice within the home, in which the ethos of the female civilising mission was reiterated.

In contrast, the scholar, Mildred A. Tuker, was concerned with women in Church tradition, and thus articulated an ecclesial Catholic feminism, which exceeded its prevalent domestic form. In her 1915 publication, *Ecce Mater*, Tuker set out the first modern Catholic case for the ordination of women (Inkpin, 1996:252). Tuker's involvement with wider Catholic feminism and with women's suffrage, and her collaboration with Hatty Baker (Inkpin, 1996:252), are evidence of mutual recognition between Christian feminists of different persuasions – both feminist and Christian – which was to recur in the Christian women's movement of the 1970s.

The second development is the formation of the Methodist Wesley Deaconess Order during the 1890s. Modelled on the Anglican establishment of Deaconess Orders, a focus on the position of women in the Methodist Church and on women's ordination also followed within Methodism. By 1922, consideration of the issue of women's ministry – centred on the existence of the diaconate of women – was on the agenda of both Anglican and Methodist churches, while Tuker had raised the question in Catholic circles.

In sum, whereas the era of the female civilising mission reached its zenith in the eventual granting of the vote to women at the end of the First World War, in the churches alone barriers remained which restricted the sphere of women's moral influence. This unfinished business was pursued in low key in the Anglican and Methodist churches, to erupt once again as a live issue during the 1960s. The St Joan's International Alliance (SJIA) was active within the Catholic church from the 1920s, in pursuing social justice issues affecting women. Before the advent of the British Christian women's movement, the SJIA was to follow Tuker's initiative by raising the issue of women's ordination during the Second Vatican Council.

*Glimpses of Eve within Church Feminism* We will conclude this section by enquiring after Eve amid 'good Christian women's' activity during the late nineteenth and early twentieth century. Though notable for her absence, we may glimpse two sightings of Eve. First, Catherine Booth – despite being an exemplar of women's preaching – was, as Inkpin puts it, 'a determined believer in the domestic and social subordination of women', asserting that God created women as equal to men, but subordinate to their husbands in punishment for Eve's sin (1996:32-3).

Second, the Catholic Women's Suffrage Society (CWSS) used as a slogan a phrase taken from a poem by one Francis Thompson: 'the Newer Eve'. As they anticipated the coming of women's suffrage and the extension of women's influence within national government, the Catholic members of the CWSS identified themselves with 'the Newer Eve' (Inkpin, 1996:154,255).[17] In contrast, Booth represents the continuing power of the traditional interpretation of the Genesis myth, against which Sharples had pitted her feminist Eve. Booth thus relied on woman restored to good repute: the rehabilitation of Eve by Miltonic means. Her approach was not to recur in the Christian women's movement of the 1970s and 1980s. In contrast, CWSS identification with Eve anticipated the focal Eve symbolic emergent within the later movement. However, as we shall see, the specific and distinctive CWSS symbolism – 'the Newer Eve' as mother of a new creation – was not to be revived in the Christian women's Eve.

Our final task in our investigation of spiritual womanhood is to look at how it acted as vehicle for discussions of female sexuality in the Victorian sexual morality debate, which began in the 1860s with the social purity campaigns. Royden perceptively grasped that traditionalist exclusion of women from the sanctuary rested upon unacknowledged male notions of women's sexuality as impure, and defiling (Heeney, 1988:125): her response was to challenge these fears in terms of spiritual womanhood, by asserting women's superior moral purity. Similarly, on encountering sexology and Marie Stopes' *Married Love*, Royden was to proclaim, 'Sex is a sacrament' (Fletcher, 1989:231). Royden's spiritualised perspectives were in tune with wider sexuality debates of the period, as our following investigation will show.

### *'First-Wave' Sexuality Debates*

Jeffrey Weeks argues against longstanding interpretations of Victorian sexual puritanism, claiming instead that the sexuality debate 'exploded' during the nineteenth century (1981:19). However, my concern is with Victorian constructions of female sexuality where earlier analyses of sexual puritanism remain relevant. My argument so far has concerned spiritual womanhood as a construction of femininity. Spiritual womanhood as a construction of sexuality is less obvious, given that women's sexuality was allotted a negative value: women who met the criteria of spiritual womanhood were constructed as *a*sexual. Given their superior spiritual and moral virtue, women were perceived as having no sexual needs of their own, their sexuality being centred upon maternity. Thus Weeks (1981:40-2) catalogues the denial of female sexuality in mid-Victorian discourse, the stereotype of women's sexual timidity and purity, and the strength of woman's maternal instinct as the given explanation for her submission to the lusts of men.[18] Victorian constructions of masculinity, however, granted men the need to express their sexuality. The resulting mismatch was resolved through the 'social vice' of prostitution.

From the 1860s, the campaign to repeal the Contagious Diseases Acts brought this 'social vice' into public view, in a debate to which women contributed. The coin of spiritual womanhood was reversed to reveal the prevalence of prostitution in Victorian society.[19] As Weeks puts it (1981:19), 'the pedestalized mother and wife depended for her purity on the degradation of the fallen woman'. The interleaving of feminism with evangelicalism and philanthropy in the female civilising mission is exemplified in the social purity campaigns.[20]

In the person of Josephine Butler, who was invited to spearhead the crusade, a contrasting Christian religiosity – both mystic and socialist – was combined with her philanthropic work among prostitutes and her feminism. In her married respectability, Butler was also an exemplar of spiritual womanhood. However, from the late 1880s, Butler parted company with the social purity movement as by this point, as Walkowitz puts it, 'feminists had lost considerable authority in the public discussion over sex to a coalition of male professional experts, conservative churchmen, and social purity advocates' (1983:55).

It will be instructive to compare Butler's feminist perspective on prostitution with more widely held views. Mainstream social purity advocates supported increased regulation of working class women's sexuality, viewing prostitutes as 'fallen women' who were primarily responsible for prostitution, and who were thus to be subjected to a penitential régime, within institutions set up for their reform. Vicinus describes the Victorian association of sexuality with fallen human nature and comments, regarding the penitential work of the Anglican sisterhoods, that religious sisters' purity was seen as a safeguard against pollution, and that 'highly controlled and pure women caring for prostitutes had a peculiar appeal and reassurance' (1985:77).

In contrast, Butler saw prostitution as a social institution existing for the benefit of men. She brought the concept of 'womankind' to feminism, and sought to unite women across boundaries of class (Forster, 1986:170). For Butler, prostitutes were sisters, not 'fallen women' (Milbank, 1987:158). When Butler protested 'Sirs, you cannot hold us in honour as long as you drag our sisters in the mire' (cited in Walkowitz, 1983:45), she gave expression to her solidarity with all womankind.[21] Walkowitz describes Butler's identification with women who, as prostitutes, were disqualified from spiritual womanhood as reliant on her feminist realisation that the sentimentalization of female influence and motherhood masked a pervasive underlying misogyny (1983:45).

Within the social purity movement, prostitutes were linked with the Magdalene rather than with Eve, the sexual, impure and fallen 'Magdalene' being compared unfavourably with the virginal, spiritual and pure Madonna. In contrast, when Butler used this figure, her reflections anticipate those of twentieth century feminist theology. Thus, in Milbank's estimation, 'The Magdalene image with which Butler works is either an example of suffering womanhood oppressed by men or the Magdalene who witnesses the resurrection appearance of Christ', while Butler portrays Mary 'as a sister to Mary Magdalene in proclaiming liberation' (1987:158)'. Butler thus anticipates themes of twentieth century feminist theology: the Christa as example of women's suffering due to male sexual abuse (Thistlethwaite, 1990:92-4); Mary Magdalene as first apostle (Fiorenza, 1975) and Mary as proclaimer of liberation (Ruether, 1979).

Eve is present as a shadowy figure, in the designation, 'fallen women'. Thus there is a clandestine meeting between Eve and spiritual womanhood in the social purity movement. However, the main effect of social purity contrasted with Butler's assertion of a single 'womankind', by reinforcing the dissociation of women of good repute from the fallen daughters of Eve. This dissociation is inherent wherever spiritual womanhood is relied upon for the rehabilitation of Eve.

However, from the 1880s 'a new sexual morality in which men lived by the same ethical precepts as women' became a central feminist demand (Bland, 1995:xiii). This new 'sexual' morality in effect elevated the asexual purity of spiritual womanhood as an appropriate standard, for men as well as women. Thus, Butler considered women's moral standards should apply to men (Milbank, 1987: 157) and this theme also found powerful expression in Christabel Pankhurst's rhetoric in her 1913 text, *The Great Scourge*, where she calls for 'Votes for women and chastity for men' (cited in Weeks, 1981:164). The same theme was implied in Royden's 'profoundly moral' claim (Fletcher, 1989:1-2), asserted in the context of the renewed sexual morality crusade within the war-time church, wherein Royden reiterated Butler's powerful opposition to Church complicity with the 'white slave traffic' of prostitution (Fletcher, 1989:102).

Control of women's sexuality, and confinement of maternity to marriage, are crucial for the patriarchal rehabilitation of Eve. In restoring woman to good repute by spiritual womanhood, she assumes an exemplary moral character, where asexuality is essential to guarantee her purity. Sexual woman is associated with Eve, while asexual woman, both spiritual and pure, is restored to good repute. Bland, (1995:49-50) makes a parallel analysis concerning the rehabilitation of Eve through spiritual womanhood, where she emphasises that for evangelicals, motherhood enabled a woman to subordinate her 'Magdalene side' or 'dangerous sexual aspect' to the 'passionless' Madonna (Cott, cited in Bland, 1995:49). While Eve's transgressions and the Fall explained women's subordination to men, motherhood provided the avenue to women's salvation.

Butler's juxtaposition of the Magdalene (Eve) with Mary anticipates one manifestation of the Eve theme in the Christian women's movement of the 1970s and 1980s. However, where Butler's exemplary spiritual womanhood has the effect of locating her as 'Madonna', 'Christian women' in the later movement chose to identify with Eve, thus signalling their dissociation from the standard of spiritual womanhood.

From the 1890s, sexological ideas began to impact upon the British sexuality debate.[22] In addition, other new forms of freethought exerted a growing influence on the discourse on sexual morality – so firmly anchored in Christian constructions of spiritual womanhood – and the new sexology. Thus, by the late nineteenth century, medicine and natural science were offering rival definitions of sexuality and morality (Weeks, 1981:141-8).

In Bland's view, 'The medical representation of femininity was ... inherently contradictory: if a woman retained her modesty she was defined by her morality; if she lost her modesty she was defined and ruled by her sexuality' (1995:60). Although Havelock Ellis acknowledged female sexuality in his sexological writings, he too stressed sexual modesty as differentiating female from male sexuality (Bland, 1995:259). My argument is that – within 'first-wave' feminism as well as more broadly – the continued use of spiritual womanhood as vehicle for the interleaved elements at play, led to a heavy investment in woman maintaining her 'modesty'. Even as the sexual morality debate was stretched to its limits in the advent of sexological ideas, being defined by modesty was considered to be a more desirable womanly state than being defined by sexuality. My concern is with women's policing of their own modesty by retaining spiritual womanhood as vehicle, rather than with the effects upon women of medical definitions of female sexuality.

Similarly, with new scientific theories, notably social Darwinism and eugenics, my concern is with their impact upon women's understanding of motherhood – the central organising principle of spiritual womanhood. By the end of the century, these new elements became interleaved with the evangelicalism, philanthropy and feminism already entwined in spiritual womanhood.[23] The eugenic and social Darwinist stress on 'mothers of the race' (Bland, 1995:70) re-sited motherhood –

including the 'spiritual motherhood' practised by single women in the wider civilising mission – within a developing Imperialist discourse of 'the nation' and the (white supremacist) 'race'. Such notions reasserted the 'naturalness' of motherhood in secular terms, thus reinforcing the longstanding theological underpinning of spiritual womanhood. Thus Ellis saw motherhood as essential, both for women themselves and for the nation (Bland, 1995:259).

Given Ellis' prominence within sexology, his views on female modesty and motherhood blended with the other new currents in nineteenth century thought, and worked to extend further the lease of life of spiritual womanhood. Thus, as Bland cautions, 'The power and influence of these sexological writings [in the years preceding the 1920s] must not be over-emphasised' (1995:257).

Both the challenge of sexology and its restricted impact upon the sexual morality debate are illustrated by correspondence in the feminist journal, the *Freewoman*, during the immediate pre-war years. Thus, prominent feminists, such as Olive Schreiner, Millicent Fawcett and Maude Royden, vehemently objected to this correspondence (Bland, 1995:265-6).[24] Yet Bland concludes that these forthright *Freewoman* sexual explorations demonstrate that contributors 'shared a common ideal of spiritualised sexual relations between men and women' in which 'the physical aspect was minimal' (Bland, 1995:280). Thus, despite the voicing of (hetero)sexual radicalism by Stella Browne in the *Freewoman*, the dominant current during the second decade of the last century was one in which sexuality was spiritualised: sexuality was perceived through spiritual womanhood, not spiritual womanhood through sexuality.[25]

When the editor, Dora Marsden, advocated the 'New Morality' of 'limited monogamy' and 'free unions' as opposed to the 'Old Morality' of 'Indissoluble Monogamy', no correspondent contested her view (Bland, 1995:280). In similar vein, Emmeline Pethwick-Lawrence wrote in *Votes for Women*, that the women's movement 'means the beginning of a new morality' especially between women and men (cited in Inkpin, 1996:136). But, in the New Morality, woman's superiority featured large in this claim of women's equality with men. The New Morality was a far cry from the more comprehensive New Moral Order envisaged by Owenism with its ideal of co-operative free unions, wherein women's moral mission was harnessed to the Utopian vision of a socialist New Jerusalem. In the free unions advocated within the New Morality, spiritualised love was the central value. As the balance between spirituality and sexuality was so strongly weighted towards spirituality, the severance between contemporary woman and Eve remained, in contrast to the Owenite Eve, 'bright picture of liberty'.

As we will see, notions of spiritualised sexuality occur in the Christian women's movement of the 1970s and 1980s, and we are therefore less concerned with the 'new sexuality' germinating within the old, than with the perpetuation of the old through its modification. Before we leave this chapter, discover that the dominant effects of the new sexuality in defining women's sexuality, which emerged during the 1920s and 1930s, can usefully be defined as a twentieth century modification of spiritual womanhood.

## 'Married Love': the Twentieth Century Modification of Spiritual Womanhood

Whereas, in the years preceding the First World War, sexology was largely subsumed within the sexual morality debate, the impact of sexological ideas about sexuality came into full effect during the 1920s and 1930s (Bland, 1995:257). As Walkowitz observes, 'the late-Victorian and Edwardian years represented a "germination" period for the formation of a "new sexuality"' (1983:52). In the 1920s and 1930s, amid the decisive break with the Victorian moral order effected by the enormity of the First World War, these seeds grew.

The principle effects of sexology were in its impact upon dominant views of heterosexual relationships within marriage.[26] The 1918 publication by Marie Stopes, *Married Love*, stands at the watershed between the late nineteenth century nexus of ideas – wherein spiritual womanhood was reconfigured in eugenic terms of motherhood as womanly duty owed to nation and race – and the new sexuality. Resistance to birth control was associated with these notions, on the grounds that birth control would interfere with the outworking of this womanly duty. Fletcher refers to Stopes' 'inflammatory effusions about the transports of the marriage bed' (1981:231). Such flowery rhetoric was effective in gaining public support for the practice of birth control within marriage. This new acceptance of married women's command of their fertility allowed a clearer separation between women's sexuality and maternity. It is also true that the self-esteem of the spinster, which in the nineteenth century had rested upon her particular contribution to spiritual motherhood within the context of the female civilising mission, was undermined by the stress upon 'married love' as the single gateway to mature adulthood.

The new sexuality gained respectability when expressed in marriage as a sexual partnership, wherein women's sexuality – with fertility now regulated by the practice of birth control – was at last acknowledged alongside men's. On the one hand, this modification was an accommodation with the delayed logic of sexology – released at last from the constraints of the sexual morality debate – to acknowledge the crucial role of sexuality in the formation of human subjectivity, female as well as male. Yet, on the other, in married sexuality, with its continued emphasis upon the nurture of children, women's particular moral qualities were carried forward into post-1920 notions of womanhood. Thus – despite the challenge to notions of woman's asexuality – it is useful for my project to view this shift as a modification of spiritual womanhood.

Modified spiritual womanhood restricted the expression of women's sexuality to the confines of marriage. Despite the rhetoric of companionate marriage, which accompanied this shift, economic conditions militated against parity between marriage partners, as most married women were economically dependent upon their husbands. In coining the term, 'modified spiritual womanhood', I wish to emphasise the continuities between the condition of married women during the years preceding the 1960s, and the domesticity and subordination recommended in the longstanding patriarchal formula for the rehabilitation of woman. However, even so limited an admission of women's sexuality created the possibility of sexuality breaking the bounds of its spiritualised confinement. This possibility began to be realised amid the cultural shift of the 1960s.

Modified spiritual womanhood was central to Eleanor Rathbone's 'new feminism' (cited in Dale and Foster, 1986:7) – including among its policies the endowment of motherhood – which sought to give financial independence to mothers (Dale and Foster, 1986:4-14). Women, including feminists, also played a major part in building the inter-war international pacifist movement (Fletcher, 1989:109-29), thus expressing moral qualities which can be seen as continuous with those of the Victorian female civilising mission. Thus, despite the 'new sexuality', spiritual womanhood underwent a further modification, so creating its particular twentieth century form, which went largely unchallenged until the 1960s.

In the following four chapters we turn to our task of the interpretation of the post-1960 British Christian women's movement, using Eve and her rehabilitation as a heuristic device. In chapter two, we begin by establishing in outline the overall dynamics of this specific historical moment.

---

## Notes

1 See Thompson (1968 [1963]) for a comprehensive study of radical activity between 1780 and 1832, which includes an account of Owenism in its interrelation with other radical currents (1968:857-87). Thompson emphasises the 'enriching of [Owen's] theory' by others, the development of the movement during Owen's absence in America between 1824 and 1829, and 'the swelling tide after Owen's return, when he found himself almost despite himself at the head of a movement which led on to the Grand National Consolidated Trades Union' (1968:858). Taylor characterises the membership of local organisations as 'democratically organised', highly resistant to the imposition of the 'paternal system' preferred by Owen himself, and 'predominantly working class, with a sprinkling of professionals and small business owners, [with] nearly all their leading activists [being] drawn from that same "respectable" sector of the working population which fuelled every other radical struggle of the period' (1983:121). By 1840 the 'Rational Society' consisted of over sixty-five branches all over the country (Taylor, 1983:120). Harrison cites the main centres of Owenite activity after 1834 as London, the Midlands, the northern industrial districts, Glasgow and Edinburgh, with London as the strongest urban base, followed by Manchester (cited in Taylor, 1983:122). Estimates of size vary from 3,000 to half a million, with an organised movement after 1835 – in contrast to Owenite-influenced schemes prior to that date – with a wider body of sympathisers who attended Owenite meetings (Taylor, 1983:300).

2 Women within the movement shared the same class profile as the men: the majority were from upper working class backgrounds, a substantial minority from lower middle class backgrounds and a tiny number from wealthy backgrounds (Taylor, 1983:57). Thus of leading Owenite women, Anna Wheeler and Fanny Wright were of wealthy backgrounds in families with a radical-liberal tradition, Eliza Sharples and Emma Martin were from middle class families, whereas Eliza Macauley and Frances Morrison were from working class backgrounds (Taylor, 1983:59,65,197,131-2,71,75). Women's lack of access to

well paid employment affected the economic standing of single women, such as Eliza Macauley, and women with children and no male breadwinner, such as Emma Martin.

3 She emphasises that self-proclaimed Owenite feminists, though voluble and influential, were in a minority among the wider female membership (Taylor, 1983:58).

4 My interpretation of Owenism as a secularising movement follows Taylor's, as the Eve theme is associated with the secularising impulse. However, Thompson states that Owen 'threw the mantle of Joanna Southcott over his shoulders' (1968:865) and, after analysing evidence concerning the millenarian 'chiliasm of the poor' (1968:878ff), concludes that 'it is premature, in the 1830s, to think of the English working people as being wholly open to secular ideology' (1968:882). In contrast, Taylor analyses the 'Doctrine of the Woman' or 'Womanpower' as an alternative Owenite strategy – to Martin's replacement of orthodox evangelical self-abnegation with radical self-determination – in which the alternative religion of Socialism took the form of a millenarian 'mystical gospel of female redemption' (Taylor, 1983:157). For Taylor, use of millenarian language, such as in the Barmby's Communist Church of the 1840s, expresses 'an intensity of aspiration' rather than 'a literal faith in millenarian change' (1983:159).

5 The Rotunda was established in Blackfriars, London, by Richard Carlile. It was a venue for radical gatherings capable of seating 2,000. Its typical clientele comprised skilled artisans (Thompson, 1968:879-80,892-5,911).

6 It is beyond the scope of my current investigation to give a detailed analysis of Owenite views on sexual relationships. Taylor places Owenite sexual behaviour in the context of 'flexible' (1983:195) sexual arrangements common among respectable working people in the early nineteenth century (1983:192-205) and Owenite ideals of freely-contracted companionate marriages within middle-class opposition to the marriage conventions of aristocratic England (1983:33-4). It would be misleading to see Owenite preaching on sexual mores in terms of post-1960 sexual libertarianism: Taylor refers to the 'inverted puritanism' of the Owenites (1983:148).

7 This concept reflects the Owenite valorising of the natural, instinctual and spontaneous over against the unnatural, artificial and constrained effects of capitalist social organisation. See Taylor (1983:41-2).

8 I use the term evangelicalism, which is appropriate in the early years of the twentieth century. As my discussion will show, the development of the Anglo-Catholic tendency in the Church of England, and the effect of differing denominational loyalties lead to a more complex pattern of Christian religiosity by the end of the nineteenth century.

9 Entitled *A Practical View of the Prevailing System of Professed Christians, in the Higher and Middle Classes of this Country, Contrasted with Real Christianity* (Gill, 1994:9).

10 Yonge's short story, 'Come to Her Kingdom' – reprinted from the *Monthly Packet* of 1889 – (Battiscombe and Laski, 1965:152-180) warns against the disastrous schemes of a young woman with private means and a High School education, who lacks male guidance from father or husband. Her ill-advised projects include renovation of housing for the poor, which suggests an implied underscoring of the doubtful nature of Dorothea Brooke's similar projects in *Middlemarch*, given their lack of any classical and theological underpinning. Whereas Eliot's aim is surely to portray this dilemma as problematic for women, Yonge's is to illustrate the dangers of inappropriate education for women, and of lack of male guidance.

11 The Unitarian tradition provided an important connecting link between women's rights activism, concurrent with the Owenite movement, and later middle-class feminism. The

South Place Unitarian Chapel provided a base for women's rights activity during the 1820s and 1830s (Taylor, 1983:62) and the initiative in forming the Langham Place Circle arose within Unitarian radicalism (Rendall, 1987a, 1987b).

12 A significant example is the ambiguous relation of the Deaconess orders to the male clergy. While many deaconesses saw themselves as in Holy Orders, the Church was reluctant to define their position (Heeney, 1988:71; Gill, 1994:167): in reality, deaconesses fulfilled subordinate roles (Heeney, 1988:70-1).

13 Thus Elizabeth Blackwell argued that women's special qualities were required in medicine (Forster, 1984:56-7), just as Nightingale's founding of nursing as a female profession took 'the Angel in the House' to the hospital ward. Similarly, Rendall (1987b:137) describes the political purpose of *The Englishwoman's Journal* as 'rooted in the experience of the different sphere of life to which domesticity and philanthropy were more central than the experience of earning a living'. My argument is that campaigns for women's education and employment gained support from those arguing on grounds of women's specific (superior) qualities – spiritual womanhood – as well as from feminists arguing in terms of equal rights, despite the tension between these two positions.

14 See Soper (1983:vi,xvi) for criticism of Mill's 'inconsistency' in arguing simultaneously on grounds of equal rights and of a distinctive 'woman's nature'. My point is that this 'inconsistency' was inherent within 'first-wave' feminism.

15 The League of the Church Militant was formed from the Church League for Women's Suffrage, after the granting of a limited Parliamentary suffrage to women. It was disbanded in 1930 when the interdenominational Society for the Equal Ministry of Women – later the Society for the Ministry of Women in the Church, (SWMC) – and the Anglican Group for the Ordination of Women (AGOW) were formed.

16 Heeney distinguishes three types of Anglican deaconess orders, the Mildmay tradition, the 'Primitive Order of Deaconess' and the 'Official' deaconess. Women in the latter group withdrew from ordinary life in the expectation of a life-long commitment, and were most likely to perceive themselves as in Holy Orders (Heeney, 1988:70-1).

17 The Newer Eve was conceived as being self-possessed mistress of her own destiny and – in terms which reflected contemporary interest in eugenics – mother of a new creation. The phrase was considered as the title of the CWSS newspaper, but rejected on the grounds that it was too provocative (Inkpin, 1996:255).

18 Weeks' argues this stereotypical view was constantly under challenge in a lively, though contradictory, Victorian discourse on female sexuality, which he traces from late eighteenth century concerns with over-population and the hyperbreeding of the poor, to controversies over public health, birth control and prostitution, to the Parliamentary Commissions of the 1830s and 1840s on employment conditions in factories and mines, where sexuality was a major preoccupation (1981:19-20). My own concern is to demonstrate that notions of spiritual womanhood shaped understandings of the ideal for women's sexuality within Victorian debates. Following my earlier argument – after Dorothy Thompson – that middle class respectability became the norm, even among the aspiring working classes, the evidence Weeks presents of middle class anxieties over sections of the population which were unable or unwilling to adopt this norm, does not contradict the case I am making.

19 The link between spiritual womanhood and prostitution was already present in eighteenth century society. Thus Gill comments, 'The new [that is eighteenth century] emphasis on female virtue did not in fact obliterate the older image of the sexually rampant woman: instead it was projected onto the fallen woman, whose existence in the form of organised

prostitution was in one sense the guarantor of bourgeois family values and property rights' (1994:28).

20 Evangelical revivals in 1859-60 and 1901-2 revitalised the influence of evangelicalism in the latter nineteenth and early twentieth century (Weeks, 1981:86-7). Walkowitz emphasises the contribution of radical working men to the social purity campaigns, alongside evangelicals and feminists (1983:44).

21 In a later generation, Maude Royden spoke in similar vein, when she described 'the intolerable sense among ... sheltered women that their own honour and immunity are secured...at the cost of the degradation...of others' (quoted in Fletcher, 1989:102).

22 Havelock Ellis was a leading sexologist, and Edward Carpenter a prominent exponent of sexology. In the 1890s, this new 'science' had marginal status within the British medical profession, and sexological writings were frequently censored, or if published, readership was restricted to members of the medical and legal professions (Bland, 1995:258).

23 These freethought disciplines could be combined with a repudiation of Christian theology and practice, or by an accommodation of theology to take account of this new scientific information. See Bland (1995: 70-1) for a succinct discussion of this point. Given the gendered nature of religiosity, for many women, Christian commitment was interleaved with the other elements involved.

24 Bland explains that hostility to the *Freewoman* was partly due to editorial criticism of the Women's Social and Political Union, of which the editors had once been members. However, she considers the sexuality debate to be the main focus of criticism of the paper.

25 Reviewing evidence of emergent lesbian identity in the same period, Bland finds evidence of the same stress upon spiritualised love in the writings of women who identified as Uranians (Bland, 1995:290-3). Bland also cites Edith Lees Ellis as stressing the importance of the sexual side of her relationships with women, just as Browne emphasized this aspect of heterosexual relationships. Her conclusion corresponds with the findings of Caroll Smith-Rosenberg and Esther Newton, cited in Walkowitz (1983:52-3). Walkowitz (1983:56) also lends weight to my argument when she asserts that, with a few exceptions such as Browne, 'public discussion of sexuality and male dominance was still couched within the terms of a "separate sphere" ideology' – in other words of spiritual womanhood as setting the desirable standard for public behaviour.

26 However, sexological discourse was not confined to marital sexuality. Thus, sexological theory resulted from a 'two-way traffic' between heterosexual observation of sexuality and (male) homosexual information (Hennegan, cited in Bland, 1995:257) and sexological naming of the homosexual, the lesbian and the frigid woman certainly pathologized these categories (Bland, 1995: 257). Some women claimed lesbian identities using sexological categories (Bland, 1995: 261-5, 290-6). Sheila Jeffreys argues, in *The Spinster and Her Enemies* (1985) that sexology also attacked the independence gained for single women during the course of the nineteenth century and correspondence in the *Freewoman,* which ridiculed sexually chaste spinsters on sexological grounds (Bland, 1995: 281-3) supports this view.

# Chapter 2

# An Overview of the Christian Women's Movement

> ...[A] women's uprising is bound to be deeply rooted in the cultural and economic life of the country where it takes place: it cannot simply be imported. (Coote and Campbell, 1987:9)

The words of Anna Coote and Beatrix Campbell are pertinent to the British Christian women's movement of the 1970s and 1980s. As we will see, the various currents of change stirring in Britain during the 1960s and 1970s, together creating the conditions in which the Christian women's movement was to emerge, were linked with wider movements in Western culture and Christianity. Yet, the particular expressions in Britain of the cultural shift of the sixties, including the currents of change within the churches, the Women's Liberation Movement, and the Christian women's movement, were distinctively British: these particular manifestations were deeply rooted in British cultural life.

This chapter provides an overview of the development of the British Christian women's movement of the 1970s and 1980s, locating the movement within its wider context of post-1960s cultural change in society and the British Christian churches.

## 'The Sixties' and the Women's Liberation Movement

'Change' was the defining characteristic of these latter twentieth century decades. Arthur Marwick prefaces his monumental re-evaluative study, *The Sixties*, with the words:

> Mention of 'the sixties' rouses strong emotions ...For some it is a golden age, for others a time when the old secure framework of morality, authority and discipline disintegrated (1998:3).

For Marwick, the sixties was neither 'the making of a counter culture' (Roszak, 1970) nor a period of 'repressive tolerance' (Marcuse, 1969). Rather, between the years of 1958 and 1974, a mainstream 'cultural revolution' was effected, as much enabled by the 'measured judgement' of those in authority (Marwick, 1998:13) as by the exuberant creativity of sixties 'counter culture'. For Marwick, the cultural revolution of the sixties 'in effect established the enduring cultural values and social behaviour for the rest of the century' (1998:806). Sara Maitland, in *Very Heaven: Looking Back at the 1960s* (1988), provides a window on this eventful decade in her sample of British women's reflections on their experiences during these years.

Currents of change began to flow, in church as in wider society, during Marwick's extended sixties. Gradually a concern with the position of women crystallised as a discrete element within each current within the churches. The point in time when these discrete elements first encountered one another was a key moment in the evolution of the Christian women's movement. 1978 was this key historical moment. There is a clear sense that, during this year, diverse initiatives connected, and the women involved came to see their projects as contributing to a broader movement. We will survey the events of this significant year to gain our first insight into the shape of the early Christian women's movement.

## 1978: a Watershed in Christian Women's Consciousness and Activity

During 1978, the presence of women's groups, responsible for a number of recent initiatives concerning the position of women in the Christian churches, became manifest. 1978 was also the year in which discrete groups first perceived themselves as part of a wider movement.

A closer look at this watershed year will make clear the extent of this plethora of activity over the position of women in the churches, and the growing connections forged between groups. In the Roman Catholic Church, Catholic feminists were among lay Catholics who submitted invited responses to the documents produced during 1978, Pastoral Paper 1 and *A Time for Building*, in preparation for a proposed National Pastoral Congress. Roman Catholic Feminists demonstrated at the 1978 Catholic bishops' conference at Westminster Cathedral, by wearing T-shirts bearing the slogans, 'Rites for Women' and 'Equal Rights in the Church', during the Eucharist (*Roman Catholic Feminist Newsletter* 7 (May 1978):2).

The World Council of Churches Community of Women and Men in the Church study was underway, and preparations were in hand for a conference on this theme to be held in Sheffield, England. 1978 was also a significant year in the Anglican campaign for the ordination of women, in anticipation of the November debate on the issue in the Church of England Synod, for the first time in over three years. Campaigners for a 'yes' vote organised a tour of Britain by Canon Sr Mary Michael O.S.H. of the Cathedral of St John the Divine, New York City, who was ordained within the American Episcopal Church. A supplement to the *Christian Action Journal*, 'Churchwomanship in a Man's World' (Champion and Kroll, 1978) was published to coincide with the visit. The tour, in April 1978, to cathedrals and churches, raised the profile of the Anglican ordination debate among women of other denominations and – through coverage in the national press – caught the attention of the wider British public. In July 1978, a vigil was organised in London, by supporters of women's ordination, to mark the Anglican Lambeth Conference.

At the 1978 Yearly Meeting of the Society of Friends in Lancaster, a national Quaker Women's Group was formed, with founder members declaring a wish to explore feminism (*Quaker Women's Group Newsletter*, 13 (Autumn 1982):7). A *Roman Catholic Feminist Newsletter* (*RCF NL*) – launched by Jackie Field when she inaugurated the Roman Catholic Feminists – was in its second year during 1978. It provided the model for Sheelagh Robinson, of the London Christian Feminists, to initiate an ecumenical *Christian Feminist Newsletter* (*CF NL*) in June 1978. Robinson canvassed potential membership by advertising in *Spare Rib* (*CF NL* 1 (May 1978)). Women members of the Alliance of Radical Methodists (ARM) published a special edition of the *ARM Reporter* concerning women's issues, entitled 'Sisters to Susannah' (Pickard and Windle, 1978). Women in the Oxford Christian Feminist Group, founded by Jo Garcia, published a feminist critique of traditional Catholic sexual morality entitled, 'On Breaking the Rules' (Nash et al, 1978).

Mary Condren edited a Student Christian Movement (SCM) pamphlet, *Why Men Priests?: Effects of Male Domination in the Church* (Condren, 1978c), inclusive of the insert, 'Announcing Funny Money', which launched a fundraising Ecumenical Feminist Trust. SCM Regional Secretaries, Trish Marsh and Caroline Smith, organised a conference entitled Nun, Witch and Playmate in November 1978 (SCM Women's Project, 1977), which attracted participants outside the student community, encouraged by publicity for the event in the recently founded *Christian Feminist Newsletter* (3 (Sep/Oct 1978):1). Participants included women who were to play a prominent role in the Christian women's movement, including Sue Dowell, Jo Garcia, Linda Hurcombe, Sara Maitland, Angela West and Elaine Willis. Marsh and Smith also produced a study pack, *Women and the Christian Future: Issues in Christian Feminism* (1981 [1978]), which circulated widely.

Finally, North American influences, in addition to Canon Sr Mary Michael's tour, were important during 1978. Thus the journalistic author, Sara Maitland, visited North America that year, to assist her research into the current surge of activity concerning women in the churches, and Jackie Field also journeyed across the Atlantic to attend the Second Women's Ordination Conference held in Baltimore, Maryland in Nov 1978.

It is clear from this catalogue that, during 1978, a great deal was happening concerning the position of women in the churches. The preceding year an interested observer had commented on 'the immense degree of cross-membership' among the Christian Parity Group, and three long standing organisations, which he considered 'unusual, even in these ecumenical days' (Bridge, 1977:54). By the end of 1978, links had expanded further, to embrace a wider number of newer groups.

Accounts of the events of 1978 create a strong impression of a growing solidarity among the various active groups and their supporters. Equally clear is the significance of the Anglican ordination debate, in providing a focus which united the nascent movement in support of Anglican campaigners – though articulated concerns were far wider than the single issue of Anglican (or Catholic) women's ordination. Through acts of solidarity a variety of – mainly women's – groups came to see their own particular concerns as contributing to a wider project which sought to develop and change the position of women in the church.

A closer look at Canon Sr Mary Michael's tour and the Lambeth Vigil, will illustrate the consolidation of the nascent movement around the focus of the Anglican campaign. Organised by the Christian Parity Group to precede the forthcoming Church of England General Synod debate in November, there was a breadth of interest and support beyond Anglican circles. Interdenominational support was expressed in the initial meeting on the tour, which was arranged by two organisations with origins in 'first-wave' Church feminism: the ecumenical Society for the Ministry of Women in the Church – founded in 1930 when the League of the Church Militant was disbanded – and the (Catholic) St Joan's International Alliance (SJIA). The preacher was the prominent Methodist advocate of women's ordination – also office-holder within the World Council of Churches – Pauline Webb. An evening meeting, jointly organised with Christian Action, included Catholic speakers. In addition, 'Churchwomanship in a Man's World', included Catholic contributions from Mary Condren and the author, Marina Warner, in addition to articles from Anglican activists, Una Kroll and Diana Collins.

The 1978 London vigil showed a similar breadth of support. An information sheet entitled 'Celebrate a Whole Priesthood' and signed by Kath Burn for the Christian Parity Group, described the vigil as co-sponsored and supported by the Ecumenical Feminist Trust, Christian Action, the Student Christian Movement, St Joan's International Alliance, the Alliance of Radical Methodists and the London Christian Feminists.

By the end of 1978, there were two significant changes in the configuration of groups within the emerging Christian women's movement. First, the defeat of a motion in favour of women's ordination at the November General Synod of the Church of England, led to reorganisation of the Anglican campaign. The Movement for the Ordination of Women (MOW) was established in place of the Anglican Group for the Ordination of Women – which had maintained a gentle presence since 1930 – and the Christian Parity Group.

Second, the launch of both the *Christian Feminist Newsletter* and the CWIRES project signalled the beginnings of an expansion of a 'second-wave' Christian women's network, from its pre-CWIRES origins within radical Christianity. We will look at these radical origins in more detail later in this chapter. In the early years of the CWIRES period, the Christian women's movement was reconfigured to include these new 'second-wave' elements alongside long-established groups. Given the importance of CWIRES for the research generating this book, we next turn to the inception and grounding of CWIRES within the nascent Christian women's movement of 1978.

**Christian Women's Information and Resources (CWIRES)**

The first CWIRES information sheet, produced in April 1979, [1] both acclaimed the importance of the events of 1978, and set out the perceived role of CWIRES:

> In the last year there has been a great increase in the number of people working for change in the position of women in the church. New groups are active locally and nationally, and the amount of material being produced is increasing. A greater exchange of material, experience and expertise is taking place internationally and between denominations ... It is now essential that these increases in activity and resources be matched with an increased effectiveness of distribution' (Marsh, 1979).

A list follows of the kind of information concerning these new groups, resources produced by groups and available study materials which CWIRES hoped to assemble and distribute, clarifying that CWIRES intended to act as a network linking these existing groups.

The document states that CWIRES trustees and members of the working group were themselves drawn from 'the many groups active in the development of churchwomanship in this country' through 'working to ...change the present position of women in the church'. Further, 'Our aim is to keep people across the country in touch with Christian feminist developments and activities' (Marsh, 1979).

Two meanings of the term 'Christian women' are evident in this first information sheet. First, the 'Christian women' of CWIRES – both working group and prospective membership – are concerned with 'the development of churchwomanship in this country' and 'change [in] the present position of women in the church'. This project is continuous with the aims of 'first-wave' Church feminism. Second, the term is infused with the 'second-wave' feminist overtones to the term 'women' as used within the Women's Liberation Movement. This second meaning locates the Christian women's movement within wider 'second-wave' feminism. Despite inherent tensions, these two understandings coexisted harmoniously in the Christian women's movement throughout the CWIRES period.

The founding of CWIRES was a purposeful event. It was to be of great significance for the melding of existing initiatives into a single movement, and for the stimulation of new initiatives during the CWIRES years. In addition, the project is invaluable in its assembling of an archive documenting the life of the movement for posterity.

The purposeful founding of CWIRES followed a considerable growth of activity within a wide range of groups, which sought closer co-operation in the pursuit of a perceived common project. The initial information sheet arose from the inaugural meeting of the CWIRES project, convened by Trish Marsh on Student Christian Movement premises in Lewisham, London, on 3 March 1979. Barbara Holden of the Alliance of Radical Methodists, Patience O'Leary of the Roman Catholic Feminists, and Una Kroll and Linda Hurcombe of the Christian Parity Group attended. Also present were Sheelagh Robinson, of the London Christian

Feminists, and Margaret Webster, founder member of the Movement for the Ordination of Women (MOW). Jo Garcia – member of the Oxford Christian Women's Group and first vice-moderator of MOW – was also at the meeting. Marsh circulated the April 1979 information sheet via the mailing lists of current radical Christian organisations and feminist groups: Christian Action, the Alliance of Radical Methodists, the St Joan's International Alliance, the Christian Parity Group, the London Christian Feminists, the Roman Catholic Feminists and the SCM Women's Project.

This account of events surrounding the launch of the CWIRES project demonstrates the existence of preceding 'radical' and 'feminist' activity, in the lives of new post-1970 groups. These radical and feminist interests, alongside a revived Church feminism, indicate the constituency from which the founders of CWIRES came, and to which they appealed, via an invitation in the information sheet, to take out membership of CWIRES.

CWIRES minutes demonstrate the importance of four links between CWIRES and preceding initiatives in the development of the CWIRES project. The connection with MOW was sufficiently strong in the early years of both projects for sharing of premises to be considered. Next, the influence of the British 'second-wave' women's movement is evident in that early plans for CWIRES as a Christian women's resource centre were modelled on the Women's Research and Resources Centre in central London.

Further, links between existing 'Christian feminist' groups in London and Oxford were central to the launch of CWIRES. Thus the Ecumenical Feminist Trust – which was immediately incorporated into CWIRES – was one expression of London Christian feminist activity, and the *Christian Feminist Newsletter* (*CF NL*) another. From its origins as a London-based publication, the *CF NL* quickly assumed a national role, and there was considerable overlap between production and readership of the *CF NL* and the CWIRES project in the early days of both projects.

Christian feminist activity in Oxford – represented by Garcia at the inaugural CWIRES meeting in London – was to be crucial for putting plans for CWIRES into action towards the end of 1979, through the forging of a fourth significant link with the CWIRES project. Relations between Oxford Christian Feminists and the Dominican Order at Blackfriars were already strong, and through the advocacy of Toni Lacey, Angela West, Jo Garcia and Trish Marsh, space for CWIRES was offered at Blackfriars and accepted.

The CWIRES project was swiftly established once premises were available. By August 1980, donations to CWIRES were flowing in from a variety of Christian women's groups.[2] With the appointment of Mary Pepper as a part-time worker, with voluntary support of members of Oxford Christian women's groups, and professional librarian advice from Katy Hambrook, the administrative support needed to serve a growing membership was in place. CWIRES was fulfilling its intended role of collecting and distributing resources generated by, and useful within, its various member groups. Between 1979 and 1992 a sizeable collection of books and papers was assembled. The final catalogue lists approximately 2,000 items, comprising books, papers and periodicals.

It is clear that, by 1978, there was a broad spectrum of group activity concerning the position of women, within and on the margins of the churches. We will now identify the distinct origins of this common concern with the position of women in the churches. Four currents within the post-1960 churches generated this impetus: post-Vatican II Catholic renewal; the World Council of Churches Community of Women and Men in the Church programme; the Catholic and Anglican debate over women's ordination, and radical Christianity. Our next task in this overview chapter is to make preliminary explorations of the emergence of a concern with women in the churches within each of these four currents.

## A Concern with the Position of Women Emerges within Four Currents in the post-1960 Churches

### *Post Vatican II Catholic Renewal: Social Justice as the Vocation of the Church in the World*

The Second Vatican Council, of 1962-1965, marked a significant fourfold shift within the hierarchy of the Roman Catholic Church. A new emphasis upon social justice as the vocation of the Church in the world infused post-Vatican II thinking. Liberation theology – emergent in Latin America from the latter half of the 1960s – gave particular content to this theme in its 'option for the poor'. The influence of liberation theology spread beyond conventional Catholicism to radical Christianity, Catholic and Protestant: the 'option for the poor' resonated with the fresh impetus given in the 1960s to movements working for social change.

Next, there was an unaccustomed receptiveness to contemporary culture. This new openness happened while the 'cultural revolution' of the sixties – with its challenge to pre-1960s cultural mores – was underway. Then there was a new ecumenical commitment, expressed in the 1964 'Decree on Ecumenism' promulgated by the Council (King, 1985:125), which was significant for Catholic relations with the Protestant churches. Finally, Vatican II brought a novel emphasis upon the role of the laity, which raised expectations among lay Catholics of a fuller role in the life and mission of the church. These heightened expectations fuelled the emergent Catholic renewal movement, through which lay Catholics sought to work out the implications of the Vatican II shift.

A member of the UK section of the St Joan's International Alliance, Ianthe Pratt, describes the post-Vatican II Catholic mood:

> The Second Vatican Council awakened in many of us an expectancy for change and renewal. We felt galvanised by the writings on the role of the laity, in particular the concept of the church as the people of God, and the new understanding of justice. ... We began to see that people could do things, could get involved in theology and being church (1994:18).

Two organisations within the Catholic renewal context – the St Joan's International Alliance (SJIA) and the Newman Association Theological Studies Group – were significant for the emergence of a specific concern with the position of women among Catholic women in Britain. Vatican II revitalised the longstanding work of the SJIA in pursuit of justice for women. The considerable achievements of the organisation from the 1920s might be seen as fulfilling Margaret Fletcher's 'Charter', through facilitating a full role for women as citizens and campaigning for justice for women. In the early 1950s, the Vatican had honoured the SJIA for its international work (Parnell, Nd). By the 1960s, Mildred Tuker's ecclesial feminism had become integrated within SJIA aims – so contrasting with the respectable distance maintained by the Catholic Women's Suffrage Society in the pre-1920 years. Thus during the council, Dr Gertrude Heinzelmann articulated 'ecclesial feminism' to the Vatican (*Catholic Citizen* (1991), 1:15-17).

Research by an active British member of the SJIA, Joan Morris, also continued the tradition of ecclesial feminism begun by Tuker. Morris – an independent scholar holding an MA in liturgical research from the (North American) University of Notre Dame – acted as Honorary Secretary of the UK section, as an international vice-president, and as editor of the *Catholic Citizen* until 1986. Her work became known in Britain in Catholic renewal, and radical Christian, circles.

In her writings, Morris recovers the history of women in authority within the Church, which she offers as a precedent for inclusion of women in positions of leadership within the contemporary Catholic episcopal hierarchy (1973,1980,1985). In contrast to Morris' arguments for women's inclusion within the Church hierarchy, new feminist elements, which combined 'second-wave' feminism with the impetus of post-Vatican II Catholic renewal, were to question Catholic hierarchical structures, rather than claim a place for women within them.

A special issue of the *Catholic Citizen* – on the eightieth anniversary of the founding of the original Catholic Women's Suffrage Society – assessed the SJIA's continuing role. The international president, Anne-Marie Pelzer, in describing the 'classical feminism for equal rights' pursued by the SJIA, and the continuing relevance of its longstanding work in promoting justice for women (*CC*, 1991, 1), demonstrates the continuing 'first-wave' ethos of the organisation. In this respect, the SJIA contrasts with other elements within the Catholic renewal milieu, which were to engage more fully with the new agenda of 'second-wave' feminism.

A focus on women also emerged from activity of the Newman Association Theological Studies Group (Pratt, 1994:15). Two different outcomes are significant. The Christian Women's Resource Centre (CWRC), founded by Ianthe Pratt at Dulwich (London), grew out of the group's publishing activities through the Lumen Religious Books Trust (Pratt, 1994:18-19).[3] Catholic women's activity thus developed early in south London through Pratt's venture.

In addition, the group initiated conferences on the position of women, in Oxford in the early 1970s. Pratt chaired a 1972 conference on Women and Religion (Pratt, 1994:19). At a second conference, held in 1973 on The Place of Women in the Church, Ianthe Pratt and the Dominican, Roger Ruston, were among the speakers. Toni Lacey was a member of a study group, which presented a paper at the conference (Wilks, 1973:16-17). Following the 1973 conference, various women's groups were convened, including the Oxford Catholic Women's Group where a specific 'second-wave' feminist ethos emerged. Thus, from the early 1970s, there was in Oxford a growing circle of interest in the predicament of women within the Catholic Church, in which both rejuvenated 'first-wave' and new 'second-wave' feminist concerns were evident.

The Blackfriars Dominican Community was involved with these early initiatives, thus the link between Christian feminists and the Dominican community in Oxford arose within the context of post-Vatican II Catholic renewal. In addition, both Lacey and West studied theology at Blackfriars and both raised women's issues in that context.

Two initiatives taken by the Church hierarchy showed a degree of responsiveness to the emergent concerns of the Catholic renewal movement. In 1976, a lay working party to the Laity Commission was set up, and a National Pastoral Congress (NPC) was staged in Liverpool in 1980. The NPC marked the highpoint in hierarchical responsiveness. By the time *Called To Serve* was issued, inviting submissions from the laity prior to the 1987 Synod on the Laity in Rome, the Laity Commission had been disbanded, and no subsequent events involving laity on the scale of the NPC were envisaged. In chapter four, we will look at the involvement of Catholic women in the Christian women's activity in relation to these various hierarchical moves, and cite evidence of the continuation of Catholic renewal activity into the 1980s, so creating the wider milieu in which the Catholic Women's Network operated.

### *The World Council of Churches*

The World Council of Churches Community of Women and Men in the Church (WCC CWMC) programme is the second post-1960 current within the churches where emerged a focus on the position of women. By April 1979, the prominence of the CWMC study and forthcoming Sheffield conference merited a mention in the initial CWIRES information sheet.

Whereas the impetus generated by Vatican II led indirectly to a focus upon the position of women, the status of women in church and theology was among the explicit founding concerns of the WCC. Two pre-1960 developments are of interest. Henrietta Visser't Hooft wrote the pamphlet, 'Eve, Where Art Thou?' during the inter-war period (Herzel, 1981:22). Further, she corresponded with Karl Barth during 1932, taking issue with his literal interpretation of Pauline epistles on the subjection of women (Herzel, 1981: 22, 160-6). Given that her husband was the first General Secretary of the World Council of Churches, Henrietta Visser't Hooft wrote from a prominent position. At the 1948 Assembly of the WCC, women present once more raised these issues with Barth (Herzel, 1981: 23).

There is a reiteration of Eliza Sharples' feminist Eve, in Visser't Hooft's concern with the effects of biblical exegesis upon the lives of contemporary women, though Visser't Hooft's Christian commitment contrasts with Sharples' freethought. Her feminist and theological use of Eve was to be reiterated in writings of the British Christian women's movement of the 1970s and 1980s.

A WCC enquiry into the function and status of women in its member churches was conducted soon after the Second World War. The response demonstrates a widespread interest in the continuing debate about women's ministry – stimulated by women's notable contribution to Christian ministry during the war years (Bliss, 1952:11) – *before* the cultural revolution of the 1960s. The study captures the historical moment where women's ministerial opportunities were expanded under wartime conditions.

Dr Kathleen Bliss, a British returned missionary, presented the findings as *The Service and Status of Women in the Churches* (Bliss, 1952). The combination of 'service' and 'status' in the choice of title echoes spiritual womanhood as vehicle for 'first-wave' Church feminism. Bliss usefully surveys the global rise of concern about women's ordination during the previous thirty years (1952:132-61). Her 1952 conclusions – that discussion of women's ministry leads to valuable re-examination of the nature of ministry, and raises the broader issue of the place of *all* women in the Church (Bliss, 1952: 161) – were to be reiterated in the Anglican ordination debate during the late 1970s and 1980s.

After 1960, three key events preceded the launch of the WCC CWMC study. The infusion of a new post-1960 consciousness led to the establishment of a Women's Desk at the 1968 Uppsala Assembly (Herzel, 1981:48-54). The subsequent election of Pauline Webb as Vice-Chairman to the Central Council (Herzel, 1981:54) helped to strengthen WCC links with churches in Britain. Webb conducted research revealing the low representation of women on WCC bodies and articulated issues concerning Methodist women (N.d., N.d.,1968 ).

The 1974 WCC consultation, Sexism in the 1970s, showed more clearly the effects of 'second-wave' feminism (Herzel, 1981:71-9; Community of Women and Men in the Church, 1978:7). Webb was among the women from 170 countries and churches who attended the consultation (King, 1985:133), giving the opening address (WCC, 1975:9-11; Webb, 1974). Una Kroll was also among the British participants.

A four-year CWMC study – aimed to broaden consideration of the issue within the member churches – was launched in 1977.[4] However, the terminology of complementarity and partnership, adopted for the broadened study, reveals a reassertion of its founding concern with women in the churches as forged within 'first-wave' Church feminism, over against the more assertive 'second-wave' consciousness evident in the 1974 consultation.

Two further WCC-inspired initiatives were significant during the CWIRES period. The Sheffield Conference of 1981 stimulated the formation of a Working Party by the British Council of Churches, set up to promote dialogue between British churches and the women's movement. The 1988 launch of a WCC-initiated Ecumenical Decade of the Churches in Solidarity with Women, was important in the life of the Christian women's movement towards the end of the CWIRES period. We will return to both initiatives in chapter four.

The CWMC programme introduced a vocabulary of community, partnership and complementarity between women and men in the church, which was current during the pre-CWIRES period. It also brought the 'second-wave' feminist term, 'sexism', into currency within Christian circles. These influences were particularly evident within the third current in the churches, the Anglican ordination debate, to which we now turn.

*Women's Ordination: Catholic and Anglican Issue, and Anglican Campaign*

As we saw in chapter one, by 1920 women were accepted for ordained ministry within the Congregationalist churches and the Unitarian denomination and, by 1922, the issue of women's ordination had been raised in the Anglican and Methodist churches – and voiced by Tuker within Roman Catholic circles. By the mid-1970s, following these precedents, women were ordained to the ministry in remaining Free Church denominations (Nash, 1979:118; *Women Speaking* (Jan-Mar, 1976):11; Church of Scotland, 1980:2).

In 1978, the Methodist ordination of women was a recently achieved reality. Methodist 'in principle' approval of women's ministry in 1966 was given prior to the rise of the 'second-wave' of feminism in Britain. The Methodist women's ordination debate, therefore, did not involve the infusion of fresh 'second-wave' feminist currents with longstanding concern over the position of women in the churches, as occurred in the Church of England, and in the Roman Catholic Church, in the late 1970s.

Women's ordination was a live topic in the renewal milieu of the post Vatican II Roman Catholic Church. Two different positions were evident from the 1970s. The Catholic ordination of women had many advocates. Thus women's ordination was a key issue in the SJIA-endorsed ecclesial feminism voiced during the Second Vatican Council. At the 1963 Fribourg meeting, Dr Gertrude Heinzelmann presented a resolution stating 'that should the Church decide to extend the priesthood to women, women would be willing and ready to respond' (*CC* (1991, 1:17). In 1976, the Vatican Congregation attempted to foreclose the issue with the 'Inter insigniores' declaration, which asserted that the Church does not have the authority to admit women to the priesthood, emphasising Christ's choice of twelve male apostles (Gössman, 1998:68).

Advocates of Catholic women's ordination did not accept 'Inter insigniores' as the final word on the matter. Responding to the Vatican declaration in the context of growing concern with the position of women in the churches, Hugh Bridge – a Catholic priest – compiled a well-researched SCM booklet, *Feminist Theology and Women Priests* (Bridge, 1977). For Bridge, women's ordination is 'a central issue' (1977:54), and his careful research led him to abandon his earlier opposition.

As already noted, the Second Women's Ordination Conference, in Baltimore, excited interest within Catholic circles in Britain. The Roman Catholic Feminists demonstrated in support of women's ordination – including Anglican women's ordination – as one means of widening women's role in the Church, but especially as a matter of justice.

Catholic advocacy of women's ordination continued throughout the 1980s. When Christine Kennally began a research MA thesis on 'The Debate about the Ordination of Women in the Roman Catholic Church Since Vatican II with Special Reference to Britain', at the University of Leeds, in 1985 (*SJIA Bulletin*, 2 (1990):5), she chose a topical subject. Members of the Catholic Women's Network showed solidarity with the Movement for the Ordination of Women (MOW) by taking part in the 1986 MOW Canterbury Pilgrimage. In 1987, an ad hoc Catholic and Anglican group organised a conference, Is the Ordination of Women Contrary to Catholic Faith? with Edmund Flood, Pia Buxton and Janet Martin Soskice among the speakers. Roman Catholic contributions were also made to the Anglican ordination debate (Doyle in Furlong (1984:28-43); Soskice in Peberdy (1988:12-21); Holdsworth in Peberdy (1988:22-29); Buxton in Peberdy (1988:61-9).

A contrasting position, regarding the Catholic ordination of women, combined criticism of women's exclusion from the priesthood with radical Catholic critique, which sought wider reformation of the hierarchical organisation of the Roman Catholic Church. Thus, the 1978 SCM pamphlet, *Why Men Priests?: Effects of Male Domination in the Church* (Condren, 1978c) gave expression to a radical Catholic anti-clericalism. As we will see in the following chapter, women's exclusion from ordination provided a focus for Condren's radical feminist critique. A critical perspective on women's progress towards ordination within the Methodist, Anglican and Roman Catholic churches also informed Jackie Field's doctoral research, begun in 1977 (Field-Bibb, 1991). In sum, there was a spectrum of views, with advocates of women's ordination within the existing hierarchy at one end, radical criticism at the other, and in between a combination of resistance to women's exclusion with advocacy of widespread reform within the Catholic Church.

Our discussion now turns to the Anglican ordination debate, which, after the formation of MOW, provided the principle focus for both Catholic and Anglican concern. The issue of women's ordination had grown in significance within the Anglican Communion throughout the 1960s and early 1970s, fuelled by the cultural shift of the 1960s which lent new impetus to the continuing and longstanding concern, so clearly documented by Bliss. From 1968, debate was encouraged at national and regional level and moves towards women's ordination occurred outside Britain in some provinces of the Anglican Communion (Gill, 1994:25,232-253). However, the polarisation between positions already established in the second decade of the century, and amplified in post-1920 Church reports, quickly re-emerged in post-1960 debates.

From the 1960s, (somewhat cautious) attention was paid to social and cultural change and to sociological and psychological disciplines of enquiry outside theology, as pertinent to the debate over women's ordination (Gill, 1994:246,250-1). Traditionalist resistance to this widening of the grounds of argument (Field-Bibb, 1991:231), reiterated earlier traditionalist resistance to Church feminist grounds for inclusion of women in ordained ministry. Thus new post-1960 considerations were mapped onto already existing 'for' and 'against' positions.[5] Temple's 'grounds of general expediency and not of fundamental principle' (cited in Heeney, 1988:128) were also reiterated, from 1966, in the statement that, despite agreement over 'no theological objections', women's ordination is considered 'inexpedient' (cited in Gill, 1994:247-248).

The 1975 Church of England General Synod – which followed debate at diocesan level – expressed this stasis by resolving 'there are no fundamental theological objections to the ordination of women to the priesthood', but voting against taking practical steps on the grounds that 'the time is not ripe' (Gill, 1994:251-252). By 1978, when the question was returned to the synod for further debate, the atmosphere among supporters of women's ordination was thus one of optimism – given precedents set elsewhere in the Anglican Communion – tempered by awareness of the entrenched position of their opponents. The subsequent MOW campaign sought to convert opponents to women's ordination, by education of opinion within the Church of England through reasoned debate (Webster, 1994; Furlong, 1991b:89-128; Gill, 1994:232-275). Witness at ordination services raised the profile of the issue.

When Una Kroll founded the ecumenical Christian Parity Group (CPG), with its associated *Christian Parity Group Newsletter*, in 1972, her action predated the Church of England synodical debates of 1975 and 1978, the events of 1978 and the formation of MOW. Rather, Kroll's initiative took place against a background of the post-1968 Anglican ordination debate, the Methodist agreement in principle of women's ordination, and post-1968 WCC events.

Kroll played a parallel role within the Church of England in the early 1970s to that of Webb in Methodism during the previous decade. However, the outcome of their respective efforts was radically different, due to the contrasting route taken in the respective ordination debates within the two churches. Both Kroll and Webb continued the project already defined by early twentieth century Church feminism – with its combination of equal rights and the particular gifts of spiritual womanhood – in their respective churches.

For Webb, World Council of Churches (WCC) terminology of sexism, complementarity and partnership was developed *after* her successful intervention in the Methodist ordination debate. In contrast, this language was available to Kroll as she became prominent through the CPG and in the writing of her book, *Flesh of My Flesh* (1975). The CPG was the first new Christian group concerned with the position of women in the churches to be formed during the rise of 'second-wave' feminism. However, as I will argue more fully, the CPG – like the WCC – owed more to 'first-wave' Church feminism than to newer 'second-wave' currents.

One further contribution to the pre-MOW Anglican ordination debate was significant for the development of academic feminist theology in Britain. Daphne Hampson, a lecturer in systematic theology at the University of St Andrews, founded the Group for the Ministry of Women in the Scottish Episcopal Church (Hampson, 1990:31). Hampson authored a letter headed, 'The Theological Case for the Ordination of Women', which was circulated by the group to members of the General Synod of the Church of England, before the crucial 1978 vote (1978). By 1980, she had left the Church and adopted a postChristian position, based on the assertion that feminism and Christianity are fundamentally incompatible.

After the formation of MOW, theological debate over women's ordination continued into the latter 1980s (Furlong, 1984; Peberdy, 1988; Dyson, 1984; Speller, 1980; Norris, 1981; Edwards, N.d.; Davis, N.d.; Baker, 1981; Holdsworth and Murphy, N.d.;. Wakelin N.d.; Nash, 1979). As I will argue more fully in the following chapters, the focus provided by the Anglican campaign, with its aim of women's inclusion in the priesthood, exerted a restraining influence on more critical perspectives. In addition, this focus actively constructed the characteristic rehabilitative ethos of the British Christian women's movement. The Anglican ordination debate both narrowed the focus to a single concern, at the expense of wider perspectives and issues, and provided a valuable unifying focus for the wider movement.

*Radical Christianity*

Of the four currents within the churches, radical Christianity showed the greatest enthusiasm for the movements of 'the sixties': the New Left, Civil Rights, peace and gay movements – and the women's movement. Radical Christian groups in Britain, Protestant as well as Catholic, articulated their faith in solidarity with British socialist groups and with liberation groups across the globe. The 'option for the poor' of liberation theology resonated with this radical Christian ethos. A populist inductive theological method, encouraging 'doing theology' from people's life experience, which grew during the 1960s and 1970s, meshed well with radical Christian concerns.

Groups formed within the denominations, such as the Alliance of Radical Methodists and (the Catholic) Pax Christi, and through ecumenical co-operation, such as Christian Action and One for Christian Renewal. Radical Christianity was a dominant force within the 1970s Student Christian Movement (SCM), given voice in *Movement,* the SCM journal launched in 1972.

The direct influence of new 'second-wave' feminist elements was most obvious in the focus on women in the churches arising in this fourth, radical current. The emergence of separate, autonomous women's groups within the wider radical Christian milieu repeated the pattern of early Women's Liberation groups. By 1978, a distinct 'second-wave' Christian feminism was evident in the new 'Christian feminist' groups, and in radical Christian publications.

Women's issues were first voiced in the Student Christian Movement (SCM). Contact between SCM in Britain and the European World Student Christian Federation Women's Project (WSCF WP) stimulated critical interest in the position of women in the churches, and in 'feminist theology'. Mary Condren was the first co-ordinator of the WSCF WP (WSCF, 1978:2), while Jo Garcia and Trish Marsh in turn acted as British contacts. A creative mutual exchange developed between initiatives led mainly by Condren, Marsh and Garcia, within Britain (and Ireland), and European-wide interest in feminist issues within the WSCF, with the WSCF Women's Project and its national SCM women's projects providing the vehicle for this exchange. Among British initiatives, the Nun, Witch and Playmate conference was preceded by a 1976 event, Women and Spirituality, where an early encounter took place between radical Christian 'second-wave' feminism and the Womanspirit feminism arising within the women's movement in Britain (*Movement* 25 (1976); 26 (1976):10; 27 (1976).

From the mid-1970s, the SCM Women's Project stimulated 'second-wave' Christian feminism in Oxford and London, alongside Catholic renewal activity. Thus, Garcia formed the Christian feminist group in Oxford while working with the SCM WP (Oxford Christian Women's Group, 1981a). The consciousness-raising focus of the group, and Garcia's involvement in the development of Women's Studies in Oxford, reflected Garcia's direct contact with the British Women's Liberation Movement, alongside her SCM WP role. As the first vice-moderator of MOW, she was also immersed in the third current moving within the churches.

By 1978, Garcia's 'second-wave' Christian feminism had developed a creative working relationship with the Oxford Catholic Women's Group. This harmonious connection anticipated widespread developments, between groups arising in the four distinct currents, during the CWIRES period.

Where Garcia was active in Oxford, during 1978 and 1979, Marsh was involved in the generation of 'second-wave' Christian feminist activity in London, and in building relationships with existing groups concerned with women in the churches. Jackie Field's 1977 launch of the Roman Catholic Feminists (RCFs) was clearly another instance of an emergent 'second-wave' Christian feminism. In founding the RCFs, Field set out to bring together Marxist and feminist sociology, with theology, by developing a network of groups to unite and support women in their fight against discrimination in the church (*RCF NL* 4 (Nov 1977). Her venture was heralded by the appearance in the Catholic press of the Marxist-inflected message, 'Roman Catholic Feminists Unite!'.

A third point of origin for 'second-wave' feminism within radical Christianity lay in the overlapping groups of the Alliance of Radical Methodists (ARM) and ONE for Christian Renewal (ONE). Judith Jenner, Janet Morley and Jen Duncan were among women active in these circles prior to 1978, who were to play significant roles in the development of 'second-wave' Christian feminism in the latter 1970s and in the early CWIRES period. Both Jenner and Duncan moved away from involvement in these radical Christian groups, preferring the milieu of autonomous Christian feminist groups (Jenner, 1979, 1981; Duncan, 1982b).

Pax Christi was a fourth group significant for Catholic members of the Christian women's movement, such as Angela West, Toni Lacey, Clare Prangley and Valerie Flessatti, during the 1980s. However, this was during the CWIRES period, not in the pre-CWIRES years.

Radical Christian publications were important in bringing feminist views to voice, prior to the circulation of regular newsletters by the various Christian women's groups, which escalated during the CWIRES period. Once again, SCM led the way. The appointment of Mary Condren as co-editor of *Movement* in 1974 was important, both for radical critique of the position of women in the church, and for the forging of a coherent movement from the variety of groups emerging within the four currents. It was also through Condren that the earliest reference to feminist theology appeared in Britain. However, it is important to note that, from 1975, Condren edited *Movement* from Dublin, and was thus at a geographical distance from developments in Britain during the latter 1970s.

From 1972, SCM pamphlets articulated Condren's radical critique alongside invited writings by American authors – including Rosemary Radford Ruether – and by women active within 1970s Christian women's groups (*Theology and Sexual Politics*, 1972; Condren, 1976b,1978c). The St Joan's International Alliance was represented in a contribution from Joan Morris (1976) and the Christian Parity Group in an article by Una Kroll (1976). Kroll later asked Condren to write an editorial introduction to 'Churchwomanship in a Man's World' (Condren, 1978a).

The 1978 special edition of the *ARM Reporter*, 'Sisters to Susannah' (Pickard and Windle, 1978), also includes an article by Kroll, while articles by Morley (1978) and Jenner (1978a,1978b) give voice to new 'second-wave' Christian perspectives. Ruth Windle – the first woman to be ordained as a Methodist minister – co-edited the supplement, and made her own confident theological contribution (1978). 'Second-wave' Christian feminist views continued to be communicated to the radical Christian readership through their own literature during the early 1980s, but texts generated directly by the Christian women's movement supplanted the early role of radical Christian publications.

## The Mood of the Movement: from Optimism to Realism

Accounts of the events of 1978 convey an overriding sense of optimism over the imminence of change regarding the position of women in the churches. This optimism continued into the early CWIRES years. Distinct movements within each of the four currents together fuelled the moment of optimism. Thus post-Vatican II impetus towards a Catholic renewal inclusive of women raised aspirations, while the WCC CWMC study, and the imminent Sheffield Conference, raised the hopes of those seeking change. The Anglican ordination of women seemed close at hand, given that Methodist women were ordained and women priested within the Anglican Communion, in dioceses outside Britain. These dynamics within the first three currents were magnified by the incipient 'second-wave' of Christian feminism, most marked in radical Christianity. The combined effect of these varied factors was that change in the position of women within the churches seemed imminent, perhaps even inevitable.

By 1984, the spirit of optimism was giving way to a new realism. The highpoint of Catholic hierarchical engagement with the laity had passed, following the National Pastoral Congress and the subsequent disbanding of the Laity Commission. The official WCC-sponsored dialogue between the Church and the women's movement had come to an end. The initial period of MOW activism had met with ever more determined opposition. Yet the focus for the Christian women's movement in the Anglican MOW campaign, with its clear objective of inclusion of women within the priesthood, remained as a clear yardstick against which progress could be measured. The single-issue campaign continued to provide a point around which the wider Christian women's movement cohered, despite the changing climate.

### 'Second-Wave' Christian Feminism during the CWIRES Period

This overview of the Christian women's movement concludes by mapping the shape of Christian feminism after the launch of CWIRES. Between 1979 and 1983, the new impetus lent by CWIRES and the *Christian Feminist Newsletter* (*CF NL*) in combination encouraged the creation of a country-wide network of 'second-wave' Christian feminist consciousness-raising (CR) groups, linked through CWIRES and the *CF NL*. The Oxford groups were involved in the wider network, groups proliferated in London, and new groups in Bristol, Cambridge, Newcastle, Sheffield and Plymouth contributed information about past and future events. The Quaker Women's Group developed a Quaker version of the CR model, making connection with the developing 'second-wave' Christian feminist network, in addition to its strong links with group activity in Oxford. The Unitarian Women's Group, formed at the Unitarian General Meeting of 1981, developed along similar lines. The Catholic Lesbian Sisterhood and the fixed-term Feminist Theology Project were also reported in the *CF NL*. This first CWIRES phase coincided with the period of optimism over change in the position of women in the churches, and with associated activity in the first three currents.

Two new networks, the Catholic Women's Network (CWN) and Women in Theology (WIT) came into being in 1984, working alongside and in liaison with one another throughout the remaining CWIRES period. CWN emerged from a wider milieu of Catholic renewal activity. WIT – like the Hartlebury weekends and the subsequent St Hilda Community – was an offshoot of MOW. In this later phase, 'second-wave' Christian feminist consciousness was combined with continuing older elements emerging from the first three currents within the Catholic CWN and the WIT-MOW milieu. Thus the organisation of activities within each network was modelled on the earlier pattern of the early CWIRES years, and the CR process of the early CWIRES groups was carried into the new networks. Both CWN and WIT combined projects of reformist activism – under conditions imposed by new realism over the imminence of change – with the development of each network as an embodied model of a reformed church. The liturgical life and theological education developed within each network were the twin components of reformed practice and theology, which CWN and WIT offered to their respective churches.

Two disparate elements were held together in the Christian women's movement of the latter CWIRES years. The first was a reinvigorated 'first-wave' Church feminism, where modified spiritual womanhood continued to act as vehicle for a muted equal rights approach, now expressed in terms of Catholic renewal or of the WCC CWMC. The second was a newer 'second-wave' Christian feminism, where the emphasis was upon women's autonomy, mutuality and sexuality, reaching beyond the terms of modified spiritual womanhood.

## Conclusion

This chapter has constructed an overview of the Christian women's movement of the 1970s and 1980s. Beginning with the context established by the cultural shift of 'the sixties', we first encountered the movement through the events of the lynchpin year of 1978. We have seen how a broad concern with the position of women in the churches was already evident by this year, grounded in the reinvigorated groups active since the 'first-wave' of Church feminism, and in new post-1970 'second-wave' groups. We have seen that the CWIRES project was a purposeful means of reconfiguring the elements present in 1978 into a recognisable, albeit variegated, Christian women's movement. 'Second-wave' consciousness-raising groups provided a useful model for the new groups of the CWIRES period. Appendix 2 contains a table providing a chronological summary of the various groups surveyed in this chapter.

We have traced the origins of 1978 activity to four distinct currents in the post-1960s churches, where a focus on women in the churches emerged, in confluence with the impact of 'second-wave' feminism. Events within these currents were influential throughout the 1970s and 1980s. Despite a shift from optimism to realism in the mid-1980s, the ongoing Anglican ordination campaign provided a focus around which the varied components of a Christian women's movement, with its combination of ongoing 'first-wave' and new 'second-wave' concerns, cohered.

Eve has been almost silent in this overview chapter. She returns in the following pages, where we consider in turn the consciousness, activity and theology of the Christian women's movement. As we will see, Eve and her rehabilitation symbolise the distinctive combination of 'first-wave' and 'second-wave' concerns within the movement of the 1970s and 1980s. We turn next, in chapter three, to our scrutiny of Eve and Christian women's consciousness.

---

## Notes

1 The publicity leaflet is reproduced as Appendix 1.

2 A second information sheet issued in January 1980, describes an information and resource service, which aims to build a collection of books, pamphlets and articles and to index resources available elsewhere. The areas in which material was sought were detailed as follows:-

1 images of women in the church and Christian history.
2 women's organisations in the churches.
3 women's perspectives on doctrine and ethics.
4 survey and interview material.
5 liturgy - language and imagery in worship.
6 women's spirituality.

7 women in the Third World churches.
8 theology of sexuality.
9 feminist theology.

Material sought was described as:-

books, pamphlets, articles or research studies
local newsletters, study sheets, services, events, reports, etc
lists of holdings in your library or collection which fall into the above categories
short reviews of books etc
lists of any books you would be prepared to lend via CWIRS
information on bookshops or other outlets selling relevant material

A catalogue of material available for loan – by collection or by post – was produced and updated periodically, and members received a copy of the current catalogue together with an occasional CWIRES newsletter.

3 Although the Christian Women's Resource Centre was officially started after the founding of CWIRES, Lumen Trust was fulfilling a similar function in collecting and distributing material on women in the churches before the CWIRES project was launched. Material was exchanged with CWIRES at an early stage.

4 The 1975 Nairobi Assembly recommended a working paper, 'The Community of Women and Men in the Church' for study in the churches (Herzel, 1981:79-83). See: *CPG NL (*Feb 1977):4, for a derived 'Questionnaire'; Tanner (1983) for an account and evaluation of the 4-year study; Webb (1979), a booklet 'for the people in the pew' entitled, *Where Are the Women?* to stimulate Methodist discussions in Britain.

5 See: Howard (1977); Mayor (1969); Woollcombe and Taylor (1975) and Moore (1978) as representative of the debate prior to the formation of MOW.

# Chapter 3

# Eve and Christian Women's Consciousness

With an overview of relevant events firmly in place, we begin our detailed investigation of the British Christian Women's Movement, taking Eve and Christian women's consciousness as the starting point of our enquiry. The Christian women's Eve is located in relation to the secular and Womanspirit – or Goddess – commitments found in the Women's Liberation Movement of the 1970s. We discover that Eve is repudiated in the wider movement. The scene then shifts to the Greenham Common Peace Camp of the 1980s, where differing strategies for the rehabilitation of Eve are identified among the women involved, including religious feminists, both Christian and Womanspirit. The legacy of 'first-wave' feminism, with its reliance upon woman's good repute is detected, alongside a 'second-wave' enthusiasm for a new constructive capacity at work in women.

We then turn our attention to the Christian women's movement itself, examining, first, the rehabilitative strategies within Catholic and Anglican elements of the movement. The juxtaposition of 'old' strategies, of good repute, with 'new' strategies, valorising women's constructive capacity, comes through clearly in the course of these investigations. We find an untrammelled response to the 'second-wave' values of women's autonomy, mutuality and sexuality in radical Christian women's consciousness. The chapter closes by demonstrating the dissemination of this 'second-wave' consciousness throughout the Christian women's movement of the second CWIRES phase, 1983-1990.

## Eve, the Goddess and the British Women's Liberation Movement

*Spare Rib*, the chosen title of a prominent British journal of the Women's Liberation Movement, implies the figure of Eve. At first sight, this choice suggests that Eliza Sharples' feminist Eve was restated in the 'second-wave' women's movement. However, as we will see, the situation was more complex.

The socialist secularising momentum, first evident in Owenism, accelerated during the nineteenth century, thus, as Rowbotham points out:

> It used to be customary to go back to Adam and Eve. ... But from the mid-nineteenth century, the main debate shifted away from the bible towards historical attempts to reconstruct the forms of the family and the position of women (1983:200).

However, where Rowbotham emphasises growing nineteenth-century socialist feminist secularism, Malmgreen comments as follows on respectable 'first-wave' feminist religiosity:

> Most English feminists were seeking, not to break free from religion, but to purge it of the oppressive accretions of centuries of patriarchal misinterpretation; hence the new woman was often a new religionist (1986:6).

Our explorations in chapter one allow these observations to be reconciled by stating that, from the 1840s, 'first-wave' feminist religiosity predominated and, consequently, secularising socialist feminism was relegated to the status of subtext.

By the rise of the 'second-wave' of feminism, these positions had become inverted: religious feminism – Christian and Womanspirit – was now relegated to subtext in a resolutely secular Women's Liberation Movement. Writing in the 1970s, Juliet Mitchell made a significant intervention in British 'second-wave' socialist feminism, with her book, *Psychoanalysis and Feminism*. Firmly anchored in the secular milieu, Mitchell suggested an alternative myth of origins. Making no mention of Eve and the Genesis myth, Mitchell also explicitly repudiates the earlier Marxist search for the historical origins of patriarchy (1974:365), claiming, rather, that 'Psychoanalysis provides the myth for us' (1974:368). Clearly the third interpretative option is at work here, in Mitchell's desire to turn her back on the Genesis myth and refuse its interpretation, as she constructs a more expansive potential for women. For Mitchell, psychoanalytic myth merely explains the power of patriarchy to reproduce itself. As a socialist feminist, she is future oriented and the new constructive capacity of woman requires no past endorsement. The impetus to break the hold of this repetitive oppressive power arises from women's present estate, not from some recovered former capacity.

Mitchell's chosen strategy is indicative of the shift in centre of gravity from feminist religiosity to secularism. The need to argue this secularist position on grounds of scriptural revisionism – including reconfigurations of the traditional interpretation of the Genesis myth – was, by the 1970s, well in the past. Malmgreen's 'new religionist' was now to be found only within the minority of religious feminists involved in either, the Christian women's movement or, the Womanspirit network. The strength of 'second-wave' feminist secularism, and of associated mistrust of Christian feminism, is illustrated by the hostile reaction at the 1983 Religion and Society History Workshop, to feminist Christians – Irene Brennan, Linda Hurcombe, Judith Maizel and Jackie Field-Bibb – who were invited to speak at the closing plenary (Religion and Society History Workshop, 1983a:9).[1]

However, the strategy of rejecting Christianity in favour of secularist socialism ignores the continuing and ongoing effects of patriarchal Christian theology and practice upon the lives of contemporary women. We have already noted that Daly and Stone – in contrast to Mitchell – reinterpreted the Genesis myth of origins as the foundation myth of patriarchy. Both authors were influential in Britain, and Stone quotes a contributor to *The Body Politic* – a collection of writings from the British Women's Liberation Movement – who writes thus: 'our culture is impregnated with the mythology of the ancient Hebrews. The original sin of Eve is still with us' (cited in Stone, 1976:252-3). For the matriarchal feminists who formed the British Womanspirit network, the power of this foundational myth was to be evacuated by a turn to the Goddess, rather than by a reconfiguration of Eve.[2] This strategy acknowledges the continuing power of the traditional interpretation of the myth, seeking to rehabilitate women from its ongoing effects through an invocation of the former capacity of the Goddess.

From her socialist and secular feminist standpoint, Rowbotham describes a feminist [Womanspirit] 'yearning towards a past potential', in which 'women's lack of possibilities in the here and now are inverted, and opposed to an abstract state of power which was mysteriously lost' (1983:202). For the women involved, Womanspirit was a vehicle for their radical religious feminism. Thus Asphodel, writing in *Goddess Shrew*, asserts the contemporary relevance of their project:

> ***Our aim in understanding the past is to influence the present.*** We see the part that male based religion and philosophy has played in demeaning and exploiting women. In exposing this we want to share our regained confidence in ourselves with other women (Matriarchy Study Group, 1977:2).

The stated aim is clearly rehabilitative. For Rowbotham, the former capacity of the Goddess has little appeal. In contrast, members of Womanspirit see themselves as restoring contemporary women to a new constructive capacity, associated with legitimate female power and women's autonomous sexuality. These qualities are symbolised and affirmed in the Goddess, figure of female power and sexuality.[3]

We return to the 'humorous sarcasm' of the title, *Spare Rib* (Stone, 1976:253) in the light of these considerations. *Spare Rib* inadvertently bridges the socialist-radical feminist divide. It evokes the socialist feminist Eve of Owenism – but from a position of confident secularism. For socialist feminists, the shift from Sharples' alternative interpretation, to Mitchell's refusal, of the Genesis myth is all-important. The title is a tongue in cheek backward glance at a longstanding source of oppression, as they exert a new-found constructive capacity in making their own liberation. For secular socialist feminists, the term 'rehabilitation' can also be discarded, as they put on their new constructive capacity while repudiating the grip of the past.

'*Spare Rib*' also evokes the radical feminist alternative interpretation of the Genesis myth, as foundation myth of patriarchy. It acknowledges – with the contributor to *Body Politic* – the continuing power of the myth in reconstructing patriarchy, and points to the religious feminist rehabilitation of women by restoring contemporary women to a new constructive capacity, already figured in a former matriarchal, female power. Thus secular socialist feminism and religious radical feminism, alike, affirm the new constructive capacity of women, activated through the Women's Liberation Movement. While socialist feminism has moved beyond rehabilitation, Womanspirit seeks to rehabilitate women from the effects of patriarchal religion, to a former capacity evident in pre-historic matriarchal female power.[4]

When Sheelagh Robinson advertised her prospective *Christian Feminist Newsletter* in *Spare Rib*, her action signalled the presence of an incipient Christian women's movement, with its own distinctive 'second-wave' appropriation of the Genesis myth of origins. Where socialist feminism ignored Eve, and Womanspirit made an alternative reading – leaving Eve her allotted position as figure of female subordination while elevating the Goddess as figure of female power – Christian women made alternative interpretations of the Genesis myth, which reconfigured Eve as a positive figure. Outside the British Christian women's movement, the moment for a 'vindication of the woman Eve' had passed. Within it, that moment arrived in the early 1970s and endured until the 1990s.

Our excursion into the Women's Liberation Movement has highlighted an unrelenting secularism, which marginalised the concerns of Christian feminists. The Womanspirit network, arising within the Women's Liberation Movement, also encountered mistrust of its focus on spirituality. Yet Womanspirit repudiation of Christianity, as irredeemably patriarchal, reinforced feminist marginalisation of Christian feminist commitments. Eve was a redundant figure for both groups within the Women's Liberation Movement. For Christian women, Eve was the symbol of their continuing engagement with Christian tradition, However, the Christian women's vindicated and rehabilitated Eve had a distinctly 'second-wave' face.

## Christian Women and the 1980s Peace Movement in Britain

### *Christian Feminists and Womanspirit at Greenham Common*

Christian feminist publications and newsletters show that the Greenham Common Peace Camp, established in 1981, was a focal event in the life of the 1980s British Christian women's movement. Greenham publicity and personal testimonies of Christian women's Greenham experiences were particularly prevalent in the *Quaker Women's Group Newsletter*, and in the life of the Feminist Theology Project. The Unitarian Women's Group organised a Peace Walk in 1983 from Greenham to the General Assembly in Oxford. Greenham activity featured among world-wide peace projects at a 1984 World Student Christian Federation (WSCF) Women's Project conference, on Women and Peace, held at Corrymeela in Northern Ireland: Carola Towle, an SCM organiser and participant in the Feminist Theology Project, helped plan the event (WSCF, 1984:20-21).

Clare Prangley, Valerie Flessati, Toni Lacey and Angela West of the Oxford Catholic Women's Group were involved in Pax Christi and related Catholic peace activity, which included setting up a Peace Preaching course in Oxford with Dominican support. Pax Christi initiated a monthly peace vigil at the Greenham Blue Gate in August 1984, and a tradition of Holy Week liturgies began in 1985, with organised participation by the Catholic Women's Network and Women in Theology. Accounts of liturgies shared at Greenham, and of peace vigils kept in solidarity elsewhere, appear in the various Christian feminist newsletters.

Women involved with Womanspirit also participated at Greenham, and practised Womanspirit ritual there. Monica Sjoo and Angela Solstice took part, with Solstice affirming the common effect of Womanspirit and Greenham Common in developing women's spirituality and political power (Summer, 1989:18). Asphodel too testifies to the growth of women's power and autonomy at Greenham, through the freeing of sexuality and religious experience. She identifies a growing 'forceful spiritual feminism', which overlaps political struggle against the missiles and for world peace, in which ritual created at Greenham worked as 'good magic' (Long, 1994:27). Teresa Shaw describes the terms 'Goddess' and 'witch' as 'respected norms' at Greenham (*Quaker Women's Group Newsletter* 40 (Aug 1989):18).

### *Greenham Common and the Rehabilitation of Eve*

Two broad interpretations of women's actions at Greenham, and in the wider Peace Movement, are clear from Christian women's writings. The first finds expression in a paper delivered by Valerie Flessati and Clare Prangley during a Wisdom of Christian Feminism lecture series (Fedouloff, 1988, 1989). Echoing sentiments of interwar feminist pacifism, with its continuing vesting of superior moral qualities in women, Flessati and Prangley argue that the care and solidarity across difference, necessary for building wholeness and peace, are inherent within the excluded experience of women (1988:8-9). They contend that this wisdom of women can only be effective in Church and world if women are included in positions of authority (1988 :10).

Flessati and Prangley's argument thus reiterates the rehabilitative strategy adopted by 'first-wave' Church feminism, by claiming a place for women on grounds of their superior spiritual qualities. In a move which parallels Maude Royden's critique of women's exclusion from the altar because of male fears of impurity, they refer to Jesus' challenge to purity laws as grounds for hope that women too will be drawn into the holy, and so become whole (Flessati and Prangley, 1988:8). In this first position, Christian women are yet again restored to good repute through the practice of modified spiritual womanhood. Realisation of the human potential for wholeness depends upon equal authority being ceded to women's specific and complementary qualities.

A contrasting second position is found in the writings of Dorothea McEwan, and members of the Quaker Women's Group. Drawing upon radical feminist analysis of male violence as principal cause and means of women's oppression, McEwan argues that violence, including the structural violence of racism, ageism and sexism, necessitates feminist challenge of male superiority with its underpinning in male violence (1989). She outlines a feminist aim of wholescale regeneration of society and Church on principles of mutuality, partnership and shared humanity. Implied in McEwan's argument is the rehabilitation of women from their inferiority and subordination, which is enforced by the patriarchal power of structural male violence. Implied also is an analysis which is also present in wider radical feminist theory: if violence and structural oppression is vested in the male, then its opposite principle – in McEwan expressed as 'mutuality, partnership and common humanity' – is vested in the female.

For many Quaker Women's Group contributors to *Bringing the Invisible into the Light* (QWG, 1986), male violence was analysed in similar terms. Testimonies and reflections support the view that 'Wars begin in the minds of men' (QWG, 1986:68) and that 'male violence ... lies at the root of the disease in our culture' (QWG, 1986:6). In contrast, the 'sweet spices' borne in the hands of women at Greenham and elsewhere bear testimony to the different way known by women of loving nurture and peace (QWG, 1986:96).

For many women at Greenham, an identification was made between female life-giving creativity in giving birth and nourishing life – symbolised in the snake and the spider spinning its web (Young, 1993:356-7) – over against violent and death-dealing male domination of women and the earth. In contrast, as Condren argues, nuclear missiles are the ultimate phallic symbol of destructive male sexuality (1989:199). In writings by McEwan and by the Quaker Women's Group, as in wider radical feminism, superior moral qualities continue to be vested in women, just as they were in the longstanding construction of spiritual womanhood. Notions of female power inherent in women – the engine of women's new constructive capacity – depend on this vesting of superior qualities in women.

There is thus a line of continuity between nineteenth century spiritual womanhood and twentieth century radical feminism, in the vesting in male and female of the inherent qualities of (negative) male sexual violence and (positive) female pacifism and nurture. The contrast between Flessati and Prangley's arguments, and radical feminist theory, lies in radical feminist emphasis on female power. Both positions seek a rehabilitation of Eve, though Flessati and Prangley rely on restoration to good repute, whereas radical feminism celebrates a new constructive capacity. The radical feminist position has wider resonance with other feminist elements gathered at Greenham, including the Womanspirit movement.

Before leaving Greenham, we will examine writings by Angela West, who was a significant presence within the British Christian women's movement. West neither identifies specific female qualities brought by women to the pacific Greenham task, nor perceives the rehabilitation of Eve as of particular importance. Her distinctive analysis of the threat of nuclear holocaust is a central theme in her early writings (West, 1981b; 1981c; 1984a). For West, the imminent end focuses attention on issues of justice within the life of contemporary communities (West, 1981b:4-5). Women, who participate in the Greenham vigil, partake in the Church's vocation to preach the gospel and work for justice, in a world where mass starvation and nuclear threat are the pressing issues, not the position of women (West, 1981b:4-5).

Thus at Greenham, we have located Christian women among the wider feminist presence. We have found, in Flessati and Prangley, evidence of continuing 'first-wave' values, where women's superior moral, peace-making qualities are invoked as a rationale for women's inclusion. The strategy, of the rehabilitation of Eve to good repute, lives on. We also found, in McEwan and the Quaker Women's Group, new 'second-wave' radical feminist perspectives, and noted that women's moral superiority is recast here in the opposition of constructive female power with destructive male violence. The strategy of the rehabilitation of Eve to a new constructive capacity is in operation here. We also clarified that the rehabilitation of Eve is not West's priority.

We now turn from Christian women's rehabilitative strategies within the Peace Movement, to strategies at work in the wider Christian women's movement. We find that 'first-wave' Church feminist strategies – congruent with Flessatti and Prangley's views – were perpetuated in Christian women's activity alongside new strategies, emergent with 'second-wave' Christian feminist consciousness. Alongside restoration of Eve to a new constructive capacity, we will encounter attempts to restore Eve to a former capacity. As we will see, Eve as Christian women's symbolic gives a firmer shape to Eve's restored capacity than may be found in Womanspirit reconstruction of the Goddess.

## Strategies for the Rehabilitation of Eve in the Christian Women's Movement

Our explorations begin with the post-Vatican II Catholic renewal movement, where a discourse of 'the feminine' emerged during the second phase of the CWIRES period, 1983-1990. This discourse coincided with the infusion of 'second-wave' Christian feminist consciousness within the Catholic Women's Network during the second CWIRES phase. We will look in more detail at this new 'second-wave' consciousness in the closing pages of this chapter. As I will show here, the effect of the Catholic 'feminine' was to resist the new direction indicated by 'second-wave' Christian feminism, by encouraging allegiance to the older rehabilitative strategy.

### *The Catholic Discourse of 'the Feminine'*

Catholic interest in 'the feminine' is reflected in events organised by the Grail Community. Regular notices and reports of events in the *Catholic Women's Network Newsletter* (*CWN NL*) show that members of the network shared this interest. Within this discourse, the feminine assumes an essential, universal quality identified with women. There is a strong association with the ecclesial feminism of the St Joan's International Alliance, as advocates of the 'feminine' seek a greater scope for women within the Church. The (patriarchal) Church is considered to have repressed feminine authority, and in excluding women – the bearers of the feminine – to have excluded particular female qualities from the ecclesial hierarchy (The Grail, 1985:2).

The work of Pia Buxton and Lavinia Byrne of the IBVM, both of whom were influential within the Catholic renewal milieu inclusive of the St Joan's International Alliance and the Catholic Women's Network, demonstrates the importance of 'the feminine' for Catholic ecclesial feminism (Buxton, 1988; Byrne, 1988). This Catholic 'feminine' is evident also in the work of Margaret Hebblethwaite – married laywoman and spiritual director – reflecting on feminine and female experience (Hebblethwaite, 1983, 1984a, 1984b; in McEwan, 1991:99-

105). Thus Hebblethwaite too argues for a fuller role for women in the Church, in order to enable more adequate symbols of the excluded feminine. She advocates the ordination of women on the grounds that exclusion of women from the priesthood causes the Church to suffer, as the qualities of God found in women cannot be represented in the male priesthood (Hebblethwaite, 1983). Though Hebblethwaite affirms feminist women as continuing the struggle of women, such as Teresa of Avila and Mary Ward, to claim their place in the life of the Church (*CWN NL* 10 (Mar 1987):4-6), she criticises feminist concern with gaining power, while recommending that women seek to serve the Church (Hebblethwaite, 1983:1149).

Thus this Catholic ecclesial feminism adopts the strategy, for the rehabilitation of Eve within the Catholic Church, of restoring women to good repute in terms of the superior spiritual qualities associated with spiritual womanhood. The discourse of 'the feminine' vests these qualities in women alone, so underpinning their plea for inclusion of women who wish to serve their Church.

Hebblethwaite claims that her distinctive project of 'finding God in motherhood and finding motherhood in God' (Hebblethwaite, 1984b:1) is a departure from the 'feminine' in favour of the 'female' (Pepper and Hebblethwaite, 1984:380). Her reflections certainly introduce an embodied maternal female sexuality, which is absent from the reflections of the religious sisters, Buxton and Byrne. Yet Hebblethwaite's use of the pronoun 'she' for God – which she claims constitutes a radical challenge to sexual stereotypes (Pepper and Hebblethwaite, 1984:380) – evokes the qualities of spiritual womanhood, with its central maternal motif. Hebblethwaite's contemporary concern with female bodily experience – which approximates wider 'second-wave' preoccupations – is effectively subsumed within the Catholic 'feminine', with its connotations of nineteenth century constructions of femininity in terms of spiritual womanhood.

Hebblethwaite herself is aware that 'while [her book] *Motherhood and God* [in speaking of God as mother and calling her "she"] takes an apparently feminist line, it differs ... from anything else currently on the Christian feminist market' (Pepper and Hebblethwaite, 1984:379). A critique of Hebblethwaite by Mary Pepper, illuminates the difference between, on the one hand, Hebblethwaite's female/feminine and the wider Catholic 'feminine' and, on the other, the 'second-wave' Christian feminism, developing even as Hebblethwaite wrote, during the initial CWIRES phase.

Two points are significant. First, though appreciative of Hebblethwaite's integration of her experience of motherhood with theology (Pepper and Hebblethwaite, 1984:373), Pepper critiques Hebblethwaite's equation of her maternal experience with an essential female experience, rather than with a particular contemporary construction of motherhood (Pepper and Hebblethwaite, 1984:373,375). Second, Pepper is critical of Hebblethwaite's eschewal of power and conflict – expressed in Hebblethwaite's statement 'I wanted *Motherhood and God* to be a book that anyone could agree with' (Pepper and Hebblethwaite, 1984:382) – in favour of service. Pepper, in contrast, claims that exercise of power – and the attendant conflict – is imperative to correct gender inequalities through radical social change (1984:374). Pepper fears that *Motherhood and God* may be used by the Church to resist change, concluding that the book is conservative in its effects, and ineffective as the radical challenge to sexual stereotypes which Hebblethwaite claims it to be (1984:378).

At issue here is the appropriate strategy for the rehabilitation of women in the churches. As Pepper's critique illustrates, the rehabilitation of women by restoration to the good repute of spiritual womanhood vests essential and superior qualities in women, and exhorts women to service, rather than to the exercise of power or authority. In contrast, Pepper's stance reflects the growing 'second-wave' feminist critique, which advocates the autonomous exercise of women's power, mutuality rather than obedient service, and critique of the constraints imposed on women's sexuality within the nuclear family.

Thus our enquiry into the Catholic feminine and its critics reveals once more 'first-wave' strategies of restoration of Eve to good repute, side by side with new 'second-wave' strategies committed to the emergence of a new constructive capacity. The Catholic discourse of 'the feminine' had its counterpart in explorations of women's sexuality in the Anglican ordination debate. Here too, we find a 'first-wave' rehabilitative strategy at play, alongside an emergent 'second-wave' Christian feminist consciousness. However, old and new elements – ideas akin to the Catholic 'feminine' and Pepper's alternative – were more closely entwined in the Anglican debate.

### *Anglican Explorations: from 'spiritualised sexuality' to 'sexuality and spirituality'*

We will examine in turn six aspects of Anglican explorations of sexuality, where old and new elements appear, beginning with the writings of Una Kroll.

*Una Kroll on Sexuality and Service* Echoes of the Catholic discourse of the feminine are found in the writings of Una Kroll, where she uses the 'womb of God' as female metaphor for God and source of affirmation of her own female bodiliness (1987). Kroll's approach contrasts with the developing 'second-wave' ethos of Women in Theology (WIT). The respect for Kroll among the founders of WIT – following her campaigning through the Christian Parity Group – is clear in Kroll being invited as keynote speaker to the inaugural meeting of the new network.

In her address, 'Veils, Mantles and Girdles' (1984), Kroll exhorts her listeners to remove 'veils' impeding their full participation in the body of Christ, to claim the 'mantles' of God-given power, and to accept the 'girdles' which bind us to service and suffering. It is notable that her text refers to veils as attitudes and fears, which impede women *and men* [my emphasis] in their full participation in the body of Christ. Her chosen images of mantles and girdles are used to convey the same message as Hebblethwaite's recommended eschewal of the exercise of power – except for power that is God-given – in favour of service. Kroll's recommendations are thus similar to those arising from the Catholic discourse of the feminine: through sexual parity women of good repute are encouraged to bring their specific contributions, which are complementary to those of men.

The second current in the churches – the World Council of Churches (WCC) Community of Women and Men in the Church programme (CWMC) – is largely absent from our consideration, in this chapter, of the development of 'second-wave' feminist consciousness. However, it is relevant at this point to clarify that 'Veils, Mantles and Girdles', demonstrates the continuing influence of this programme on Kroll's thinking. Terminology introduced in the CWMC study appears in Kroll's *Flesh of My Flesh* (1975), where she combines vocabulary of 'sexism' and 'complementarity' with her prior commitment to 'Christian parity', in advocating 'sexual parity' in Church and society. Her subsequent concern with 'churchwomanship in a man's world' (Champion and Kroll, 1978) also reflects the terms of the WCC debate.

In short, Kroll continues Maude Royden's Church feminist project. Despite her use of the new 'second-wave' concept of 'sexism', the importance of 'complementarity' belies her perpetuation of the rehabilitative strategy associated with spiritual womanhood, in that women's special qualities complement those of men. Sexual 'complementarity' echoes 'the ideal relationship between the sexes...based on love, commitment, monogamy and mutual respect' (Bland, 1995:281) of pre-1920 'spiritualised sexuality'. However, in place of the assumed moral *superiority* of spiritual womanhood, Kroll asserts the *parity* of women's distinct qualities with those of men: Kroll's even-handed insistence upon sexual parity, is one example of the intertwining of old and new.

*Collins: Optimism at the Threshold Between Old and New* Diana Collins is poised at the threshold between old and new. She penned 'The Rehabilitation of Eve' during the heightened moment of Canon Sr Mary Michael's 1978 tour. Collins draws a parallel between the new consciousness of women in renewed spiritual searching over the last hundred years – thus both 'first' and 'second-wave' – and the female element of humanity in Eve, who acted as an instrument of new consciousness and in whom spirituality and sexuality were associated (1978:5). Thus Collins makes a positive assessment of the emergent new consciousness as arising through the connection of spirituality and sexuality. For Collins, making this connection requires that rejection of the feminine be ended: the Anglican ordination of women provides one opportunity for this termination.

This association of spirituality and sexuality acts as meeting point for old and new rehabilitative strategies, reflecting both the reinvigoration of 'first-wave' Church feminism, and the emergence of 'second-wave' Christian feminism. The old strategy of restoring women to good repute perpetuates the spiritualised sexuality characteristic of pre-1920 New Morality, while 'spirituality and sexuality' also points the way to a different, 'second-wave' Christian feminist accommodation between these two elements.

On the one hand, optimism over social change, following the 1960s cultural shift and the rise of the British 'second-wave' women's movement, are reflected in Collins' positive attitude towards changes in women's lives over the last one hundred years (1978:4). Evidently, she anticipates this moving current soon to embrace the Anglican ordination of women. On the other hand, her reliance upon women's 'special feminine contribution to the whole' (1978:4), as ground for her subsequent advocacy of woman as 'instrument of new consciousness', implies a contrasting ground to her thinking. Her phrase suggests that Collins herself is closer to the 'spiritualised sexuality' of the New Morality, than to explorations of women's autonomy, mutuality and sexuality, in the consciousness-raising of the 'second-wave' women's movement. In short, Collins stands at the threshold between the old and the new, as she both reiterates the old rehabilitative strategy, where the 'special feminine contribution' features large, and anticipates the newer strategies which 'second-wave' Christian feminism brings into play.

*Court: A New and 'Positive' Sexuality* A counterpoint to Collins' optimism is provided in writings on women and ordination by Gillian Court (1979, 1980). Like Royden before her, Court articulates the insight that the Anglican ordination debate revealed a distrust of women's sexuality to lie at the heart of opposition to women's ordination. For Court, the block is rooted in the 'exclusion of the female from the concept of God', in the power of the priesthood and in rejection of the goodness of human sexuality (1979:1). The time has now come, Court urges, for men and women to face questions of the use and abuse of sexual power and for women to declare a positive sexuality (1979:5).

Court's connection of male opposition with women's sexuality, her linking of women's exclusion with the use and abuse of sexual power and her expression of the need for a positive women's sexuality, signal her 'second-wave' Christian feminist consciousness. Court's positive sexuality implies a move beyond the spiritualised sexuality of spiritual womanhood, with its celebration of women's superior moral qualities. Where Collins asserts the benefits of women's 'spirituality and sexuality' as uncontroversial, Court is alert to the power conflicts which will arise with the declaration of a positive women's sexuality.

*Old and New Alongside at Hartlebury* Hartlebury weekends on the theme, In the Image of God, were convened during 1982 and 1983, by a group including Diana McClatchey, Janet Morley and Jill Robson. The weekends were advertised in both the *Christian Feminist Newsletter* and the *MOW Newsletter*. A focus upon sexuality and spirituality emerged at Hartlebury, which was to be explored in both 'old' and 'new' ways.

The 'old' was present in initiatives taken by Jill Robson – a Catholic participant at the meetings – who brought to Hartlebury previous experience of a women's group interested in sexuality and spirituality (Robson, 1981, 1982e). Robson's emphasis on women's sexuality experienced in pregnancy, labour and mothering as source of spiritual insight was similar to themes explored by Kroll (1987) and by Hebblethwaite (Robson, 1982a:8-16 cf Hebblethwaite, 1984a:17; Robson, 1982c:1-7, 1982d). Certainly Hartlebury explorations of women's sexuality from the experience of motherhood, like Kroll's 'womb of God' and the Catholic 'feminine', remained within the parameters of the rehabilitative strategy based on modified spiritual womanhood.

However, the 'new' was also emerging at Hartlebury, in Janet Morley's explorations of women's images of God, and the effects of excluding female identity and experience from thinking about God (*CF NL* 15:6). Morley saw Hartlebury as 'an attempt to broaden and deepen the issues thrown up by the debate about women's ordination', by exploring both women's spirituality and the female imagery hidden within the Christian tradition (*CF NL* 17 (Spr 1982):17). As we will see, in her later work Morley developed the Hartlebury theme of 'In the Image of God' to recommend a positive celebration of the feminine. But Morley's understanding of the feminine was infused with 'second-wave' notions of women's autonomy, mutuality and sexuality. Morley was to move from women as image of God, to recovery of the neglected tradition of imaging God through the feminine, viewing sexuality as suggestive of language for addressing God (1988a:5). Her explorations in this respect exceed the prescribed maternal sexual purity of modified spiritual womanhood.

*The Anglican Ordination Debate: Three Positions on Sex and Gender* Morley's work belongs within a new discourse about 'sexuality and spirituality', emergent in the Anglican ordination debate, which develops the critical awareness already present in Court's early writings. It will be helpful to locate this new discourse in relation to two other positions.

First, advocates of fixed, distinct, eternal and complementary masculine and feminine identities – often citing Jungian concepts – argue two contradictory and incompatible cases. On one side, traditionalists argued that priesthood was a gendered male role, from which women should continue to be excluded. On the other, the 'old' Church feminist argument for the inclusion of women's essential feminine qualities within the priesthood – the rehabilitative strategy reliant on women's good repute – was perpetuated.

Kate Mertes, of the Oxford Christian feminists, makes cogent criticism of this conservative use of Jungian theory, arguing that socially conditioned characteristics are treated as eternal realities (1984c:12-14). Similarly, Henriette Santer attempted to widen the debate by presenting research evidence demonstrating the construction – and thus variability – of gender and sex roles (in Furlong, 1984:139-49).

This shift in the grounds of the debate opens the way to a second position, explicit in the work of Susan Dowell and Elaine Storkey and, as we will see in later chapters, implicit in Mertes. Here a move is made away from grounds of women's distinctive moral qualities to claim sameness between women and men, which demands expression in the dissolution of fixed gendered roles.

Thus Elaine Storkey (1988), while criticising women being defined in terms of their sexuality (1988:49-50) and the ascription of fixed feminine and masculine identities and roles, asserts that men and women are 'together made in God's image' (Storkey, 1988:56). In similar vein, Susan Dowell (1991:153-9) argues for the integration of sexuality and spirituality in place of the trinity of virgin, wife and whore. For Dowell, when women are acknowledged as fully human and made in God's image they will be able to live, as men do, in both sensual and domestic, and spiritual and intellectual spheres (1991:160).

Storkey and Dowell alike side-step the declaration of a distinctive and positive women's sexuality made by Morley, who places a specific emphasis upon *women* as in the image of God. Thus two 'new' strategies arose with 'second-wave' feminist consciousness, one asserting sexual equality and the other sexual difference. *Both* strategies moved beyond the confines of women's 'good repute'. Later, we will see that the position of asserting sexual equality relies on the strategy of the rehabilitation of Eve by her restoration to a scripturally-defined former capacity; but this runs ahead of our present investigation. The emphasis of the following section – 'the new takes shape' – is on the emerging focus on women's difference.

*The Anglican Ordination Debate: the New Takes Shape* Monica Furlong, when prefacing her collections of contributions to the ordination debate, *Feminine in the Church* (1984) and *Mirror to the Church* (1988a), links the misogyny revealed during the synodical ordination debates to negative male attitudes towards women's sexuality (1984:1,2, 1988a:7-9). Her key insight is that placing 'pure' woman on a pedestal conceals a 'profound hostility' to women (Furlong, 1984:1-2).

Furlong's argument helps to pinpoint a significant hidden cost attached to the rehabilitative strategy, which seeks to restore women to good repute. 'First-wave' Church feminists chose to identify with woman as 'pure', using this ascribed purity as vehicle for extending the female mission into the ministry of the Church. In contrast, Furlong emphasises the constriction imposed by the male-defined duality, in which women are depicted as either depraved or pure (1988a:5). The 'profound hostility', which she identifies, effectively polices the boundaries within which spiritual womanhood may operate. Inherent in Furlong's argument is the conviction that women, who are now coming to voice and protesting against their prior silence and invisibility (Furlong, 1984:1-2, 1988a:1-6), cannot avoid repudiating 'purity' in favour of the declaration of a positive sexuality advocated by Court: the limited potential of the pedestal has by now been fully exploited. In her rejection of male-defined duality, her 'protest' evokes 'second-wave' assertion of women's autonomy, mutuality and a 'positive sexuality', in place of subservience within marriage.

As we will see later, in chapter four, it is at this point that the British Christian women's Eve assumes her characteristic shape. As we found in chapter one, Mary was implicit within spiritual womanhood, and thus she is implicit also in its residual notions of purity and pedestals – so decisively rejected by Furlong. The Christian women's Eve figures the repudiation of these options together with the 'old' rehabilitative strategy associated with good repute, in favour of the women's autonomy, mutuality and sexuality associated with 'second-wave' feminist consciousness. Eve symbolises the demand for inclusion of this new woman in the life of the institutional churches.

As we saw in chapter two, this new consciousness was to the fore in the founding of Women in Theology (WIT). In her inaugural address, Kroll expresses reservations about WIT's founding aims (1984:9). She does not clarify the exact nature of these, but her expressed desire to see WIT 'built upon Gospel foundations' (Kroll, 1984:9) suggests they concern WIT's making women's experience – rather than 'male sources' of Scripture and tradition (*CF NL* 22 (Aut 1983):14) – the central focus of theological training. The difference between 'old' and 'new' – attributable to the effects of 'second-wave' Christian feminist consciousness-raising during the early CWIRES years – is clearly visible.

Thus, in sum, we have found 'old' strategies of Eve's restoration to good repute juxtaposed with emergent new strategies within the Anglican context. We have distinguished two kinds of 'new' strategy: reliance on women's sameness to men, as basis for a call for equal treatment, and a contrasting stress on women's difference. Resort to women's difference is linked with the rehabilitation of Eve to a new constructive capacity while, as we will see, reliance on sameness is linked to the rehabilitation of Eve to a former capacity. We now turn to the fourth current – radical Christianity – and investigate Christian women's consciousness in this context.

### *Radical Christian Women's Consciousness: Autonomy, Mutuality and Sexuality*

Women who identified with radical Christianity showed a greater openness to 'second-wave' feminist consciousness than women located solely within the other three currents within the churches. As we saw in chapter two, Mary Condren's pre-CWIRES writings are an important precursor of 'second-wave' consciousness. Condren's call for women's inclusion is informed by North American and European, as well as British, 'second-wave' feminism. It is a different call to Christian women's expressions of a reinvigorated Church feminism, arising within the other three currents. Condren's rehabilitative strategy acknowledges the ongoing effects of patriarchal Christianity, and exhorts women to forsake the subservience of femininity, in favour of a new constructive capacity characterised by women's autonomy, mutuality and sexuality.

Domination of women, hierarchy and ecclesial control of sexuality – opposite principles to women's autonomy, mutuality and sexuality – are the targets of her critique of Catholic celibate male clericalism, which finds its focus in the issue of women priests, Catholic and Anglican. The campaign for women's ordination is not her prime concern – although she supports this move as a matter of justice (Condren, 1972:22, 1976a:21) and as a means of feminization of Church and society (1978a). For Condren, 'feminization' requires the inclusion of women who demonstrate the characteristics named here as autonomy and mutuality, as opposed to 'feminine' servitude to men. Rather than claiming women's heritage within the institutional Church, Condren perceives a prophetic role for Christianity in unmasking the structural injustice of patriarchy, and transforming the Church from its current sanctification of the existing social order, to a feminized 'beautitudinal community' (1978a).

Condren's commitment to women's autonomy is clear from her scathing critique of male regulation and control of women's religious communities (1972:22), while her opposition to hierarchy is also well articulated (1978b:2). Women's sexuality is central to her analysis of the patriarchal subjection of women and the earth. Condren asserts that Christian exorcism of the Mother Goddess in the Virgin Mother requires of women that they renounce their sexuality in the imitation of Mary (1976a:21). Traditional exclusion of the sexual from the religious sphere through the elevation of male celibacy – which is threatened by the advent of women priests – is, in Condren's view, the underlying reason for clerical resistance to women's ordination (1978b:2).

By the last pre-CWIRES year, 1978, others joined Condren in giving voice to the new consciousness of 'second-wave' feminism. Thus, in 'Sisters to Susannah', Janet Morley makes a spirited apologist statement on behalf of the Women's Liberation Movement (1978:2), while Judith Jenner argues for mutuality, in her critique of the male hierarchy of the Methodist Church (1978b). Jenner also offers 'An Introduction to Feminist Theology' in which she eschews hierarchical approaches in church and theology in favour of mutuality (1978a). Like Condren's earlier 'introduction to feminist theology' (1976a), Jenner's approach is indebted to North American feminist theology, being based on the 1972 Grailville papers – which she learned of through reading Mary Daly's *Beyond God the Father* (FTP, N.d.:1.1).

The fruits of Jo Garcia's Christian feminist consciousness-raising in Oxford were also evident in the *New Blackfriars* article, 'On Breaking the Rules' (Nash et al, 1978) which, in its feminist critique of traditional Catholic sexual morality, proclaims a new consciousness concerning women's sexuality. Arguing the ethical necessity of breaking traditional rules (Nash et al, 1978) the authors assert that recent social change requires redefinition of acceptable sexual practice 'between persons of either sex, married or not' (Nash et al, 1978:563-4). Their affirmation of sexual practice outside marriage, thus challenges the terms set by modified spiritual womanhood.

Tensions between feminist women and the male-defined ethos of radical activity stimulated the development of separate women's groups (Jenner, 1981; Duncan, in *CF NL* 16 (Aut 1981):16-18). The point at issue was the contrast between the authoritarian style of radical Christianity (West and Ruston, 1981) and the participative, consensual ways of working within the Peace Movement and the Women's Movement (Jenner, 1981:4; Duncan, 1982a, 1982b). In consequence, by 1983 'second-wave' Christian feminism had relinquished its base in radical Christian organisations: the CWIRES/*Christian Feminist Newsletter*-based Christian feminist network was now its home.

Thus women within radical Christianity were the first to embrace the new feminist consciousness emerging in the Women's Liberation Movement. In the pre-CWIRES years they gave expression to this consciousness in radical Christian publications. But their experience there ran parallel to that of women of the New

Left: they felt the need of separate women's groups to overcome resistance to women's issues in male-dominated radical structures. Women's radical Christian impulse was redirected into the burgeoning Christian feminist network of the early CWIRES years.

This 'second-wave' consciousness was carried over into the networks of the second CWIRES phase, 1983-1990: Catholic Women's Network and Women in Theology. Condren departed the British scene for North America at the beginning of the CWIRES period. However, her work, and the scattered examples of a new Christian feminist consciousness which became visible during 1978, were precursors of the 'second-wave' Christian feminism which was to infuse the Christian women's movement during the CWIRES period. Our final task in this chapter is to examine this infusion in more detail.

### *'Second-Wave' Christian Feminist Consciousness: Autonomy, Mutuality and Sexuality*

We prepare the ground by scrutinising two kinds of evidence: first, of a continuing concern with the position of women in the churches during the initial CWIRES phase and, second, of close networking between groups – important because this facilitated the infusion of 'second-wave' Christian feminist consciousness throughout the movement. We begin by tracing a commitment to women's autonomy and mutuality in three representative Christian women's groups: the East London Christian Feminists, the Feminist Theology Project and the Quaker Women's Group. Next, we encounter evidence of a 'second-wave' Christian feminist consciousness of women's sexuality – already highlighted in my analysis of 'spirituality and sexuality in the context of the Anglican debate' – which is then set in the context of contemporary assessments of the importance of 'second-wave' feminism for current theorising of sexuality. The considerable Christian women's engagement with issues of women's sexuality – in which lesbian contributions played a key role – is then demonstrated. Finally, we examine the moves towards Womanspirit by a minority of those involved in the Christian women's movement.

Our overall purpose is to establish that a 'second-wave' Christian feminist consciousness, characterised by a focus on women's autonomy, mutuality and sexuality, was extant by the start of the second CWIRES phase. Further we find that this 'second-wave' consciousness infused, rather than displaced, the defining concern of the incipient movement of 1978 – the position of women in the church. Thus concern continued to define the project of the Christian women's movement throughout the CWIRES period.

*Continuing Concern with the Position of Women in the Church* Concern about the position of women in the churches continued alongside the spread of 'second-wave' feminist consciousness-raising among Christian women's groups. Some groups contributing to the *Christian Feminist Newsletter*, such as the Cambridge Ecumenical Discussion Group on Women and the Church, and the Newcastle Ordination of Women Group (NOW), were involved in the Anglican ordination issue, while the Bristol New Room Community was an experimental liturgical community arising within radical Christianity. The Stockton Ecumenical Women's Study Group may well have been formed in response to the WCC Community of Women and Men in the Church study.

Of the new groups developing in London, initial meetings of the South London Christian Feminists brought together liturgical experiment – so developing Ianthe Pratt's pioneering work in early Catholic renewal activity – and solidarity with the Anglican ordination campaign. The West London Christian Feminists became involved in the issue of inclusive liturgical language. Books by Bliss, on women's service and status within the churches (1952), and Kroll, on sexual parity (1975), were included in the newsletter as recommended reading. Concern with women in the churches was shown also in both the East London Christian Feminists (Morley, 1980) and the Feminist Theology Project (FTP, N.d.:1.6-1.7).

Thus – as had happened in Oxford during the pre-CWIRES years – the 'second-wave' impetus, gaining momentum within these groups, infused and informed the concern with the position of women in the church arising in the first three currents. As we saw in chapter two, both elements were already present in the founding concerns of the CWIRES project: our investigations here demonstrate their continuing interleaving during the initial CWIRES phase. Some women who played a significant part in the development of 'second-wave' consciousness – notably Jenner and Duncan – were not primarily concerned with change in the position of women in the churches: but they were in a minority. By the second phase of the CWIRES period, members of Catholic Women's Network were influenced by 'second-wave' Christian feminism, as well as by the Catholic discourse of the feminine, while – as we have seen – 'second -wave' consciousness is central to the founding ethos of WIT.

*Networking Between Groups* Links between the variety of groups, connected through CWIRES and the *Christian Feminist Newsletter*, are important because the infusion of 'second-wave' consciousness, beyond the CR of individual groups, depended upon them. An annual Christian feminist conference was established with responsibility for the newsletter.[5] Members of the Oxford Christian women's groups played an active part in the network centred upon CWIRES and the *CF NL* through overlap in membership with the CWIRES project, representation at the annual Christian feminist conferences, and reporting of Oxford events in the *CF NL*.

Given Jenner's northern location in Sheffield, her initiative in founding the Feminist Theology Project was independent of developments in Oxford and London, though the FTP soon joined with the wider activity encouraged by CWIRES and the *CF NL*. The FTP was important in strengthening links between groups during the first CWIRES phase, as the project provided a meeting place for women involved in groups scattered across the country, who were aware of one another through reports in the *CF NL*. The FTP also directly influenced formation of both the Sheffield Christian Feminists and the Plymouth Women's Theology

Group (PWTG), both of which made major contributions to the production of the *CF NL*.

The Quaker Women's Group was linked with CWIRES and the developing Christian feminist network of the initial CWIRES phase, by exchange of newsletters, with the Feminist Theology Project, and with the Oxford Christian Feminists. A stated aim of the QWG was 'to share information through our own resources and those of other women's groups' (*QWG NL* 12 (Aug 1982):9). Similarly, the Unitarian Women's Group made contact with CWIRES early in its life and members became involved with the Movement for the Ordination of Women, with one member – Ann Arthur – becoming an active participant in the St Hilda Community.

*Women's Autonomy and Mutuality* The growth in a distinctive 'second-wave' Christian feminist consciousness, stimulated by the combined effect of the CWIRES project and the *Christian Feminist Newsletter*, can be seen in the lives of the representative groups: the East London Christian Feminists; the Feminist Theology Project; and the Quaker Women's Group. The East London Christian Feminists were active early during the first CWIRES phase, the fixed term Feminist Theology Project ran from 1980 to 1982, while the Quaker Women's Group was active throughout the CWIRES period.

'Second-wave' priorities of women's autonomy and mutuality are clear in the process of these groups. Thus Morley (1980) and Duncan (*CF NL* 9 (Mar 1980):10) emphasise the shared leadership style of the East London Christian Feminists, where rotating leadership and 'leaderless' sessions were favoured (Morley, 1980). Jenner's FTP guidelines for the Feminist Theology Project (FTP) show her commitment to autonomy and mutuality (Jenner, 1978a, 1978b, 1981:4), in suggesting that theology will be examined in the light of the Women's Movement, by working with women's own experience (Feminist Theology Project, N.d.:1.1). The FTP publication, *Our Stories*, presents ample evidence that this commitment was pursued during the life of the project in member-led experiential and discursive sessions (FTP, N.d.).

Similar priorities are evident in the life of the Quaker Women's Group (QWG). Newsletter accounts of meetings emphasise mutual support in the sharing of experience and attention to peace issues, in which the consciousness-raising (CR) practice of the wider women's movement is fused with the Quaker practice of meeting in silence. QWG commitment to women's autonomy and mutuality is well illustrated in their 1986 Swarthmore presentation at Yearly Meeting, and the associated publication, *Bringing the Invisible into the Light* (Quaker Women's Group, 1986).

Presentation and book provide a window on the CR process of the group. The group assessment was that what was said privately in the first QWG meetings had been said publicly at Swarthmore (*QWG NL* 28 (Aug 1986):16). Through a group presentation of members' own experience of sexist oppression, which was owned by the group as a whole rather than by its individual contributors, QWG practice of women's autonomy and mutuality was made visible to the wider Society of Friends.

Having examined evidence for women's autonomy and mutuality as focal points in British Christian women's consciousness, we turn to recent evaluations of the theorising of sexuality within 'second-wave' feminism. This broader context will help establish the significance of our following investigation of sexuality as the third focal point within British Christian women's consciousness.

*'Second-wave' Contributions to the Theorising of Sexuality* New feminist scholarship emphasises the cultural construction of sexuality, and so differs from the normative heterosexuality of sexology, with its base in biology and psychology (Jackson and Scott, 1996:2). Such feminist scholarship differs also from advocacy of normative heterosexuality, based upon traditional theological grounds, which we have already noted in the context of the Anglican ordination debate. Lesbian practice has shaped contemporary theories of sexuality, in contrast to its former construction and interpretation through the restrictive sexological category, 'Uranian', with its tendency towards the spiritualised sexuality characterising the wider 'sexual morality' debate, at the turn of the twentieth century (Bland, 1995:290-3). Contemporary scholarship on sexuality is heavily indebted to 'second-wave' feminist theory and practice, where women's control of their own sexuality is seen as essential to women's autonomy and mutuality (Jackson and Scott, 1996; Vance, 1992; Snitow et al, 1984).

Gayle Rubin refers to a cultural heritage of 'sex negativity' (cited in Jackson and Scott, 1996:26). This heritage met with effective challenge in the cultural shift of the 1960s, leading to what Jackson and Scott describe as a contemporary revering of sexuality as 'gateway to ecstasy, enlightenment and emancipation' (1996:26). This book spotlights Christian women's consciousness, at the historical moment where women in the churches were caught in the contradiction between lingering 'sex negativity' – focused particularly clearly in the Catholic and Anglican women's ordination debate – and growing 'second-wave' feminist consciousness with its stress upon women's autonomy, mutuality and sexuality).

Jackson (1993:225) defines sexuality as 'feelings and actions connected with erotic desire'. Erotic desire described in women's terms is frequently associated with the whole body and with wider creativity, rather than mirroring the male tendency to restrict sexuality to genital activity. Further, the limits imposed by 'compulsory heterosexuality' (Rich, 1980) may be exceeded by erotic desire. In my discussion of the three focal points of 'second-wave' Christian feminist consciousness, I give particular attention to sexuality, interpreted in this wider sense. This broadening of the meaning of sexuality moves in a different direction to the spiritualising tendencies associated with spiritual womanhood. It is congruent with the trajectory begun in Gillian Court's 'declaration of a positive sexuality', which leads away from the spiritualised sexuality of Hartlebury towards Linda Hurcombe's 'exploration of the spiritual aspects of the erotic', in her book, *Sex and God* (1987:6). We now investigate the discourse on sexuality, which developed during the life of the Christian women's movement.

***Women's Sexuality*** In 1978, the fledgling *Christian Feminist Newsletter* printed 'the seven demands of the Women's Liberation Movement', while advertising a London Christian Feminists meeting dedicated to this subject. The statement: 'The Women's Liberation Movement asserts a woman's right to define her own sexuality' prefaced the demands (*CF NL* 2 (Jul 1978):2).[6] 'Second-wave' Christian women evidently shared the wider feminist desire to 'talk about their sexuality in their own terms' (Coote and Campbell, 1987:11). Thus when the East London Christian Feminists discussed 'sexuality and spirituality', in contrast to the (assumed marital) maternity of Hartlebury, their focus was pornography and abortion, and acknowledgement of differences in members' sexual orientation (Morley, 1980).

Jenner (1980a) describes sexuality as one of three important issues, and – like Condren – portrays the link between spirituality and sensuality as problematic in religious contexts. Within the Feminist Theology Project this problematic was addressed in explorations of sexuality. Thus *Our Stories,* describes women's bodily experience and sexuality as significant themes, pursued in 'discussions on sexuality [which] were shared within the context of women's stories', so challenging women's enforced silence about female sexuality (FTP, N.d.:5.1).

Women's sexuality also preoccupied the Quaker Women's Group (QWG) in its preparation for Swarthmore, finding expression in the resulting presentation and publication, *Bringing the Invisible into the Light* (QWG, 1986). Analysis of male violence and women's work for peace, at Greenham and elsewhere, frames explorations of women's sexuality. Thus male sexual violence expressed as pornography was a concern (QWG, 1986:58-65). Writings on maternity – again in contrast with Hartlebury – stress its confining effects upon women (QWG, 1986:v,45,84-7) while affirming a positive women's sexuality in childbirth (QWG, 1986:39) and in lesbian identity (QWG, 1986:92). A broadened appreciation of women's sexuality – the 'erotic desire' associated with the whole body and with wider creativity – is expressed in women's redefinition of the identity, 'woman' (QWG, 1986:66-7), and in the affirmation of women's creativity (QWG, 1986:22)

Concurrent with QWG preparations for Swarthmore, Sara Maitland commented on similar qualities within the Oxford Women's Theology Seminar, during the second CWIRES phase. Thus she remarks on the 'rich, informal, affectionate and supportive' atmosphere, of the 'relaxed and shared space' of the Oxford Women's Theology Seminar, which she found to be a stimulus to creativity (Maitland, 1984). Her connection between creativity and (broadly interpreted) 'erotic desire', finds many echoes within Christian feminist literature.

Women's autonomous sexuality is important in Patricia Duncker's paper to the Oxford Women's Theology Seminar, 'John Milton's Reading of Genesis', where she makes a powerful critique of the Milton's legitimation of male power (1984). Duncker's 'second-wave' consciousness is evident in her analysis of the buttressing of heterosexuality, marriage and motherhood in *Paradise Lost* (1984:9,17), and in her conclusion that women's autonomous control of their own sexuality is essential in resisting these means of male control (1984:25).

This theme recurs in Catholic women's criticism of Catholic reinforcement of women's traditional role (West, 1980a:1-2; McEwan, 1991: 248-9). Several contributors to *Women Experiencing Church* describe acting on their own authority, counter to Church pronouncements on marriage, divorce and sexuality (Birtchnell in McEwan (1991:19); Clancy in McEwan (1991:48-52); Price in McEwan (1991:187-198); Petrie in McEwan (1991:199-203); Owsianka in McEwan (1991:205-216); Shackle in McEwan (1991:217-224); Norris in McEwan (1991:231-3)).

At first sight the declaration of a positive women's sexuality – palpable in the Anglican campaign – is not immediately obvious within the Catholic Women's Network. Sexuality was an explicit focus within the manifesto of the early Roman Catholic Feminists, which is absent in the 1987 CWN Position Paper.[7] However, in addressing CWN founding aims – building a network between women seeking change in their position in the Church; transformation of liturgy; and women's theological education – CWN was as open to 'second-wave' emphasis on women's sexuality, autonomy and mutuality, as it was to the discourse of 'the feminine'. A similar openness to women's sexuality was shown in Women in Theology, with its parallel concern with building a new network, where liturgy and women's theological education were of central importance. Support by members of both networks, for study days exploring sexuality, bears out this claim (Walsh, McEwan and Brewster, 1987; Fedouloff, 1988:19-28).

The emergence of lesbian identity was significant for 'second-wave' understanding of women's sexuality. Thus *Our Stories* describes the emergence of lesbian identity within the Feminist Theology Project (FTP, N.d.:5.2,1.6-1.7). The vocal presence of lesbian women within the group challenged assumptions of a heterosexual norm, and raised awareness of the active process of creating sexual identity, common to all women. *Our Stories* states:

> Most of us move between [heterosexual and lesbian identity]...For women, sexuality is more than heterosexual versus lesbian identity. It is about reclaiming our bodies, … and releasing ourselves from what we have been conditioned to believe …To break the mould, to see ourselves anew, that is the converting moment. …it is the fact that we have examined and questioned our sexual identities …which is recreative (FTP, N.d:5:2).

The Catholic Lesbian Sisterhood (CLS) with its *Catholic Lesbian Sisterhood Newsletter* (*CLS NL*), founded by Maggie Redding in 1979, was an explicit lesbian presence within the Catholic Church (Redding, 1983). The *CLS NL* documents this emergence of Catholic lesbian identity, and pastoral support given by the group chaplain, Sr. Liz Rees. The group also established links with the growing Christian feminist network through CWIRES and the *CF NL*.

Elaine Willis played a key role in lesbians coming to voice and visibility within both the Christian women's movement and the Gay Christian Movement (GCM). Thus, when Jo Garcia raised the issue of the invisibility of lesbians within Christian feminism (*CF NL* 16 (Aut 1981):14), Willis responded with a critique of the heterosexual norm of Christian feminism, arguing that many heterosexual

Christian feminists are unprepared to work for lesbian liberation, for fear of compromising their heterosexual privileges and status (*CF NL* 17 (Spr 1982):10). Among the women active within GCM who were also involved in Christian women's groups, Willis – like Corinna Smart – was involved with the Feminist Theology Project.

Willis was instrumental in Sheila Briggs being invited to give the 1984 annual address (GCM Annual Report 1985:7). The address provided a stimulus to lesbian involvement in the movement, which was recognised in the 1986 change in name to the Lesbian and Gay Christian Movement (LGCM). In her contribution to *Sex and God*, Briggs writes:

> Feminist justice must oppose compulsory heterosexuality as fiercely as Luther did the exaltation of celibacy (1987:275).

Given her Black British origins and standpoint in North American academic theology, Briggs' voice helped break the silence over lesbian sexuality and identity within the GCM (Willis, 1982a).

By the latter 1980s, lesbians and lesbian identity were also more visible within the Christian women's movement, for example in the WIT Community Day, 'Female Sexuality - Seeking New Models', co-organised by Judy Foskett after attending a conference on homosexuality in Amsterdam. By the end of the CWIRES period, the CLS and CWN had set up a regular dialogue.

However, *Our Stories*' portrayal of a harmonious Christian feminist 'lesbian continuum' (Rich, 1980) was contradicted by evidence of tensions between heterosexual and lesbian perspectives and commitments.[8] In sum, the evidence suggests continuing heterosexual dominance within Christian feminism, but that the effect of emergent lesbian identity was nevertheless to problematise 'compulsory heterosexuality' within the movement.

*Traffic at the Boundary with Womanspirit* Our final task in this chapter is to identify exchanges between the 'second-wave' Womanspirit network – where women's autonomy, mutuality and sexuality were likewise strongly affirmed – and a minority of those within the Christian women's movement. In general, Christian women during the 1970s and 1980s were largely ignorant of and little interested in Womanspirit, with North American writings by Christ, Starhawk and Budapest, included in *Womanspirit Rising* (Christ and Plaskow, 1979), being more influential than contact with British Womanspirit. The low awareness of British Womanspirit is exemplified in Garcia and Maitland's *Walking on the Water* (1983). Although the book concerns women and spirituality, and includes contributions from women in the British women's movement alongside Christian women's contributions, women within Womanspirit were not invited to contribute. Though Garcia was aware of Sjoo's work (*CF NL* 16 (Aut 1981):15), and included a reproduction of one of Sjoo's paintings, the editors were unaware of the Matriarchy Study Group (interview with Garcia 14 March 1999). Similarly, West's critique of Goddess religion (West, 1982a) was a response to *Womanspirit Rising*: West had no contact with British Womanspirit.

In contrast, members of the Matriarchy Study Group, Sheila Redmond and Mary Coghill, demonstrate a comprehensive awareness of developments in the Christian women's movement (1983:6-13). However, they refer to a 'strong split between christian and non-christian groups' (Redmond and Coghill, 1983:7), demonstrating a Womanspirit suspicion of Christian women's reformist concern with the position of women in the church. They conclude that, due to Christian feminist allegiance to the denominational churches, 'no revolution in thought and practice can therefore emerge' (Redmond and Coghill, 1983:14). In their review of *Map of a New Country* (Maitland, 1983), Coghill and Redmond criticise Maitland for ignoring the oppressive history of the Church, for her 'carping references to the women's movement', for her opposition to women's ordination and for her silence regarding the Goddess (1984:7-8). Their review of *Walking on the Water* (Garcia and Maitland, 1983) criticises the failure to request an MSG response to West's critique of Goddess religion (Coghill and Redmond, 1984:7; West, 1982a). Asphodel alone took a distinctive stance, in her perception of the Christian women's movement and Womanspirit as a common project, in accordance with Christ and Plaskow's inclusive view of feminist theology (1979).

However, there were exceptions among Christian women. Thus Jen Duncan was involved in both the Christian women's movement and Womanspirit, and Linda Hurcombe (1987) combined involvement with the Anglican women's ordination issue and explorations of the Goddess. The artist. Meinrad Craighead, worked on the Christian/Womanspirit boundary (Craighead, N.d:5; Maitland, 1983:178-182,188; *Signum* 30 (April 1975):1-12; Garcia and Maitland, 1983:91; Hurcombe, 1987:cover). Towards the end of the CWIRES period, Jan Berry – Women in Theology member and URC minister – co-taught Christian and Womanspirit feminist theology at dayschools in the North East of England.

When women in the Quaker Women's Group (QWG) affirm women's closeness with a female God and share in the divine (QWG, 1986:23,30-5,51), while criticising the oppressive effects of the male God as Father (QWG, 1986:36-40), they describe a spirituality which is akin to that of Womanspirit. Following the 1986 Swarthmore presentation, members of the QWG made a substantial engagement with Womanspirit. A similar openness to Womanspirit was found in members of the Unitarian Women's Group (UWG). While for the QWG, this expression of 'second-wave' feminist consciousness took place outside Quaker meetings, as will be seen in the following chapter, parallel explorations within the UWG took place within Unitarian denomination.

Thus, in sum, a 'second-wave' Christian feminist consciousness, with women's autonomy, mutuality and sexuality as major concerns, diffused through the Christian women's movement during the CWIRES period. As in the wider women's movement, lesbian perspectives were an important element in the new discourse on sexuality. The continuing concern with the position of women in the church is a major reason for the sparse contact between the Christian women's movement and the Womanspirit network, despite their common 'second-wave' feminist consciousness.

## Conclusion

This chapter has revealed Eve as figure of the Christian women's fusion of an agenda arising from unfinished 'first-wave' feminism with a new 'second-wave' feminist consciousness, centred on an unequivocal affirmation of women's autonomy, mutuality and sexuality. The Christian women's Eve has been located in relation to the new constructive capacity embodied in the Women's Liberation Movement, both in socialist feminist repudiation of the Genesis myth of origins, and in radical feminist definition of the biblical story of Eve as the foundation myth of patriarchy. For Womanspirit feminists, the former capacity of the Goddess is a potent resource for the rehabilitation of woman, so undoing the damage wrought by the patriarchal myth. Eve and the Goddess, respectively, symbolise the two aspects of British religious feminism: Christianity and Womanspirit.

Greenham Common provides a setting where contrasting Christian women's strategies for the rehabilitation of woman – reliant, respectively, on 'first-wave' good repute, and the gender-specific constructive capacity of radical feminism – are in play. Strategies at work in the Christian women's movement itself have been identified as continuing reliance on good repute, in the Catholic discourse of the feminine, and at work in the Anglican milieu, interwoven with emergent 'second-wave' strategies, which demand 'positive affirmation of women's sexuality', autonomy and mutuality.

We have examined evidence of the diffusion of 'second-wave' consciousness throughout the movement, from its radical Christian origins, and of the continuing impetus towards reform in the institutional Catholic and Anglican churches. We have noted the low key exchanges between Christian feminism and Womanspirit, which are complicated by Christian women's reformism, but least problematic on the boundary between Womanspirit and Christian women in the Quaker and Unitarian traditions of Old Dissent.

With the fusion of old and new Christian women's consciousness firmly in view, we now turn to the relationship between Christian women and their denominational churches. In chapter four, our quest leads us to Eve and Christian women's activity.

---

## Notes

1 See Hurcombe (1987:8) and Obelkevich et al (1987:9) for comment upon this hostility; see Religion and Society History Workshop (1983a; 1983b) for details of this event, which was attended by 700 participants, and Obelkevich et al (1987) for published papers first presented at this workshop. The History Workshop was a significant presence within the British New Left, which was influential in the growth of socialist history, and in the subsequent development of women's history – including the work of Rowbotham and Taylor. Women's activity within the workshop was a point of origin for the first Women's Liberation Conference (Coote and Campbell, 1987:12-13). Reaction to

feminist Christians at this event is thus a significant barometer of socialist feminist attitudes at the juncture of the first and second phases of the CWIRES period.

2 The Womanspirit network is also termed the 'Goddess movement', 'women's spirituality movement' or 'feminist spirituality movement' (Long, 1994). See Long (1994:13-14) for an account by Asphodel – founder member and self-styled 'grandmother of the women's spirituality movement' in Britain – of the formation of the Matriarchy Study Group (MSG) in 1975, and later the Matriarchy Research and Reclaim Network (MRRN), by women involved with the Women's Liberation Movement.

3 Womanspirit ritual and art express the close relation between women's sexuality and women's empowerment. Thus see Summer (1989:35-41) re a Leicester Womanspirit group ritual, where the centrality of women's sexuality to the raising of power is clear. See also Sjoo, in *Women Speaking (WS)* (Apr-Jun 1979):10 re her 1968 painting, 'God Giving Birth' and representations of the Goddess and her sites, eg at Avebury; See Tell, in *WS* (Apr-Jun 1979):10; Long, 1981:52-3 re work by Marika Tell and Beverly Skinner. See Long, 1981:50-53, and Sjoo and Tell in *WS* (Apr-Jun 1979):9-10) re a mobile Woman-Magic exhibition of Womanspirit art.

4 My argument focuses upon religious radical feminism, because Womanspirit is of greatest relevance to my own investigation. I am not, however, implying that radical feminism is equated with religious feminism. Many radical feminists involved in the 'second-wave' women's movement were secular in their commitments, and felt no need to turn to the Goddess as figure of the female power fuelling their new constructive capacity.

The extent to which Womanspirit feminists relied upon the veracity of a historical period of matriarchy, is a matter of debate. As the above quote from Asphodel makes clear, the purpose of Womanspirit was for women to realise their 'new constructive capacity' in the present: the 'former capacity' of matriarchal female power was an encouragement to do so, rather than a blueprint confining the contemporary shape of female power.

5 This conference lost support after 1984, reflecting the declining importance of the *CF NL* to the Christian women's movement, in relation to the second phase networks, CWN and WIT. Three stages are discernible in the life of the newsletter: Sheelagh Robinson produced issues 1-9 (1978-80), then an annual *CF NL* meeting was established and issues 10-15 (1980-81) were produced by a collective responsible to the meeting. In stage 3 responsibility for production passed in turn between local groups. The Plymouth Women's Theology Group took over responsibility for the *CF NL* from 1985.

6 These demands were drawn up by the National Women's Co-ordinating Committee, which came into being through National Women's Liberation Conferences held during the 1970s, the first at Ruskin College, Oxford in Feb 1970:

1. Equal pay for equal work.
2. Equal opportunities and equal education.
3. Free contraception and abortion on demand.
4. Free community-controlled child care.
5. Legal and financial independence for women.
6. An end to discrimination against lesbians.
7. Freedom for all women from intimidation by the threat or use of violence or sexual coercion, regardless of marital status. An end to the laws, assumptions and institutions that perpetuate male dominance and men's aggression towards women.'

7 Thus the RCF manifesto (Appendix 4) speaks of 'polarisation of female sexuality' between nuns and married women, and 'inappropriate' Church teaching on contraception

and abortion. The RCFs contested Catholic rulings on contraception and abortion and challenged negative attitudes to women and female sexuality among male Roman Catholic celibates. In contrast, the CWN Position Paper (Appendix 4) makes no explicit reference to sexuality, contraception or abortion.

8 In tune with the *Our Stories* citation, Janet Morley commented on the harmonious relations between Christian feminist heterosexual and lesbian women, in contrast with the high profile split in the wider women's movement during the 1970s and 1980s (interview with Janet Morley, 5 Jun 1996). However, three incidents are instructive concerning inherent tensions:

First, a letter in the *CF NL* from a lesbian woman (*CF NL* 31 (Nov 1986):2-3) prompted a reply written from an evangelical perspective, declaring that homosexuality is a sin, and that the *CF NL*, though clearly feminist, is certainly not Christian (*CF NL* 32 (Spring 1987):4-5) (See Elaine Ambrose in Keay (1987:260-79) for expression of a similar evangelical perspective on lesbianism). This view was countered by Sara Maitland's forceful criticism of the *CF NL* for printing this letter, and her assertion, on grounds of the 'official' position of the women's movement as expressed in the (already-mentioned) 'seven demands', that an anti-lesbian position is necessarily anti-feminist (*CF NL* 33 (Summer 1987):3).

Second, a similar tension is evident in *QWG NL* correspondence over newcomers' misperception – arising from the ease of physical contact between members of the group – of the QWG as predominantly lesbian (*QWG NL* 30 (Feb 1987):4-7, 31 (May 1987):7,10-11, 32 (Aug 1987):10-11).

Third, a 1989 CWN workshop on sexual orientation gave expression to unresolved differences and tensions between lesbian and heterosexual women (*CWN NL* 22 (Mar 1990):4-5).

# Chapter 4

# Eve and Christian Women's Activity

> Two attitudes to women emerge ... from a study of the history of the Church. One is that woman is Eve, the temptress ... the incarnation of sensuality. The other attitude, which revolved around the cult of the Virgin Mary, ... put woman on a pedestal, as a 'pure' being ... as mother, and therefore [as] sexually taboo. (Furlong, 1984:1)

> [The Oxford Women's Liturgy] combine[s] creative imagination with an acceptance of and confrontation with the reality of sexual discrimination within the Church. [Such liturgies] can also so strengthen women while offering a route back into the institutional church that we can return with gifts in our hands, empowered by the experience of the desert. The Church needs the creative and innovative power of women's worship, I believe, more than it needs a few more priests – of whatever sex – doing the things that priests have always done (Maitland, 1983:111).

In this chapter on Christian women's activity, our focus is the rehabilitative ethos of the Christian women's movement. We find that the central project of the Christian women's movement was the rehabilitation of Eve within the Christian churches. The emphasis here is on the term, 'rehabilitation', taking up the clue embedded in Diana Collins' choice of title, 'The Rehabilitation of Eve' (1978). In this chapter, we put aside the improvised heuristic device for analysis of Christian women's rehabilitative *strategies* – restoration to good repute, to a former capacity or to a new constructive capacity – in favour of a focus on the rehabilitative *ethos* of the movement. Nor are we concerned with assessing the outcome of Christian women's rehabilitative activity in the churches. Rather, our task is to establish the centrality of this rehabilitative ethos within the Christian women's movement, and to demonstrate the considerable commitment made to the rehabilitative project. Establishing this rehabilitative ethos is important for interpretation of Christian women's theology, in the following chapter.

We proceed on four different fronts. First, we examine the development of the explicit Eve theme in relation to Christian women's activity. We discover that the identification of contemporary women with Eve arises within the Anglican context of church-based rehabilitative activity, but that this Eve symbolic strikes a chord within the wider movement. Our following analysis, in this chapter, investigates the attempted rehabilitation of Eve in Christian women's activity, either in enthusiastic response to moves made within the denominations, or in shaping their own distinctive initiatives towards the institutional churches.

Thus our second line of enquiry reveals that, concurrent with the first CWIRES phase, the radical critique of the Christian churches arising in pre-CWIRES 'second-wave' feminism, within the radical Christian current, was eclipsed by widespread optimism over the imminence of change, within the first three currents in the churches. Collins' (1978) polemic, that Eve be rehabilitated through the Anglican ordination of women, epitomises the early spirit of optimism that such a rehabilitation of women in the churches was imminent. This optimism was fuelled by denominational initiatives concerning the position of women in the churches arising within the first two currents – post Vatican II Catholic renewal and the World Council of Churches Community of Women and Men in the Church programme. We make brief examination of these initiatives, and of Christian women's perspectives and responses, as reflected in CWIRES.

We find that the optimistic and enthusiastic response to these denominational initiatives – palpable within the myriad activities of 1978 – continued, during the initial CWIRES phase, side by side with the development of a distinct 'second-wave' Christian feminist consciousness. This optimism gradually gave way to realism over anticipated change within the churches. Thus, by the second CWIRES phase, a confident and pervasive 'second-wave' Christian feminist consciousness was combined with a new realism. We chart the shift from optimism to realism in the first two currents within the churches, and also in the conflict-ridden context of the third current – the Anglican ordination debate.

Our third line of investigation exposes the pivotal role played by the ongoing Anglican ordination campaign, both in providing a common focus for the disparate groups and projects represented within the British Christian women's movement of the 1970s and 1980s, and in forming its rehabilitative ethos. The, as yet unfinished, Anglican campaign helped to maintain this rehabilitative ethos, in the face of the shift from optimism over expected change to realism over the strength of resistance.

Finally, we distinguish contrasting forms of Christian women's activity in relation to discrete denominational churches. Beginning with 'second-wave' feminism in the traditions of Old Dissent, we find that the rehabilitative ethos of the wider movement is absent from relations between the Quaker Women's Group (QWG) and the Unitarian Women's Group (UWG) and their respective denominations. Nevertheless, shared 'second-wave' Christian feminist consciousness creates and maintains the links between the QWG and UWG, and the wider Christian women's movement. In the networks of the second CWIRES phase – Catholic Women's Network and Women in Theology – Christian women's 'second-wave' feminist consciousness is harnessed to the central rehabilitative project. The Quaker Women's Group slips these traces. In contrast – due to denominational differences between the Society of Friends and Unitarianism – members of the Unitarian Women's Group assumed a mainstream position within their denomination, without recourse to any prior 'rehabilitation'.

Next, we encounter the – principally Anglican – expression of the moment of optimism, in terms of Christian feminism bearing gifts to the institutional churches, and the – principally Catholic – renewed critique of the church, which arose in the moment of realism. We find that both gift and renewed critique are harnessed to a dominant rehabilitative ethos. Finally, we encounter the most creative expression of this yoking, of 'second-wave' Christian feminist consciousness with Christian women's rehabilitative ethos, in the practice of liturgical experimentation within the movement. This distinctive liturgy was central to the 'model of renewed church' developed in the Catholic Women's Network and Women in Theology during the second CWIRES phase. Yet the strength of commitment to the rehabilitation of Eve, within the institutional churches, meant that the British Christian women's 'model of renewed church' contrasted with the 'autonomous' identity assumed in the North American Women-Church movement.

We begin by identifying the emergence of the Christian women's Eve amidst rehabilitative activity within the Anglican Church.

## Eve and Christian Women's Activity

Both Diana Collins, in 'The Rehabilitation of Eve' (1978), and Susan Dowell and Linda Hurcombe, in *Dispossessed Daughters of Eve* (1987), imply a link between Eve and contemporary women within the Anglican Church. Collins argues that exclusion of the feminine leads to an – somewhat bizarre – 'emasculated', inward-looking and uncreative spirituality (1978:5). She makes an alternative interpretation of the Genesis myth, when she looks to women to provide the missing feminine element, so evident in Eve. This element is capable of restoring Christian spirituality to an outgoing creative capacity linked with sexuality, in which the 'bread of living faith' may be offered rather than 'the stones of tradition' (1978:5). Clearly, in Collins scheme, to rehabilitate Eve is also to rehabilitate contemporary women within Christianity. In contrast, Dowell and Hurcombe's chosen title stresses the link between the current dispossession of contemporary women within the Church of England, and the identification of women as daughters of Eve in the traditional interpretation of the Genesis myth.

Susan Ashbrook Harvey effectively juxtaposes traditional and alternative interpretations, in her conference paper 'Eve and Mary: Images of Women', when she argues that Eve/Mary images simultaneously confine women by defining them, and empower women as '"dispossessed daughters of Eve" ... to battle against or with' these images (1981:1-2). Thus Harvey suggests an empowering potential, for women, in images of Eve and Mary. Her recommendation was not new, as the older rehabilitative strategy, of restoring women to good repute through spiritual womanhood, had effectively taken the empowering potential of Mary images to its limit, albeit these images were recast in Protestant terms through Milton's domestic and subordinate Eve.

However, it was the potential of Eve which was exploited by women caught up in the Anglican ordination campaign, while identification with the image of Mary, in lingering expectations of spiritual womanhood, was decisively rejected. Thus when Monica Furlong repudiates the purity of spiritual womanhood in favour of Court's positive sexuality, she makes this choice of Eve, not Mary. Furlong pinpoints the confining effects of both figures of the Eve/Mary pair, in the text cited as first epigraph to this chapter, where she complains that women in the Church are preached at in the image of Eve and Mary (1988a:13), and in her 1981 Movement for the Ordination of Women (MOW) dramatic production, *After Eve*. Yet when, following *Another After Eve*, members of the MOW dramatic group name themselves Eve's Lot, their chosen identification expresses Anglican women's decisive rejection of the 'stigma of Eve' (Furlong, 1988a:1).

In Furlong's writing and activity, the link between women's sexuality and the figure of Eve is made explicit in a nexus of elements. Women's protest against their prior silence and invisibility now includes rejection of the stigma of Eve and the purity of spiritual womanhood, as opposite facets of a male-defined duality. Though Furlong argues in terms of the Catholic Eve/Mary pair, she effectively rejects also both the culpable and domestic (monstrous and angelic) facets of the Miltonic Protestant Eve. Anglican women's identification with Eve signals their declaration of a positive sexuality.

Although Janet Morley makes no direct reference to Eve, her (Genesis-derived) theme of women as in the image of God, with its explicit reference to women's sexuality, was developed with full awareness of the link forged between Eve and sexuality in the context of the Anglican ordination debate. She contributed to both of Furlong's collections (Morley, 1984a,1988c) and, as participant at both the 1981 conference, where Harvey's paper was delivered, and at Hartlebury, was aware of both Dowell and Hurcombe's book and Harvey's work. This evidence suggests two things. Anglican identification between contemporary women and Eve is implied in Morley's notion of women in the image of God, and there is an implied reconfiguration of Eve as positive model for contemporary women, in Morley's focus on women in the image of God. Similarly, given Hurcombe's co-authorship of *Dispossessed Daughters of Eve* (Dowell and Hurcombe, 1987) and her continuing involvement in the Anglican ordination campaign, Eve as figure of a positive women's sexuality may also be implied in her investigation of women's sexuality and spirituality, in *Sex and God* (1987).

Given the pivotal role played by the Anglican ordination campaign within the Christian women's movement, the identification between Eve and contemporary Christian women gained currency outside the Anglican debate. Thus, in an early editorial to the *Catholic Women's Network Newsletter*, Pat Pinsent comments that 'Eve is re-examining her role!' (*CWN NL* 2 (Mar 1985):1), so identifying Eve with contemporary women in the Catholic Women's Network. Pinsent reconfigures Eve, so giving an alternative interpretation congruent with the rehabilitative aims of Catholic Christian women's activity, in which women re-examine their role in the church. Pinsent thus reiterates, in Catholic form, the reconfigured Anglican Eve, figure of women's positive sexuality.

Pinsent is versed in seventeenth century literature, and her comment is prefaced with an reference to the Miltonic Eve (*CWN NL* 2 (Mar 1985):1). It is instructive to compare Pinsents's allusion with the sophisticated rejection of Milton's Protestant reworking of the foundation myth of patriarchy in *Paradise Lost*, by Patricia Duncker, in her Oxford paper (1984). Unlike Pinsent, Duncker makes no explicit reference to the Miltonic Eve when she perceives Protestant linking of the institutions of heterosexuality, marriage and motherhood as reinscribing patriarchal control of women – in our terms, reinscribing the traditional interpretation. Duncker – in contrast to Pinsent – is little concerned with change in the position of women in the churches. Her radical feminist rehabilitative strategy relies on the new constructive capacity of women's autonomy and sexuality, without recourse to a reconfiguration of Eve and the Genesis myth. Thus Pinsent – like the Anglican members of Eve's Lot, and their wider following – uses Eve to endorse the Christian women's project, whereas Duncker represents a radical feminist alternative.

We now turn to the first three currents and to the optimism, and subsequent realism, over change in the position of women in the churches, within them. The initial CWIRES information sheet (Marsh, 1979; reproduced as Appendix 1) bears testimony both to increasing activity, and palpable optimism over imminent change, during the year of 1978. Preoccupation with change in the position of women in the churches – rather than the fourth current radicalism of Condren's critique of Christianity or Jenner's feminist consciousness – was the central concern. We examine the shift from optimism to realism, in the relations between Christian women and their churches, considering each current in turn. These dynamics are hereby mapped onto the time-span of the CWIRES period, during which, as we have already seen, 'second-wave' Christian feminist consciousness diffused throughout the Christian women's movement.

## From Optimism to Realism: Aspirations Towards the Rehabilitation of Eve Arising Within the First Three Currents in the Churches

### *Post-Vatican II Catholic Renewal*

The shift from optimism to realism happened most quickly in the first current: post-Vatican II Catholic renewal.

*The Laity Commission and the National Pastoral Congress* The founding of the Laity Commission (LC) and the National Pastoral Congress (NPC), held in Liverpool in 1980, signalled a brief moment of openness on the part of the Catholic hierarchy towards lay involvement in defining the contemporary agenda for post-Vatican II Catholic renewal. This openness to lay views created an ideal opportunity, for – necessarily lay – women, to place on the agenda change in the position of women within the Catholic Church. Catholic groups involved in the Christian women's movement seized the moment.

An LC working party, with a brief to assess the position of women within the church, made widespread consultation with Catholic women, in the years between 1976 and 1981. The eventual report, *Why Can't A Woman Be More Like a Man?* (LC, 1982), defined as 'pastoral challenge' the need for the Church to oppose discrimination against women in Church and society (LC, 1982:28).

Discussion documents– the 1978 Pastoral Paper 1 and *A Time for Building* – preceded the 1980 NPC, while the bishops' message, *The Easter People*, was written in response to the NPC Congress report. Ianthe Pratt attended the Congress and chaired a group concerning the role of women in the church, which firmly recommended a wider role for women. Documents on women and justice were submitted to the NPC by the Oxford Catholic Feminists, under the name of the Oxford Women's Theology Group, and by the Roman Catholic Feminists. Here, and in surrounding discussions, a sharper 'second-wave' consciousness was articulated, placing justice for women in the context of the creation of a just society through radical change.

The 1980 National Pastoral Congress was a watershed, as it marked a high point in optimism concerning the effects of lay consultation in setting the agenda for continued post-Vatican II Catholic renewal, and in lay participation in pursuit of this aim. However, the Congress generated a flood of demands for renewal, extending far beyond those the Church was prepared to accommodate. It was not to be repeated. Despite the stated intention of the LC report, to stimulate discussion within the Church in England and Wales, the LC, too, was wound up soon after its 1982 report was published, with responsibility for lay matters being then vested in the Bishops' Conference. From that point on, as demonstrated by the 1987 (episcopal) Synod on the Laity, lay matters were to be discussed exclusively by the bishops though the invitation of lay submissions continued.

The principal response to hierarchical entrenchment, on the part of Catholic Christian women, was to persist in articulating, to the bishops, lay views developed within post-Vatican II Catholic renewal, including those on change in the position of women. Attendance of 300 people at a (lay-convened) 1986 Laity Consultation in Oxford timed to precede the 1987 synod, with Margaret Hebblethwaite as speaker, provides one illustration of this stance.

*The Catholic Women's Network: Born as Optimism Turns to Realism* The initiative to form the Catholic Women's Network (CWN) followed the disbanding of the LC, and experience of the restrictive processes of subsequent consultation by the Bishops' Conference. Mary Warrener and Jenny Bond, former members of the LC working party, were among those who joined the new network, as were members of the Oxford Catholic Women's Group, such as Toni Lacey, and London Catholic feminists, such as Alexina Murphy.

The CWN continued to represent the views of those working for change in the position of women to the bishops, partly through membership of the National Board of Catholic Women (NBCW). Thus in 1987 the CWN was granted membership of the NBCW, which had been set up in the 1930s as a consultative body to the Bishops' Conference of England and Wales. The CWN took its place alongside representatives of about twenty women's organisations, including the St Joan's International Alliance (SJIA). In 1988, representatives of CWN and SJIA on the board were appointed to a committee, which made quarterly briefings on women's issues to the Bishops' Conference. Regular reports of NBCW activity appeared in the newsletter.

The shift from optimism to realism is evident in CWN expectations concerning their Position Paper, produced for the bishops in response to the document, *Called To Serve*, which invited submissions from the laity prior to the 1987 Rome synod. The CWN AGM, in March 1987, formally adopted the resulting eight-page document before its submission. When Pat Pinsent subsequently commented that the synod had produced 'nothing of significance' (*CWN NL* 12 (Dec 1987):11), realism about the likely impact of the Position Paper is clear, evident also in newsletter correspondence. A similar realism was at work when the Catholic Lesbian Sisterhood issued their three-page report in response to *Called to Serve*, to Bishops in England and Wales.

*CWN: Rehabilitation of Women within the Church and 'Second-wave' Consciousness* The elements held in tension within the CWN are well expressed in the Position Paper, being epitomised in its opening reference to CWN as 'a sign of hope and reconciliation', providing a place where a programme of change for the Church can be developed (CWN, 1987:1). The ethos of the Catholic Women's Network, with its continued commitment to rehabilitation of women within the institutional Catholic Church, always held in tension with 'second-wave' Christian feminist consciousness, was shaped within the shift from optimism to realism over change in the position of women. During the second CWIRES phase, CWN attempted a determined rehabilitation of Catholic women within the church, instigated as the LC/NPC-inspired optimism over the imminence of change began its decline.

The stated CWN aims are to seek full participation of women in the church – including a full role in the liturgical celebration of the Eucharist – the use of inclusive language and the promotion of lay involvement and witness in the church (Appendix 4). In its early years, CWN continued to press for the rehabilitation of women within the Catholic Church. However, the 'second-wave' Christian feminist consciousness, represented at the NPC by the Roman Catholic Feminists and the Oxford Catholic Feminists, developed further in subsequent years. Formed in the face of a diminishing response from the Bishops, but with a growing 'second-wave' Christian feminist consciousness, the women of CWN set out to sustain one another during the continuing uphill task.

'Second-wave' consciousness is at work where the Position Paper, refers to 'development of base communities' and 'an egalitarian ministry of all the baptised' (Appendix 4), which contrasts with the project of women's rehabilitation within existing church structures. As we will discover in the closing pages of this chapter, this consciousness was expressed in the liturgical life of CWN, though the newer 'second-wave' impetus never displaced CWN commitment to rehabilitation within the institutional church.

Consideration of two interrelated issues – 'women and justice' and women's ordination – reveals the disparate elements in tension. Given the Vatican II declaration of social justice as the vocation of the church in the world, claims made upon the hierarchy on behalf of women could be made in terms of social justice. Thus the CWN Position Paper argues that the Church must support the self-determination of women, along with that of other marginalised groups and that 'the equality of women within the Church is a justice issue' (Appendix 4). The CWN approach, reiterates the claim made by the Oxford group in their NPC leaflet, 'Women and Justice' (Oxford Women's Theology Group, 1980a).

Looking specifically at the ordination issue, the plea for justice was capable of uniting the longstanding ecclesial feminism continued in the SJIA, continued in support for women's ordination among advocates of the Catholic feminine, such as Buxton (1988) and Hebblethwaite (1983), with those in the middle-ground, such as Pratt (*CF NL* 11 (Aug 1980):4-5) and Murphy (Holdsworth and Murphy, N.d.), together with radical 'second-wave' voices, such as those of Field and the RCFs, in their claim of 'Equal Rites for Women' (*RCF NL* 7 (May 1978):2), and even Condren (1976a:21). The CWN statement, in its reference to both Catholic women's ordination and renewed non-hierarchical ministry (Appendix 4), and internal CWN debates on the matter, in the *CWN NL*, demonstrate this point.

*Angela West: a Constrasting Response* Hierarchical entrenchment engendered a contrasting response, in the work of Angela West, of the Oxford Christian feminists, to the CWN strategy of continuing to press the case of women. For West, the ineffectiveness of the Oxford Catholic Women's Group NPC submission 'Women and Justice' – ignored by bishops and removed from bookstalls at the congress – marked a turning point away from direct engagement with the Catholic hierarchy (West, 1982b:5), in favour of women's autonomous discernment, in practice and theology, of the Church's mission to the world. After this turning point, West wrote her distinctive feminist theology, with the Oxford Women's Liturgy and the Greenham Vigil as focal points for her reflections. In addition, she was influenced by radical Catholicism through both theological education at Blackfriars and involvement in Pax Christi. We will revisit West's work in the following chapter.

Later in this chapter, we will encounter the liturgical life of the Oxford Women's Liturgy, and of the CWN, enabling us to uncover further evidence of the fusion of reformist activism within the institutional Church and autonomous women's liturgical practice. But first we turn to the second of the currents in the churches: the World Council of Churches Community of Women and Men in the Church programme and the British dialogue arising from it between the church and the women's movement. Here we encounter, once more, a surge of optimism from 1978 into the mid-1980s, which then gives way to a realism over the expected pace of change.

### *The WCC-Initiated 'Dialogue between the Churches and the Women's Movement'*

A parallel moment of openness to the position of women in British denominational churches arose from the WCC Community of Women and Men in the Church programme, over a broadly similar period to Catholic explorations through the LC and NPC.

*Sheffield and the British Council of Churches Working Group* The location of the 1981 WCC CWMC consultation in Sheffield raised the profile of the CWMC programme within British member churches (Parvey, 1983; Crawford and Kinnamon, 1983; Frost, 1980; Braithwaite, 1981). Already brought to the attention of the Christian women of CWIRES by the April 1979 information sheet, the Sheffield Consultation was advertised in the *Christian Feminist Newsletter*, and Janet Morley and Jen Duncan of the East London Christian feminists attended as observers.

Following the Sheffield consultation, the British Council of Churches (BCC) urged member churches to engage with the CWMC programme and to enter into dialogue with the women's movement. A BCC CWMC ecumenical working group of women and men was established, with a brief to monitor and facilitate this process (BCC, 1984:1).

A strong link with the Christian women's movement was established when Janet Morley was appointed as Secretary to the BCC working group (BCC, 1984:1). Already involved in the East London Christian feminists and in the Feminist Theology Project, Morley – as an Anglican married to a Methodist minister – was also closely involved in the life of two denominational churches. As Secretary of the BCC working group, she acted as spokeswoman on behalf of the women's movement to the churches. Morley also participated in a range of Christian women's activity and events (BCC, 1984:11-12), the progress of the ecumenical working group being reported in the *CF NL*.

In the event, the project was cut short in April 1984, before the brief was fulfilled, as a working group recommendation that a permanent BCC CWMC desk be established failed to gain the necessary financial support from the member churches (Morley, 1985a). This lack of support for long-term developments followed considerable activity within the churches between 1981 and 1984, in relation to the CWMC study, in some cases initiated by members of the BCC working group. We will make a brief survey of the effects of this activity, as monitored by the BCC working group, looking at denominational churches in turn.

The WCC CWMC study attracted some interest among Catholics involved in post-Vatican II renewal (Braithwaite, 1981:1,2), but its main impact was on non-Catholic denominations. In the Methodist Church, the United Reformed Church (URC), the Church of Scotland (COS) and the Baptist Union (BU) exclusion of women from ministry was not an issue, thus the CWMC programme focused attention on broader issues concerning women and men in denominational life.[1] With the exception of the Methodist Church, there was little involvement of women in these denominations in the Christian women's movement, which inevitably leads to a paucity of evidence concerning denominational developments within CWIRES. However, some documents produced by the denominational churches in the course of the WCC-inspired dialogue are held in CWIRES, and these are open to our scrutiny.

*The Baptist Union* (BU) produced two documents for use within local congregations. A Department of Mission working group on women within the BU, which included Roger Nunn – the Baptist representative on the BCC working group – among its members, produced a study pack, *"Free Indeed"?* (BU, 1983). The Department of Ministry issued *Man and Woman in the Church* (Beasley-Murray, 1983), which surveys biblical evidence concerning the relation between man and woman, and concludes that redeemed man and woman are to live in partnership, for which the reformed tradition provides the necessary conditions.

*The Church of Scotland* Maidie Hart – the Church of Scotland representative on the BCC working group – acted as Vice-Convenor of a church committee on the Role of Men and Women in Church and Society, which reported to the Assembly of 1980 (COS, 1980). When, Anne Hepburn at a 1982 Women's Guild meeting, used a prayer referring to God as 'Mother', the intensity of response led to the setting up of a joint Women's Guild/Panel of Doctrine Study Group, which offered its report, *The Motherhood of God*, to the General Assembly (Lewis, 1984). The prayer concerned was written by the URC minister and hymn writer, Brian Wren.

The varied members of the study group reached agreement on two points: that traditional language for God may be complemented by mother language 'in ways consistent with Scripture's richness and variety' (Lewis, 1984:61), and that God the Father is neither exclusively male nor masculine (Lewis, 1984:64). However, members differed on whether mother language could be used as a mode of address, or should be restricted to that which we say *about* God (Lewis, 1984:61-3). While a minority were happy to attribute motherly qualities to the Father, but considered it illegitimate to call God 'Mother', the majority felt it would help develop the community of women and men, to acknowledge that God resembles the female and motherly (Lewis, 1984:64-6).

Thus the study group worked similar terrain to that explored at Hartlebury, and by Hebblethwaite (1984b). In confining their consideration of God in the feminine to God as Mother, the group stayed closer to Robson's and Hebblethwaite's theological reflections on motherhood, than to Morley's broader explorations of feminine imagery, with her appreciation of a women's sexuality which exceeds maternity. Even these restricted explorations, in which God is associated with the good repute of spiritual womanhood, were unacceptable to a minority within the study group. For the sake of these members – who were prepared to add these gendered qualities to the male God as Father but not to address God as Mother – the potential of God as Mother affirmed by the majority – as by Hebblethwaite and Robson – was likely to be taken no further. With God the Father as pre-eminent, neither an acknowledgement of God as female and motherly, nor 'second-wave' Christian feminist imaging of God beyond the terms of modified spiritual womanhood, may be realised.

*The United Reformed Church and the Methodist Church* A URC CWMC group produced a leaflet, *Why Bother?*, for circulation to local churches, together with a questionnaire to explore the situation of women and men within the URC, including representation of women on Church committees. The leaflet expressed both a commitment to increased use of women's talents within the URC, and support for the introduction of inclusive liturgical language (BCC, 1984:15). The Methodist Church established an inter-Divisional Consultation on the CWMC in 1984 (BCC, 1984:14).

*Christian Women in Dialogue with the Churches* During her term as Secretary to the BCC working group, Morley was instrumental in the republication of the United Churches of Canada's *Guidelines for Inclusive Language*, as 'Bad Language in Church' ('Bad Language in Church', 1983). Prior to the 'dialogue', in the context of revision of a Methodist and URC hymnbook, Morley had been among women active within radical Methodism and in the 'second-wave' Christian feminism of the initial CWIRES phase, who raised the issue of inclusive liturgical language. Together with Judith Maizel – the Methodist representative on the BCC group – Morley had made representations to the Methodist hymnbook committee (Maizel, 1980). The representations were put together at a series of workshops on Women and Worship, held at Notting Hill Methodist Church in West London during 1980 and 1981, co-organised by Maizel – then an SCM organiser based in Birmingham – and Barbara Holden of the East London Christian feminists. The workshops were advertised in the *Christian Feminist Newsletter*.

Correspondence generated by 'Bad Language in Church' prompted Morley to reflect on the reasons for resistance to inclusive liturgical language (Morley (1984b). The experience strengthened her interest in feminine imagery for God, begun at Hartlebury. We will encounter the impact on Morley's contribution to the liturgical life of Women in Theology, and the St Hilda Community, in the closing pages of this chapter.

Janet Morley, like Kate Mertes of the Oxford Christian feminists, was a prominent spokeswoman for the women's movement in the dialogue with the churches. Thus Morley addressed theological students in Oxford and at Cuddesdon (1983a, 1985b), while Mertes gave a number of papers to general audiences (1982, 1984a, 1984b, 1984c).

*The Dialogue within Evangelical Christianity* The dialogue between the churches and the women's movement eventually extended into evangelical Christianity – the self-identified evangelical wings of mainstream denominations. The formation of the charitable trust, Men, Women and God, after a 1985 conference of that title, and the publication of conference papers is significant. A newsletter, the *Men, Women and God* newsletter, edited by Veronica Zundel, recommended study material and publicised events, which were also advertised in Christian feminist mailings.

The aim of the trust, as expressed by John Stott, Director of the London Institute for Contemporary Christianity, was to facilitate positive engagement between evangelical Christianity and feminism, through 'a double listening, both to the voice of feminists and to the voice of God' (cited in Keay, 1987:vii). The notion of listening to feminism is also found in Lavinia Byrne's argument for a Catholic 'feminine' (1988:xi). In both Stott and Byrne this notion belies a desire to maintain a distance from feminism as popularly perceived within the churches, beyond the Christian women's movement and its sympathisers.

As we discovered in chapter three, whereas many Catholic women in the centre ground of the movement – such as Pratt, Pinsent and Murphy – were comfortable with 'second-wave' Christian feminism, others – such as Hebblethwaite and Byrne – actively resisted it, preferring the Catholic discourse of the feminine. From Roman Catholicism to evangelicalism, a belated but widespread acceptance of the demands of 'first-wave' ecclesial feminism, coupled with suspicion of (secularising) 'second-wave' feminism, underpinned the stance of 'listening to feminism'.

Myrtle Langley and Elaine Storkey – both among the speakers at the Men Women and God conference – were principal spokeswomen for feminism to the evangelical audience of the 1980s. Thus, in *Equal Woman*, Langley urges evangelical Christians to re-examine their attitudes to the ministry and place of women in the Church (1983:9), whereas Storkey, in *What's Right with Feminism?* (1985), argues for Christian feminism as an alternative to both Christian anti-feminism and secular feminism. Both authors identify a heritage for contemporary evangelical feminists within 'first-wave' feminism (Langley, 1983:23-113,113-4; Storkey, 1985:133-59).

Langley's argument is made in terms of WCC CWMC terminology of complementarity between women and men, while her assertion of the need for a whole ministry of equal women and men (1983:117-178) is effectively an argument for partnership. Storkey too argues for the equality of women with men, on the grounds that both are made in the image of God, and advocates partnership between the sexes. As we have already seen, Storkey moves away from the notion of ascribed gender roles. However, by invoking 'first-wave' feminism as evangelical heritage, there is a tendency to reinforce modified spiritual womanhood within the evangelical dialogue with the women's movement. Egalitarian arguments advanced by Langley and Storkey regarding partnership in ministry – like 'first-wave' arguments asserting New Morality – may become linked with, and undermined by, a continuing norm of modified spiritual womanhood, in which moral qualities of nurture are vested in women, and leadership qualities are vested in men.

*Dialogue Terminated* The dialogue came to an abrupt halt with the premature end to the BCC working party in April 1984. Though individual churches replied to Morley's subsequent request for finances by stating they had set up their own CWMC groups (Morley, 1985a), the ability to make independent evaluation of the effectiveness of denominational initiatives was lost. The working party brief to identify priorities and to offer co-ordination between denominations was also left unfulfilled. The BCC working party report of March 1984 had begun to assess women's marginalisation by analysis of pastoral care, mission, unity and theology (BCC, 1984:3-7; Morley, 1985a), but this analysis was in turn marginalised by the project's premature end.

One positive outcome of the BCC working party was that Morley's contact with groups across the Christian women's movement, in her role as Secretary, helped to cement links between them. After the demise of the working party, Morley pursued questions raised in the final BCC report, together with her enquiry into feminine imagery for God, through her active involvement with Women in Theology. However, apart from Morley and Mertes, and also Maizel regarding revision of the Methodist hymnbook, there was no widespread participation by women involved in the Christian women's movement in the WCC-initiated dialogue. Effort expended by the Christian women's movement as a whole within the WCC dialogue was less widespread than that of Catholic women responding to the Laity Commission and the National Pastoral Congress.

*The Ecumenical Decade of the Churches in Solidarity with Women* The launch of this WCC decade, in 1988 – towards the end of the CWIRES period – illuminates the relation between the churches and the women's movement at this time. Initiative towards the decade came from an Ecumenical Forum of European Christian Women (EFECW). We find the second CWIRES phase networks, Catholic Women's Network and Women in Theology, acting in concert with other groups, just as elements within the incipient movement of 1978 had worked together during Canon Sr Mary Michael's tour. An Ecumenical Forum of Christian Women's Organisations (EFCWO) drew the groups together. Jean Mayland – member of the Movement for the Ordination of Women (MOW), organiser of the 1981 WCC Sheffield conference and member of the BCC working party – played a co-ordinating role, also serving as President of the EFECW. CWN and WIT participated in the organisation of a Liverpool conference, Celebrating Women, to launch the new decade (EFCWO, 1987). The Quaker Women's Group and Unitarian Women's Group were also involved, alongside women active in MOW, EFECW and the BCC Women's Inter-Church Committee.

Where the CWMC dialogue had risen on a high tide of Christian women's optimism in the early CWIRES period, and the churches for a time took note of this force, by the launch of the new decade in 1988, there was less responsiveness within the denominational Church hierarchies. The CWMC language of complementarity and partnership resonated with reinvigorated 'first-wave' feminism, with its demand for full inclusion of women, and their distinctive gifts, in church life. Despite the radicalising influence of Sexism in the Seventies, the subsequent CWMC programme was largely conducted in terms arising from 'first-wave' Church feminism.

In contrast, the language of 'churches acting in solidarity with women' demanded a response to 'second-wave' feminism, by taking action in solidarity with women in their autonomy, mutuality and sexuality. The churches were as unready for this demand in 1988 as they had been to receive 'first-wave' demands in the second decade of the century. The Ecumenical Decade began, as it was to continue, with women organising events largely attended by women, on the margins of mainstream church life.

Thus the sense of anticipation expressed in the 1979 CWIRES information sheet, over the role of the WCC study in bringing change in the position of women in the church, was not realised in any dramatic way. By the mid-1980s, the aspirations of women involved in the Christian women's movement, towards the rehabilitation of Eve within the denominational churches, had undergone a shift from optimism to realism within the WCC CWMC dialogue, thus mirroring events in post-Vatican II Catholic renewal.

We now turn to the third current, the Anglican ordination debate, where we find a similar shift from optimism to realism.

*The Anglican Ordination Debate*

Within the Anglican Church, the women's ordination debate dominated the dialogue between church and women's movement. The debate marked out a public arena for the attempted rehabilitation of Eve. In 1981, writing in *Dispossessed Daughters of Eve*, Dowell and Hurcombe give testimony to the 'devastating let-down' in the November 1978 vote against the ordination of women (1987:vii). Their book attempts to bridge the gulf between the Church and 'the longing for change among Christian women' (1987:xiii), by bringing their feminism – newly-'forced' into connection with church, liturgy and theology (1987:vii) – into the longstanding dialogue between advocates and opponents of women's ordination. Feminists caught up in the debate were well aware of the wider issues at stake. Thus Dowell and Hurcombe refer to women's ordination as 'the tip of an iceberg' (1987:xiv) while, for Furlong, the issue is the 'narrow end' of a lively Church of England debate, the 'broad end' involving a full evaluation of women within Church and society (1984:1). However, in the Anglican Church, women's ordination provided Christian women's principal focus.

As, during the early 1980s, windows of opportunity had closed in both post-Vatican II Catholic renewal and the WCC dialogue, so, and concurrently, the Anglican ordination debate reached a stasis. Thus Dowell and Hurcombe, in the preface to the second edition of their book, refer to 'alarming retrenchments' and 'polarisation' within the debate (1987:xiv) in the years since 1981. Similarly, polarisation is already implied when Furlong states that *Feminine in the Church* attempts to bring into play 'new ideas' concerning the wider issues surrounding women's ordination, rather than to 'reiterate defensive postures' (1984;1). By 1988, in *Mirror to the Church*, Furlong's aim in highlighting women's continuing exclusion (1988:1) is to draw attention to the gulf between the Church and Christian women, rather than to bridge it. Thus the new optimism of the early MOW years gave way to a renewed realism over retrenchment and polarisation in the third current also.

In sum, within the first three currents – post-Vatican II Catholic renewal, the WCC Community of Women and Men in the Church programme, and the Anglican ordination debate – windows of opportunity for change in the position of women in the churches had closed by the mid-1980s. With this closure, the optimism of women in the Christian women's movement over the imminence of change gradually gave way to realism over the strength of resistance. The moment of optimism broadly coincided with the first phase of the CWIRES period, and the moment of realism with the second CWIRES phase.

However, we now turn our attention to the pivotal role played by the Movement for the Ordination of Women (MOW) campaign, in keeping alive Christian women's aspirations towards change in their position in the churches. Despite the shift to realism, this focus perpetuated the rehabilitative ethos of the Christian women's movement during the second CWIRES phase.

## The Anglican Ordination Debate and Christian Women's Rehabilitative Ethos

Retrenchment and polarisation, though never threatening the continuation of the MOW campaign, necessarily raised the question as to its most appropriate stance and strategy. The MOW newsletter, *Chrysalis*, reflects varying views within the MOW spectrum, in response to the stalemate reached. Thus Jean Mayland argues for patient waiting for a positive Synod decision (*Chrysalis* (Oct 1987):4-5), whereas Penny Nairne, a Lay Reader, describes herself as 'radicalised', and prepared to enter grey areas of canonical legality (*Chrysalis* (Oct 1987):5-6).

When Hannah Ward states that she is now committed to building up women's Christian community, irrespective of Synod decisions (*Chrysalis* (Oct 1987):6-7), she speaks as an active member of both Women in Theology (WIT) and the St Hilda Community. As member of MOW, Ward also remains fully committed to the Anglican campaign for women's ordination within the Church of England.

Ward epitomises the combination of the two elements held together during the second CWIRES phase, in both WIT and the Catholic Women's Network (CWN). At the end of this chapter, we will examine more closely the building up of Christian women's 'community' in the second CWIRES phase. Here our concern is the influence of the Anglican ordination campaign – a constant presence throughout the CWIRES period – on the ethos of the wider Christian women's movement. We have already seen the pivotal effect of the pre-MOW Anglican campaign as a focal point for the incipient movement during 1978, bringing disparate groups, emerging within the four currents in the churches, into a single Christian women's movement. Solidarity with the Anglican campaign continued to strengthen links between the groups, fostered through CWIRES and the *CF NL*: it is significant that MOW too came out of the ferment of 1978.

The continuing presence of the MOW campaign, during the second CWIRES phase, as the impetus from the first two currents declined, helped to maintain a focus on change in the position of women in the churches, alongside Ward's project of building up women's Christian community. Thus commitment to the rehabilitation of Eve within the institutional churches was maintained. When CWN and WIT built up their group life, inclusive of liturgical experiment, they created a model of reformed church, not an alternative to the institutional churches.

In the face of retrenchment and polarisation, the Anglican campaign lent hope to members of CWN who sought change in the Catholic Church, but faced retrenchment. CWN and WIT, together with the Oxford Christian feminists, the Quaker Women's Group and Unitarian Women's Group, continued to act as a single Christian women's movement during the second CWIRES phase.

Our enquiry now moves to activity initiated by Christian women towards their denominations: the Quaker and Unitarian traditions, and the Catholic and Anglican denominational churches. We begin with the traditions of Old Dissent, turning our attention to the Quaker Women's Group (QWG) and the Unitarian Women's Group (UWG). Both arose in direct response to the British women's movement, within dissenting denominations with a radical ethos, rather than within one the first three currents in the churches. In consequence, they are largely absent from our preceding discussion of the shift from optimism to realism within these currents. The openness of both groups towards Womanspirit, noted in the previous chapter, can here be placed in the context of relations, respectively, between the Quaker Women's Group with the Society of Friends, and the Unitarian Women's Group with the Unitarian denomination.

## Christian Women's Activity in Relation to the Denominational Churches

### *'Second-wave' Feminism in Traditions of Old Dissent: the QWG and UWG in Relation to Their Respective Denominations*

There are many similarities in relations between the QWG and UWG with, respectively, the Society of Friends, and the Unitarian denomination. The two groups were formed in a similar way: the QWG at the 1978 Yearly Meeting of the Society of Friends and the UWG at the 1981 Unitarian General Assembly. From their inception, each group had a strong awareness of both the 'second-wave' women's movement and – through contact with CWIRES and the *CF NL* – the 'second-wave' Christian feminism of the early CWIRES years.

Both groups identified a feminist tradition within their own denomination, and saw their activity as continuing this tradition within the context of the British 'second-wave' women's movement. Finally, QWG and UWG openness to Womanspirit is congruent with these denominational traditions of 'Old Dissent', where the emphasis is upon the Inner Light of religious experience and religious freethought, in contrast with the imposition of traditional Christian doctrine.

Early in the group's life, Sarah Darby observed the group to be 'a Quaker branch of the feminist movement, rather than a feminist branch of the Quaker movement' (*QWG NL* 10 (Jan 1982):3). Thus the group was involved in feminist consciousness-raising and in activism outside the Society of Friends, notably at Greenham. In contrast to demands made by Christian women in the Roman Catholic, Anglican and Methodist churches, sexist language was the sole issue raised by the QWG within their denomination, in the form of an Advice and Query presented to Yearly Meeting (YM) in 1981 (QWG, 1980). However, the inception of the group at YM, QWG preparation of a meeting, exhibition or event on successive years at YM, and the use of Quaker meeting houses for QWG meetings, anchored the group within the life of the Society of Friends.

*Bringing the Invisible into the Light* (QWG, 1986) – the QWG presentation given on 3 Aug 1986 in the Great Hall of the University of Exeter – presented the Society of Friends with an expression of 'second-wave' feminist consciousness of sexism, rather than with an agenda for reform of the Society.[2] The Swarthmore presentation also portrays a contradictory record in the historical relationship between Quakerism and feminism. Thus the involvement of Quakers in 'first-wave' feminism is cited. Lucretia Mott, the American abolitionist and women's suffragist, is named, and encouragement given to Josephine Butler, by English Quakers – Margaret Tanner, Mary Carpenter and Mary Priestman – to assume leadership of the campaign to abolish the Contagious Diseases Acts, is noted (QWG, 1986:1-3). Butler's acknowledgement of the leading Quaker role in the campaign is cited (QWG, 1986:1).

However, the QWG conclude the Society has yet to respond to Lucretia Mott's feminist challenge (QWG, 1986:9-10). They portray a Quaker 'herstory' of women's equality – given form in separate nineteenth century Women's and Men's Yearly meetings – which is gradually displaced in the exercise of male temporal authority, following the 'logical and inevitable' (QWG, 1986:18) amalgamation of women's and men's meetings (QWG, 1986:11-20).

British Quaker 'first-wave' feminism relied upon spiritual womanhood as vehicle, rather than emphasising women's rights. The British feminist heritage, claimed by the QWG, was ambivalent as, although it made a major contribution to the expansion of the female mission beyond the home, it was nevertheless heavily implicated in spiritual womanhood. In consequence, Quaker women were subject to male temporal authority. 'Second-wave' QWG feminists emphatically reject these terms, even as they lay claim to an assumed heritage of women's equality, embodied in once-separate women's and men's meetings.

Women in the UWG were in a different relationship to their denomination. As we saw in chapter two, there is a Unitarian tradition of 'first-wave' 'Church' – or denominational – feminism, given that the first women ordained to the ministry belonged within the Unitarian denomination. Given the strength of this Unitarian tradition in women's ministry, it is unsurprising that Unitarian ministers – Helen Campbell, Joy Croft, Celia Midgely and later Ann Arthur – were prominent among the UWG membership, and that it was a minister, Helen Campbell, who first raised women's issues within Unitarianism.

Nineteenth century Unitarian women also played a prominent role in the development of the women's rights tradition, albeit without abandoning the feminist vehicle of spiritual womanhood. Thus members of the UWG had a stronger feminist tradition to invoke in comparison with QWG feminists. Whereas Catholic and Anglican adherents to reinvigorated 'first-wave' Church feminism were typically wary of new 'second-wave' feminist concerns, members of the UWG were open to these, just as their forebears had been open to women's rights activism.

Taken together, these two aspects of a Unitarian feminist tradition led to UWG members working more closely within the life of the Unitarian denomination, and in individual churches where members were active. The founding concerns of the UWG – exploration of being both women and Unitarians; exploration of the effects of sexism in Church and society; education of Unitarians about sexism; re-evaluation within Unitarian thought of emotions, experience and caring, and recovery of contributions made by earlier generations of Unitarian women (*UWG NL* 1 (Jan 1982):2-3) – show both 'second-wave' consciousness and orientation towards the mainstream of their denomination.

This same combination of 'second-wave' consciousness and denominational orientation is expressed in *Growing Together: the Report of the Unitarian Working Party on Feminist Theology* (UWPFT) (UWPFT, 1985). Set up by the 1982 Unitarian General Assembly, with a brief 'to consider the possible implications of feminist theology in connection with the thought and worship of our denomination' (UWPFT, 1985:ii). UWG members, Joy Croft, Ann Arthur and Celia Midgley, were appointed to the group, with Croft as convenor, together with Arthur Long, Peter Sampson and Len Smith.

The report gives working definitions of feminism, as adding women's perspectives to the traditional male half of the story, and of feminist theology as consciousness-raising, use of inclusive language, deeper appreciation of feminine values and concepts, and doing, sharing and experiencing as well as rational discussion (UWPFT, 1985:ii-iv). In chapter five, we will encounter a similar experiential approach to feminist theology in Judith Jenner's initiative, the Feminist Theology Project. *Growing Together* also presents research findings on the tradition of women's ministry, and the nineteenth century Unitarian contribution to female emancipation (UWPFT, 1985:4.3-4.6). The report shows awareness of developments outside Unitarianism, in its inclusion of: Sara Maitland's article, reprinted from the BU publication, *"Free Indeed"?* (UWPFT, 1985:1.1-1.5); material from the SCM study pack, *Women and the Christian Future* (UWPFT, 1985:6.2-6.3) and excerpts from Morley's BCC report (UWPFT, 1985:7.1-7.5). UWG members also contributed to a second Unitarian publication, produced in 1987: *Crying Out Loud,* 'an anthology of poetry and prose on women's spiritual insight and experience' (*UWG NL* 15 (Aug 1987):2).

UWG members were active within individual church congregations. Thus Dawn Buckle writes of leading a service 'about feminism' in her local congregation, drawing on material supplied by Ann Arthur and Joy Croft (*UWG NL* 2 (Apr 1982):2-3), while Celia Kerr led a 'Bread and Roses' service, to coincide with the ordination of Audrey Vincent in Cleveland, Ohio, and as a tribute to Vincent's ministerial training in Edinburgh (*UWG NL* 14 (Sep 1986):2-3). Kerr reflects on the restrictive aspects of gender expectations, and asserted that Vincent had given the congregation both the Bread of the (male) Logos and the Roses of 'womanly enthusiasm, love and laughter' (*UWG NL* 14 (Sep 1986):2-3). In addition, a sermon given by Helen Campbell (1981) provides an example of feminist preaching to a Unitarian congregation. During her stay in Edinburgh, Audrey Vincent introduced the UWG to an American text, *Feminism From the*

*Pulpit,* written by a Californian minister, Marjorie Newlin Leeming (*UWG NL* 2 (Apr 1982):4).

This UWG combination of 'second-wave' consciousness and denominational orientation thus contrasts with the 'second-wave' consciousness of the QWG. Whereas the principal QWG engagement with their denomination, in the Swarthmore presentation, was made in response to an invitation from the Society of Friends, *Growing Together* was the result of a UWG initiative taken within the Unitarian denomination.

In sum, Christian women who belonged within the traditions of Old Dissent, were more open to 'second-wave' feminism than were many women in the Free Churches, due to respective Quaker and Unitarian feminist traditions. Members of the QWG and UWG were drawn towards the broader Christian women's movement by 'second-wave' Christian feminist consciousness, rather than by commitment to a rehabilitation of Eve within their denominations. However, the close involvement of members of the UWG in the life and structures of the Unitarian denomination provided a model of the rehabilitation of Eve within the denominational churches.

Moving on from Old Dissent, we explore a Christian women's theme which emerged strongly during the initial CWIRES phase, thus coincident with both the moment of optimism and the diffusion of 'second-wave' Christian feminist consciousness: Christian feminism as gift to the Church.

### *Optimism: Christian Women Bear Gifts to the Church*

During the moment of optimism, some Christian women – like their 'first-wave' forebears – came to see their movement as bringing valuable gifts to the church. Sara Maitland's words, from *Map of the New Country,* appearing as the second epigraph to this chapter, show that liturgical expression of 'second-wave' Christian feminist consciousness was crucial in this bearing of gifts. Our investigation thus moves to the development of liturgy within the 'second-wave' Christian feminism of the initial CWIRES phase. From this vantage point we will interpret Christian women's gifts to the Church, as expressive of optimism concerning change in the position of women in the churches.

*Christian Women's Liturgy* Liturgical experiment developed within post-Vatican II Catholic renewal (Pratt, 1994:18-19). Following the November 1978 synod vote, Una Kroll encouraged a similar process within the Anglican ordination campaign, urging full use of existing opportunities for developing and experimenting with liturgy, including the ministry of women (*CPG NL* (Nov 1978); Maitland, 1983:112). Kroll's overriding concern was to resist the American Episcopalian precedent of illegal ordinations of women. Thus liturgical experiment within, respectively, the Anglican women's ordination current, and the post-Vatican II Catholic renewal current, developed as a legitimate aspect of institutional life in both the Anglican and Roman Catholic churches.

Movement for the Ordination of Women (MOW) vigils at ordination services, which included 'wilderness liturgies' such as a responsorial sermon written by Bridget Rees (B. Rees, 1983; MOW, 1984b), reflected the development of experimental liturgy within MOW. Liturgy, together with pilgrimages and meetings, marked the widespread MOW celebration of the work and ministry of women through the ages in May 1983 at Juliantide (MOW, 1983a, 1983b). A Eucharist of thanksgiving at Westminster Abbey marked the fortieth anniversary of the ordination of Li Tim Oi, in Jan 1984. Li Tim Oi was present, and Canon Sr. Mary Michael Simpson and Kath Burn were among the thirteen women ordained abroad who attended the service (MOW, 1984a). A sister event, in Sheffield, celebrated with an experimental liturgy.

The Christian Parity Group (CPG) had pioneered Kroll's project. Services of rejoicing for the ministry of Christian women were organised for a day of action, on 29 April 1979, initiated by American Catholics in support of women's ordination. When the Roman Catholic Feminists (RCFs) described events organised in Britain for that day – in which they also participated – their newsletter used more combative language than the *CPG NL*: their text refers to solidarity with the American Eucharistic Hunger Strike held in protest against male-domination of church structures (*RCF NL* 10 (Mar 1979):2; *RCF NL* 11 (Apr 1979):1-2). Similarly, when Dowell and Hurcombe describe the burning of texts expressing misogynistic traditions (1987:95-6) during one liturgy organised at St Botolph's, Aldgate in London, it is clear that a 'second-wave' Christian feminist consciousness had found liturgical expression.

In addition to its clarity over sexism in the church, 'second-wave' Christian feminist liturgy celebrated women's autonomy, mutuality and sexuality. These elements were present in a liturgy created by the East London Christian Feminists, in which Jesus' washing of the disciples' feet was sacramentalised, by women washing each others hands (Maitland, 1983:110). Janet Morley, who was involved in its creation, had begun to appreciate the potential of experimental liturgy during her participation in the Feminist Theology Project (FTP, N.d.:2.3,4.3-4.4).

The regular Oxford Women's Mass, or Liturgy, which began in 1981, grew from Oxford Christian women's activity in Blackfriars-supported Catholic renewal, SCM-initiated 'second-wave' Christian feminism, and the Anglican ordination debate. Before its inception, Kroll had spoken on liturgy to the Oxford Christian feminist group founded by Garcia. Whereas the fate of the 'Women and Justice' leaflet at the NPC was significant for West's turn towards women's liturgy (West, 1982b:5), Garcia comments on the response met when seeking reform in Anglican liturgical practice: 'We took our harp to the party, and no-one asked us to play – again and again' (discussion in Women's Liturgy Group, 14 March 1999). In the monthly liturgy, a space was created where such 'play' was encouraged and appreciated.

Women's preaching was a central focus in the early years of the liturgy (West, 1982b:6; Oxford Christian Women's Group, 1982e). Sermons were preached by women active in the loose network of Oxford Christian Women's Groups (OCWG) – Catholics, Anglicans and even one Quaker, Sarah Darby – and by guest speakers.

Dominican support, in supplying a celebrant for the Mass (West, 1982b:6), gradually gave way to a group celebration in the form of an agape. In the early years, the Women's Mass was radical in its inclusion of women as preachers and assistants in eucharistic celebration, rather than in liturgical experiment: liturgies were traditional in both style and language (OCWG, 1981b, 1981c, 1981d). Liz Campbell's 'Women's Agape Celebration' (OCWG, 1982d) then became the most frequently used form.

A more experimental approach to the Oxford Women's Liturgy grew through creating liturgy for the Greenham Peace Vigil, and through encounter with 'second-wave' liturgies created elsewhere in the Christian women's movement. During liturgies shared at Christian feminist conferences, including WIT or CWN study days, members of the Oxford network experienced practices such as anointing one another with oil as a mutual blessing, and symbolising tension and difference by marking boundaries with ribbon.

The Oxford Women's Liturgy became a focal point for the Oxford network, beyond meetings of its constituent groups. West (1982b:6,13) describes the inauguration of the liturgy as marking a shift from consciousness-raising group to eucharistic community as the focus of Oxford Christian feminist activity. For many other participants, the monthly liturgy allowed the expression of raised 'second-wave' feminist consciousness, initially in feminist preaching within a traditional 'Women's Mass', and later in experimental liturgies, combining new feminist symbols with traditional Christian symbolism. Thus Liz Campbell, speaking on 'Women's Spirituality' in the BBC Radio 4 series, *Lighten Our Darkness* (Campbell, 1984), could describe the Oxford Women's Liturgy as expressive of a distinctive women's spirituality, arising from women's exclusion within the church. Her insight returns us to Maitland's opening epigraph.

*Liturgy as Crucible for Women's Gifts*[3] With the Oxford Women's Liturgy in mind, Maitland envisages women's experience of 'the desert' as bringing forth 'creative and innovative worship' which women bring as gifts into 'the institutional church' (1983:111). In Maitland's perception, Christian women's gifts are combined with a perceived prophetic critique of the church, recalling it to its 'own roots' and to its 'central truth', which is Jesus (1983:5).

Maitland's core claim is that the 'mutual ministry' of 'an institutional model of sisterhood', which 'is already becoming a historical, material reality' [among Christian women], is needed by the churches (1983:48). Given their experience of this model, it is Christian women's 'service... ministry ...[and] collective vocation' to offer it to the whole body (Maitland, 1983:48).

Maitland's reference to 'sisterhood' signals the effects of 'second-wave' concern with women's autonomy, mutuality and sexuality. Maitland was involved in CWIRES and the network based around the *Christian Feminist Newsletter* as she wrote these words (Maitland, 1983:43-5,153,208). It is therefore likely that her concept of 'mutual ministry' is modelled on groups of the early CWIRES years – in particular on the 'creative and innovative' practices of the Oxford Women's Liturgy. It is likely also that her 'institutional model of sisterhood' implies the style of CWIRES and of the annual *CF NL* Christian feminist conferences. Her model of sisterhood is created by the 'special blend of love and ['second-wave' feminist] theory' of 'un-structured, anti-hierarchic' ['second-wave'] Christian feminist groups (1983:45). Thus it is from the 'relaxed and shared space' of 'rich, informal, affectionate and supportive' groups – her experience of the Oxford Women's Theology Seminar (Maitland, 1984) – with their associated innovative creativity that the model of mutual ministry derives. Given the association of creativity with sexuality in post-'second-wave' theory, affirmation of women's sexuality is implied in Maitland's observation.

Other Christian women make similar arguments. Thus Janet Morley affirms mutuality in the group life of the East London Christian Feminists (1980) and, in a Women's Liturgy sermon, offers the mutuality of Christian feminist groups as a valuable model for the wider Christian community (1982a). Similarly, Kate Mertes draws on Morley's sermon to offer the collective authority practised in Christian feminist groups as a useful model for denominational and ecumenical groups (1984d). When Ann Hoad – soon to become the first vice-chair of WIT – in *Feminine in the Church*, depicts the gifts offered by Christian feminists as the pain and desire of women (Hoad, 1984:116) she, too, implies women's sexuality among the 'hidden treasures' (Hoad, 1984:115) of women's autonomy and mutuality.

*Dispossessed Daughters of Eve* (Dowell and Hurcombe, 1987 [1981]) is offered in the spirit of gift, in its attempt to bridge the gulf between church and Christian women's aspirations. The related notion of Christian women's prophecy to the institutional churches as an aspect of their gift (Morley, 1982:7, 1983a:10; Mertes, 1984d:6; Hoad, 1984:116) is developed in this earlier text. Thus Dowell and Hurcombe portray themselves as prophetic voices identified, in their opening pages, with the unheeded Cassandra, (1987:1), concluding their book with the hopeful image of the Apollo of patriarchal religion rebuilding, with Cassandra, both 'temple' and world (1987:131). Maitland, too, refers to women's 'prophetic insight into mutual ministry' (1983:47), claiming that the model of mutual ministry is 'infinitely nearer to the most orthodox Christian teachings on community and ministry', than current church practices (1983:45).

Thus, during the moment of optimism, these Christian women's writings show confidence in the value to the institutional churches of gifts born in the crucible of 'second-wave' Christian feminist consciousness-raising, given liturgical expression, and offered to the churches so that they may, in Maitland's image, enter a 'New Country'. It is also clear that when Christian women claim a prophetic role, they also speak with confidence of '*re*building' (Dowell and Hurcombe, 1987:131), '*re*claiming' (Morley, 1982:7), or of providing 'a way *back* to the Christian truth of service, equality, justice and the renunciation of power through love' (Maitland, 1983:190, 193-4). It is in this sense – that the way *forward* to the New Country, which they map, is also the way *back* to a kernel of Christian truth – that Christian women claim their insights as prophetic for the institutional churches, and thus as central to renewal.

It will be helpful to relate this notion of prophetic gift to our earlier findings on differing strategies for the rehabilitation of Eve within the churches. The notion of gift evokes 'first-wave' Church feminism with its reliance upon the superior moral qualities associated with spiritual womanhood. As we have seen, this tradition, with its emphasis upon women's service within the churches, was perpetuated in the discourse of the Catholic feminine and in aspects of Anglican explorations at Hartlebury, also reflected in the broader ordination debate.

Where does Maitland, with her 'service... ministry ...[and] collective vocation' of Christian women, stand in relation to this 'first-wave heritage? Maitland includes within her remit a wide swathe of women's activities in the churches. In her broad study of lay women's church organisations, women's religious communities, admission of women to ministry and priesthood and women employed by the churches, she examines the continuing tradition of women's service to the Church. She credits this tradition with allowing women's capacities to be proven and with fostering women's aspirations for inclusion in substantive, as opposed to auxiliary, Church ministry. However, when Maitland speaks of Christian women making prophetic critique of the institutional Church, which goes beyond a mere demand for inclusion of women within existing structures (1983:4-5), she in effect shifts away from these 'first-wave', Church feminist, grounds of argument.

Yet Maitland blurs the distinction she effectively makes between 'first-wave' notions of women's service to the church, and affirmation of 'second-wave' women's autonomy, mutuality and sexuality, as a prophetic calling to the church. Thus she lumps old and new together when she claims that women, throughout the swathe of activity surveyed, 'can build a base from which they can demonstrate new patterns of mutual ministry' (1983:29). Her rendering of Christian women's 'gift' attempts to superimpose the experience of 'second-wave' Christian feminists upon the older tradition of women's service. In contrast, the analysis offered here differentiates reinvigorated 'first-wave' strands of Church feminism from newer 'second-wave' elements.

Morley implies a similar differentiation (1985b). When she describes women in ministry as choosing between a distinct – subordinate – feminine ministry, taking male ministry as their model, or taking up a feminist position (1985b:1-4), Morley makes explicit the link between feminine gifts – offered in terms of spiritual womanhood – and women's subordination. In contrast, her (recommended) 'feminist' position, with its rejection of male ministry as model, implies women's autonomy, mutuality and sexuality as resources for women's ministry.

In sum, the notion of Christian women's gift to the Church is derived from 'first-wave' Church feminist proffering the qualities of spiritual womanhood to the church. However, the new concerns of 'second-wave' feminism, emerging alongside the revitalisation of 'first-wave' strands, injected new challenge into the received notion of gift to the church. In offering 'second-wave' models of mutual ministry and collective authority as prophetic gift, with the associated agenda for change within the institutional churches, 'first-wave' vocabulary was adapted to express 'second-wave' demands.

During the second CWIRES phase, as optimism gave way to realism, a new conception of the Catholic Women's Network and Women in Theology as models of reformed church displaced the notion of gift. The move to realism was also evident in renewed critique of the churches. Our final task in this chapter is to evaluate these later developments in Christian women's activity.

*Realism: Renewed Critique of the Church*

The moment of realism stimulated a renewed critique of the Catholic Church, reiterating themes, of clerical hierarchy and exclusion of women and sexuality, found in Condren's 1970s writings (Walsh, McEwan and Brewster, 1987; Thomas, 1992; Mertes, 1986; McEwan, 1991). Compared to Condren's dissemination of her ideas through *Movement* pamphlets, by the late 1980s a number of speakers addressed a growing audience, either through adult-education courses on women and religion, such as the *Wisdom of Christian Feminism* series, or at study days, mainly organised by CWN and/or WIT. Some of these papers were simultaneously published (Walsh, McEwan and Brewster, 1987; Fedouloff, 1988, 1989), others subsequently appeared in early editions of the journal, *Feminist Theology*.

Yet this critique of celibate clerical authority is closer to the Anglican feminist awareness of male distrust of women's sexuality, which we encountered in chapter three and the opening pages of this chapter, than to Condren's radical consciousness. Where Condren looked beyond the institutional church to the construction of her envisaged feminized 'beautitudinal community' (1978a), renewed critique of the latter 1980s is focused on reform of the institutional Catholic Church. Thus Walsh advocates rethinking compulsory clerical celibacy and the place of sexuality (Walsh, McEwan and Brewster, 1987:7-8), and McEwan calls for an end to the celibate priesthood (Walsh, McEwan and Brewster, 1987: 28-9), while Brewster challenges the Church to recognise and address its misogyny (Walsh, McEwan and Brewster, 1987:39).

In similar vein, Thomas, in advocating return to an egalitarian Christ-based model of authority, of early Church origins, appeals for reform of the institutional Catholic Church (1992). Mertes' analysis of post-Vatican II revisions to canon law, as perpetuating women's longstanding exclusion from jurisdiction, concerns women's status within the institutional Catholic Church (1986:5). In addition, a number of Catholic and Anglican commentators seek improved employment conditions for women working for the churches, criticising the underlying attitudes to women revealed by existing practices. Thus, writing in *Women Experiencing Church*, Thomas, 'Willis' and McEwan document their experience of being undervalued and underpaid while in church employment (McEwan, 1991:89-95, 107-129, 131-9), while similar themes are pursued elsewhere by Robson, (in Furlong, 1988a:106-123), McCurry (in Furlong, 1988a:39-46) and Borrowdale (1988, 1989).

*Women Experiencing Church* (McEwan, 1991) documents women's alienation from the church, so constructing a powerful case for reform. The CWN Position Paper and the earlier report of the Laity Commission (CWN, 1987:1; LC, 1982:9) refer to Catholic women's felt alienation from their church, and many contributors were involved in CWN or its wider Catholic renewal milieu: McEwan's text assembles detailed evidence of their felt alienation. McEwan herself speaks in terms, similar to Condren's, of 'transformation' rather than reformation of religion (1991:247) being more important than the survival of the institution (1991:252), anticipating that the systemic problem revealed in the writings (1991:254) will be resolved in the rise of 'feminist liberation faith communities' (1991:263). However, McEwan's desire for democratic reform underlies her argument (1991:248-9) that women's oppression within the Church stems from required obedience to canon law, which women have no part in making or amending. Her vision of women's equal participation in the churches (1991:261) sets the context for her reference to the building of democratic, inclusive communities of mutually affirming 'believers' (1991:252) wherein ordained/lay distinctions are ended (1991:250-1). When McEwan envisions social transformation through building inclusive neighbourhood communities, concerned with global issues of peace and development (1991:263:4) she demonstrates a radical consciousness similar to that of Condren. But when she urges the churches to respond to this historic moment (1991:263), on the grounds that 'Christianity is a fundamentally egalitarian religion' capable of working through democratic institutions (1991:264), she frames her vision in terms which are close to the predominant rehabilitative ethos of the British Christian women's movement. Sociological interpretation – Condren's key tool in analysis of the oppressive social effects of Christian religion – is valued by McEwan also, but as a means of building partnership between Church and society (1991:264). In effect, though McEwan, among Christian women writers of the second CWIRES phase, comes closest to Condren's radical revisioning, she is closer still to Anglican renditions of Christian women's prophetic gift. McEwan's 'gift' is a blueprint for a reformed Catholic Church relocated within a new – democratic and just – global order.

We have established that the moment of realism was expressed in renewed Christian women's critique of the Catholic, and to a lesser extent Anglican, Church, but that the direction of this critique was towards reform of the institutional churches. We conclude our investigation of Christian women's activity by encountering Catholic Women's Network (CWN) and Women in Theology (WIT) as models of a reformed church.

### *CWN and WIT as Models of a Reformed Church*

The second CWIRES phase saw the decline of the earlier network, based on the *Christian Feminist Newsletter* during the initial CWIRES phase, while CWN and WIT grew in strength. In addition, Christian women's activity continued in Oxford, in the Quaker Women's Group and in the Unitarian Women's Group throughout the CWIRES period. CWN and WIT embodied models of a reformed church, receptive to the 'prophetic' insights of 'second-wave' Christian feminism. The two networks demonstrated in their group life how their respective churches would be transformed by receiving this gift.

CWN and WIT modelled a rehabilitation of Eve within the institutional churches, thus – despite the climate of realism – perpetuating the rehabilitative ethos of the British Christian women's movement, by pursuing reformist aims within their respective churches. 'Second-wave' Christian feminist consciousness, now common currency within the Christian women's movement, was yoked with this rehabilitative project of full inclusion of women within the institutional churches. Comparison of the liturgical life of CWN and WIT with that of the North American Women-Church movement – developing concurrently with the second CWIRES phase – reveals the centrality of this rehabilitative ethos.

Liturgy was a founding CWN concern, the new network drawing upon members' experience of liturgical experiment within the Catholic renewal movement, and in the life of the South London Christian Feminists. The newsletter gives ample evidence of the liturgical life of CWN. The 1987 launch of the Association for Inclusive Language (AIL) also drew upon Catholic women's liturgy, both within CWN and prior to the formation of the network. Educational material was distributed by the Christian Women's Resource Centre in Dulwich, London, with the support of various groups, including the St Joan's International Alliance (AIL, 1988a, 1988b:1).

Similarly, when WIT was formed, members brought with them prior experience of 'second-wave' liturgical experiment in the Feminist Theology Project, the East London Christian Feminists and in the Movement for the Ordination of Women. Facilitated by Janet Morley, Hannah Ward and Bridget Rees, liturgy assumed a central part in the life of WIT. A WIT liturgy group was established, with Morley and Ward as active members, and a framework for liturgy created in the group, included in the mailing (WIT, N.d), encouraged sharing and reporting of group liturgies. Liturgical material was later gathered from a variety of sources for a joint WIT and MOW publication, *Celebrating Women* (Morley and Ward, 1986). The breadth of interest in feminist liturgical material is clear from the sale of 2,500 copies in two months, followed by a reprint and production of a mainstream American edition. Unsurprisingly, WIT was invited to prepare liturgy for the launch of the WCC Ecumenical Decade (WIT, 1988:1). This process was continued in the life of the experimental worship group, formed as an offshoot of MOW: the St Hilda Community (SHC) (Fageol, 1989; Furlong, 1991a), as reflected in the collection of liturgies, *Women Included* (SHC, 1991).

Janet Morley also published *All Desires Known* (1988a), an anthology of her own liturgical writing. Morley's substantial contribution to liturgical development, in WIT and the St Hilda Community, reflected her resolve to counter the negative formative effect of exclusive liturgical language (Morley, 1984a; Morley and Ward, 1986:2) by positive liturgical celebration of the feminine, and of women as in the image of God (Morley, 1984a:70).

Thus a legacy of published material gives testimony to the abundance of liturgical experiment. Much ground had been travelled since Una Kroll's exhortation in 1978, and Maitland's comment on the lack of 'widely disseminated spirituality and worship tools' in Britain (1983:112). Liturgies not only use inclusive language, but also embody 'second-wave' Christian feminist consciousness, affirming women's autonomy, mutuality and sexuality through mutual leadership, and through expression of sensuality and emotion.

Women in the British Christian women's movement were aware of the developing North American Women-Church movement. Certainly, Rosemary Radford Ruether, author of *Women-Church* (1988), was well known to British Christian women. Her articles appeared in 1970s SCM publications and in the *CWN NL* of the 1980s; she was principal speaker at the 1983 conference, Women, Men and Power (Women, Men and Power, 1983) and other events; and she supported the incipient CWN (Murphy, 1992:42,44). The joint CWN/WIT organised debate between Ruether and Hampson further raised Ruether's profile within the British movement (Hampson and Ruether, 1987).

More specifically, an article written by Ruether on Women-Church appeared in the newsletter (*CWN NL* 17 (Dec 1988):6-7). Members of WIT were also aware of Women-Church, as Bridget Rees attended their conference at Cincinnati in October 1987, with WIT support. In addition, Suzanne Fageol refers to the St Hilda Community using a *Women-Church* liturgy (Fageol, 1991:21).

However, despite similarities between concurrent British and North American developments, there was a fundamental difference between the British rehabilitative ethos and the emphasis upon separate organisation in Ruether's portrait of the North American Women-Church movement. Certainly, comparison of liturgical language in *Women-Church* (Ruether, 1988) with texts from *Celebrating Women* (Morley and Ward, 1986) or *Women Included* (St Hilda Community, 1991) reveals close similarities, in the expression of 'second-wave' consciousness of women's autonomy, mutuality and sexuality. Ann Hoad – an architect of WIT's vision of theological education (Hoad, 1983) – places the 'Christian feminist community' both 'within and on the edge of the Church' (1984:114) just as Ruether places Women-Church both within and on the edges of existing church institutions (1988:62).

Yet when Hoad writes that separatism diminishes the Christian feminist community (1984:114), she expresses the British project – reiterated in the title of the St Hilda Community publication *Women Included* – that women be fully included in the institutional church. In contrast, Ruether speaks of a necessary separatist stage (1988:59-60), represented in the independent bases of Women-Church, which are outside institutional control (1988:62-3). Hoad's talk of Christian feminist striving on the margins (1984:114) speaks of renewal of the institution. But when Ruether speaks of Women-Church, as a (separatist) feminist exodus within and on the edge of church, she speaks of a feminist counterculture (1988:62) located within the tradition of 'spirit-filled community'.

For Ruether, 'spirit-filled community' and 'historical institution' are conflicting models of church in tension (1988:11-23), whereas Hoad (1984:113-4) explicitly rejects Ruether's countercultural strategy, in favour of working for the inclusion of women within the priesthood of the Church of England. Thus 'second-wave' Christian feminist liturgy, even as it celebrates women's autonomy, mutuality and sexuality, seeks to return the fruits of this autonomous creation to the institutional churches. The debate about women's ministry further illustrates the contrast between British Christian women's project of rehabilitative inclusion, and Women-Church separatism (Hoad, 1984; Williams in Furlong, 1984:11-27; J. and G.

Muddiman in Peberdy, 1988:30-48; Baker in Peberdy, 1988:49-60). CWN and WIT are not the different model of church, found in Ruether's portrait of Women-Church, but models of reformed institutional churches.

**Conclusion**

We began by establishing Eve as figure of Christian women's decisive stand on women's sexuality, and with it autonomy and mutuality, siting the origin of this figure within the Anglican women's ordination debate. We have also seen how the Anglican debate and campaign provided a pivotal focus for the wider Christian women's movement. This focal position accounts for the wider resonance of the Eve figure within the movement.

The chapter marks out a significant shift in mood over the CWIRES period. We have seen the optimism, over the immanence of change in the position of women in the churches – already palpable in 1978 – gradually subsiding during the first CWIRES phase, 1978-1983. As optimism subsided, realism concerning resistance to change set the dominant tone of the latter CWIRES years, 1984-1990.

During the moment of optimism, there was a plethora of activity regarding the position of women in the churches. We have reviewed the mass of evidence of initiatives taken both in denominational structures and by Christian women. It is principally at this point in the book that the impact of the second current in the churches, the WCC Community of Women and Men in the Church programme, comes under scrutiny. The shift from optimism to realism frames our investigation of Christian women as bearers of gifts to the Church. We have seen how 'first-wave' and 'second-wave' notions are entwined in this notion, how Christian women's liturgy acted as crucible, shaping the 'gift', and how the networks of the second CWIRES phase, Catholic Women's Network, and Women in Theology, embodied models of reformed denominational churches. Our investigation of the renewed critique, particularly of the Catholic Church, which accompanied the shift to realism, found the criticism marked with Christian women's rehabilitative ethos.

We have also clarified that Christian women in the Quaker and Unitarian traditions of Old Dissent sat most lightly to the rehabilitative project. We have investigated the respective feminist heritage within the two traditions, and established that feminist consciousness sustained their link with the wider Christian women's movement and – together with their grounding in traditions that sit lightly to doctrine – opened their way also to links with Womanspirit.

We now turn to our next task. Bearing within our grasp the complexities of Christian women's consciousness and activity, we focus our gaze on Christian women's theology. Here the Eve theme appears more frequently, in writings that grapple with the ambiguous position of women in Christian theology. In chapter five, we investigate Eve and Christian women's theology.

## Notes

[1] In the Church of Scotland, eldership and ministry were opened to women in 1966 and 1968 respectively (COS, 1980:2). The component churches of the URC had opened ordination to women in 1918 and 1962 respectively: see Fletcher (1989: 129,152-3) re the 1918 ordination of Constance Todd for ministry at the Congregationalist City Temple, and Nash (1979:118) for reference to Congregationalist to Presbyterian ordinations of women. The BU had accepted women for ordination from the 1920s, and in 1974 had discontinued the separate ministry of deaconesses (*WS* (Jan-Mar 1976):11).

[2] The influence of the WCC dialogue is evident in John Crompton – the Quaker member of the BCC working group – requesting written contributions from the QWG on the position of women in the Society of Friends (*QWG NL* 15 (April 1983):4-5). It seems likely that the Swarthmore invitation arose in the context of the BCC dialogue.

[3] I am indebted to Jan Berry for the notion of liturgy as crucible.

# Chapter 5

# Eve and Christian Women's Theology

> Feminist theology challenges the distorted pictures of God, Christ and the Holy Spirit which have been transmitted through the historical process of patriarchy. It suggests that there is a hitherto unrevealed truth about the nature of God, the person of Christ and the work of the Holy Spirit which has been missed, suppressed and ignored because male theologians have predominated in the institutions of the Churches. ...
>
> A theology which proclaims by its words and deeds that women and men are different from each other yet alike by reasons of their shared humanity is a whole theology. We need to move eagerly towards the day when we can transcend our differences and discover that, 'in Christ there is …neither male nor female, for you are all one in Christ Jesus' (Kroll, 1976:20).

It is clear from our explorations, in the previous two chapters, that significant developments in Christian women's consciousness and activity occurred during the 1970s and 1980s, and that these can usefully be understood as an attempted rehabilitation of Eve within the institutional churches. Our task in this chapter is to examine the theological explorations, which accompanied this surge in Christian women's consciousness and activity. We find that the principal aim of Christian women's theology was to provide theological justification for the rehabilitation of Eve within the Christian churches, by correcting patriarchal distortions of the foundational gospel message.

In chapter six, we will investigate the relationship between the emergent genre of feminist theology, concurrently being crafted by (principally) North American feminist theologians, and Christian women's theology. The term 'feminist theology' was also current in Britain, though – as we will see – in every case this usage was derived from North American sources. We begin this chapter by clarifying British use of the term 'feminist theology' in relation to the Christian women's consciousness and activity, analysed in the previous two chapters, and to the Christian women's theology investigated in the current chapter.

Our next task is to identify the dominant concern of British Christian women's theology as the offering of a corrective to the patriarchal theology of the institutional churches: the citation from an early article by Una Kroll encapsulates this corrective – and rehabilitative – intention. However, we also detect a minority genre, which keeps a critical distance from the central rehabilitative project. We then make a comprehensive analysis of theological arguments involving Eve, as she appears within the CWIRES material. We examine both the minority of writings, which go beyond the predominant rehabilitative project, and the majority of writings, which contribute to it. Our exploration at this point follows on from the opening discussion of chapter four, 'Eve and Christian Women's Activity', where we established the importance of Eve, as figure of Christian women's rehabilitative project within the churches.

The chapter closes with detailed attention to the outstanding contributions of two women, whose committed participation in the Christian women's movement of the 1970s and 1980s included original theological writing, namely Janet Morley and Angela West. We have already encountered the breadth of Morley's involvement in the constituent groups of the Christian women's movement, culminating in her formative role within Women in Theology. Similarly, we have noted West's presence in early Catholic women's initiatives in Oxford, and in the subsequent development of the Oxford Women's Liturgy, with its pivotal role in wider Oxford Christian feminist activity.

We find that Morley gives expression to the dominant ethos of the Christian women's movement, where 'second-wave' Christian feminist consciousness is harnessed to the rehabilitative project of women's full inclusion within the institutional churches. In contrast, West's is an original and distinctive voice, always informed by the lively theological debate centring on the Blackfriars Dominican community, and by her experiences in Pax Christi and at Greenham, as well as by her involvement with the Christian women's movement. Though West's is a significant Christian women's voice, her theology is never a straightforward expression of Catholic concerns within the mainstream of the British Christian women's movement.

We turn to the British appearance of the term 'feminist theology'. Our aim is to clarify the interrelation of 'feminist theology' with Christian women's consciousness, activity and theology.

## 'Feminist Theology' and Christian Women's Consciousness, Activity and Theology

For many Christian women, the term feminist theology was remote from their central concern with the position of women in the churches. For others, feminist theology was associated with their consciousness, or with their activity, rather than with theological writings – our main preoccupation in this chapter. Others still saw their own theological writings as feminist theology. Thus four stances towards feminist theology co-exist within the Christian women's movement: detachment from feminist theology; feminist theology as consciousness; feminist theology as activity; and feminist theology as theological writing. Here we will examine, in turn, examples of the first three stances.

Jo Garcia provides a significant example of a prominent member of the Christian women's movement, who was little interested in the development of feminist theology. Garcia was closely associated with the broader British women's movement, with the development of 'second-wave' Christian feminist consciousness, and – as the first Vice-Moderator of the Movement for the

Ordination of Women – was also committed to Christian women's activity. Yet she chose not to join Women in Theology (WIT). Garcia explained her reason as being that WIT was concerned with the development of feminist theology and, as a feminist sociologist, she had little interest in this area (interview with Jo Garcia, 14 March, 1999). Jo Garcia, like Angela West, was a member of the Oxford Christian Feminist Group, which at one point in its development acted as a Writing Group. After the group article (Nash et al, 1978), Garcia's writing took the form of *Walking on the Water* (Garcia and Maitland, 1983), where writings on women's spirituality were collected, not only from the members of the Christian women's movement, but also from women active in the wider British women's movement. In contrast, West's subsequent writing was theological.

Feminist theology as 'second-wave' Christian feminist consciousness-raising (CR) finds its strongest example in the writings of Judith Jenner, and the practice of the Feminist Theology Project (FTP). As we saw in chapter three, Jenner's approach replicated a pre-existing North American model of feminist theology, which was documented in the Grailville papers. Here, feminist theology is understood as a form of 'doing theology' from women's experience. Thus, describing her initial response to reading the Grailville papers, Jenner states the material 'blew [her] mind', as it comprised 'impressions from women ... within varying theological traditions [who] were struggling to free them for women by listening to each other. Women had come together to do theology beginning with their experience as women' (FTP, N.d.:1.1).

Though Jenner made clear the implications for Church and theology of her radical feminist approach, (1978b, 1979) her main energies were directed towards neither reformist activism within the institutional churches, nor dialogue with 'male' theology. Rather, feminist theology, like CR, effected the rehabilitation of women by restoration to a new constructive capacity, reflected in the 'new creation' of feminist theology (FTP, N.d.:7.2). For Jenner, the varied FTP methodology is a means of generating change in women themselves, which will drive change in broader social reality. Thus she describes the 'new creation' of feminist theology as women redefining themselves and defining their own alternatives within social analysis, biblical knowledge and Church traditions (FTP, N.d.:7.4). Thus, for Jenner, feminist theology as CR is sufficient: that is what it is all about.

Jenner was not deeply committed to defending the naming of this new process as 'theology': the process is more significant than its naming. One aim of the fixed-term FTP, and of its publication, was to encourage similar experimentation in other groups. While experience within the FTP was diffused through the 'second-wave' CR groups of the initial CWIRES phase, the Plymouth Women's Theology Group apart, there is no evidence that these groups perceived their group life in Jenner's terms as 'feminist theology'. Nonetheless, given its high profile within the Christian women's movement, the FTP brought the term feminist theology into currency during the CWIRES period.

Similar Quaker and Unitarian versions of feminist theology as CR are evident. Quaker suspicion of theology (*QWG NL* 15 (Apr 1983):1) affected the Quaker

Women's Group stance towards feminist theology. However, the group responded to the method of 'doing theology' from women's life experiences, affirming the approach as a 'creative source of spiritual growth and action' (*QWG NL* 15 (Apr 1983):1). Similarly, the preface to *Growing Together* emphasises the congruence between 'doing theology' and openness to members' religious experience in the Unitarian tradition, and informs its readers that 'feminist theology is something to do, not to read about' (Unitarian Working Party on Feminist Theology, 1985:ii).

Aspects of Christian women's activity may – like consciousness – be taken to comprise feminist theology. Thus the efforts of the Unitarian working party on feminist theology – given the denominational status of the group – may be construed as Christian women's activity. Similarly, articulation of 'second-wave' Christian feminism as gift to the church, renewed critique of the church, and development of models of a reformed church in the life of the Catholic Women's Network and Women in Theology are, in one sense, feminist theology. These Christian women's activities, and associated writings, are expressions of a practical feminist theology, which is concerned to reform the faith communities comprising the institutional churches.

Liturgy provides a meeting point between feminist theology as consciousness, activity and theology. The development of liturgy informed by Christian women's 'second-wave' feminist consciousness, in the context of their activity in the churches, acted as a crucible in which was generated Christian women's theological reflection on God in relation to women and men. We will investigate the theological fruits of this process, in the liturgical writing of Janet Morley, later in this chapter.

Having clarified meanings of the term feminist theology within the Christian women's movement, in relation to consciousness and activity, we proceed to our analysis of Christian women's theology. We examine evidence that the prime concern was to offer a corrective to the patriarchal theology of the institutional churches. But first, we encounter the minority genre, which mounted a critique of institutional religion accompanied by re-visioning and construction of alternatives, thus maintaining a distance from the central rehabilitative project of the movement.

## Christian Women's Theology: Minority and Majority Projects Distinguished

### *A Minority Genre: Critique of Institutional Religion*

Writings by Judith Jenner and Elaine Willis are significant to this minority genre of critique of institutional religion, while doctoral research, by Mary Condren and Jacqueline Field-Bibb, makes substantial contributions. *Our Stories* (FTP, N.d.) gives the fullest available account of Jenner's understanding and practice of feminist theology.[1] For Jenner, the 'new creation' of feminist theology does not involve the rehabilitation of women within the institutional churches. Elaine Willis, whose catalytic effect in the emergence of lesbian identity within the Christian women's movement we encountered in chapter three, makes a powerful statement of lesbian iconoclasm in her contribution to *Sex and God*, 'Nothing is Sacred, All is Profane' (1987). For Willis, lesbian identity involves a reconstruction of spirituality, in which she smashes internalised, repressive icons of the Godhead, and refuses further talk to or of God (1987:107-8). Thus Willis severs her previous links with Christian theology and practice, so locating herself outside the Christian women's rehabilitative project.

Condren's radical critique also exceeds the aims of the rehabilitative project within the institutional churches. As Eve features large in Condren's work, we will examine her writings in the course of our later discussion of the theological development of the Christian women's Eve theme. Field-Bibb brings a critical consciousness, similar to that of Condren, to her doctoral research on women's move towards priesthood in the Methodist, Anglican and Roman Catholic churches. However, given her research subject, and the publication of her work before the Anglican ordination of women was authorised, Field-Bibb's *Women Towards Priesthood* (1991) has been widely misconstrued as a contribution to the Anglican (and Catholic) ordination debate, and thus as sharing Christian women's rehabilitative aim. It is more accurate to view Field-Bibb's project as exceeding this focused end.

Certainly Field-Bibb applies sociological and psychoanalytic critical theory to analyse opposition to the priesting of women within the three churches. She also uses Elisabeth Schussler Fiorenza's critical feminist theology as interpretative tool to elucidate 'the theologising of dominant trends to impede the liberating impulses of women' (Field-Bibb, 1991:247). Yet Field-Bibb's study begins with the encounter between Jesus and the Samaritan woman (John 4), where Jesus states that the hour will come when she will worship neither on this mountain nor in Jerusalem (1991:1). Significantly, Field-Bibb interprets Jesus' statement as meaning that 'Religion and its liturgical celebration are delocalised and *deinstitutionalised*' [my emphasis] (1991:1). For Field-Bibb, this Johannine exchange contradicts the Christian institution and its roles acting as 'focus and locus' of the praxis of Jesus in the lives of women (1991:1). Clearly her intention is not the rehabilitation of women within the institutional churches. Rather, her study traces the movement of women towards ministry 'under the Enlightenment banner of equality', analysing both male resistance to this move, and the reason for the chosen direction of women's impetus, given its contradiction of the Johannine exchange (1991:1).

Field-Bibb concludes, from her multi-faceted analysis, that androcentric institutions require femininity to act as differentiator, so placing women – who are culturally constructed as feminine – as 'a constant "other" to this socio-historical androcentric trajectory' (1991:266).[2] She argues that the male priest as *persona Christi* relies upon female representation of the Church and upon mariology, and that woman is therefore required to differentiate the divine (Field-Bibb, 1991:264-5): 'Man becomes God, and woman provides the difference' (1991:265). Field-Bibb finds little of value for women in this traditional Catholicism symbolism, recommending instead that women make use of the superior symbols offered by feminist theology, based on feminist theory, which allows 'a rediscovery and re-presentation of symbols' of women's identity (1991:267).

Field-Bibb's argument makes clear that she recommends women move beyond the 'focus and locus' of the institutional church. Her notion of feminist theology is thus closer to that of Condren, than to the central corrective project of the Christian women's movement. Field-Bibb's contention that, in the various reviews of her book, Condren alone understood her purpose, lends support to this interpretation (interview with Jacqueline Field-Bibb, 4 Jan 1997; Condren, 1992).

However, Jenner, Willis, Condren and Field-Bibb – together with Sheila Briggs and Martha Lynne Nielson, whose writings appear in our following consideration of the theological Eve theme – represent a minority genre within the Christian women's movement. The majority of theological writings offer their corrective of Christian theology from within the institutional churches.

### *The Majority Concern: a Corrective to Patriarchal Theology*

The epigraph chosen for this chapter is taken from Una Kroll's contribution to the SCM pamphlet offering an introduction to feminist theology: *For the Banished Children of Eve*. In the first paragraph cited, Kroll takes Condren's proffered term, feminist theology, and crafts a clear statement of its function as corrective to patriarchal distortions to truth about the nature of God, resulting from male dominance within the institutional church. Her (pre-CWIRES) statement anticipates a widespread consensus within Christian women's theology, which was to grow during the CWIRES period. However, Kroll's following paragraph is more representative of her predominantly 'first-wave' approach, and her reliance upon the WCC-derived terminology of complementarity and partnership. During the CWIRES period, as we will see, alternative strategies take shape to Kroll's recommended notion of shared humanity, where sexual difference is transcended in Christ.

Feminist theology as corrective of patriarchal theology is implied in 'weak' form, in arguments stressing the benefits of the inclusion of women in the churches, and in strong form, beginning with Kroll's 1976 article. We will look first at three instances of the weak form. Thus Collins asserts that the rejection of women leads to an uncreative spirituality, associated with the stones of tradition. The ordination of women will act as necessary corrective, by incorporating women's new consciousness into the bread of living faith offered by the Church (1978:5).

Similarly, feminist theology as corrective is implied in the notion of Christian feminism as gift to the church (Maitland, 1983; Morley, 1982; Mertes, 1984d). Recovery of women's traditions within Christianity – the unacknowledged legacy of women's gifts to the Church – was also a significant form of corrective activity (Morris, 1973, Unitarian Working Party on Feminist Theology, 1985:4.3-4.4; Fedouloff, 1989:18-21, 22-4; Pinsent, 1992). It is noticeable that recovery of women's traditions by British Christian women concentrate on women within the institutional churches. In contrast, Ruether (1992; Ruether and McLaughlin, 1979) stresses the importance of recovery from within marginalised 'spirit-filled' traditions, as well as from within institutional structures.

Three 'strong' arguments appear, in addition to that of Kroll. Thus, in *Dispossessed Daughters of Eve*, Dowell and Hurcombe name feminist theology as corrective to patriarchal theology and practice (1987:55-68). Similarly Mertes, in 'Tensions Between Theologians and the Women's Movement', describes a contest between feminist theology and traditional theology (Mertes, 1984c:1).

An exchange between West and Jenner, during the life of the Feminist Theology Project (FTP), led West to a comparable definition of feminist theology as corrective to patriarchal theology. Taking issue with the experimental style of the FTP, West exhorts feminists to favour coherent thought and effective organisation, arguing that Jenner's all-embracing approach endangers the potential of feminist theology as a tool to counter patriarchal theology (FTP, N.d.:7.4). West warns that the inclusive FTP process risks reducing feminists to 'the silence of incoherence' and confirming 'the powerlessness that patriarchy confers on us' (CW correspondence, 31 Jan 1983 [unlisted]:2).[3] In an earlier text, West perceives feminist theology as emergent from women's groups (West and Ruston, 1981:459-60). We will return to West's distinctive contribution to feminist theology in the final section of the chapter.

We will now investigate Eve, as a significant figure in the attempt, by Christian women's theology, to correct patriarchal distortions underlying the exclusion of women in the institutional churches. We return to the Eve theme within the CWIRES material, examining its use within Christian women's theology. We clarify first Eve's appearance in the minority genre, working outside the project of the rehabilitation of women within the institutional churches, then turn to the majority project, where the two aspects of Kroll's original definition of feminist theology are both perpetuated and countered.

## Eve in Christian Women's Theology

Within the CWIRES references, Eve appears as partner in four different couples. She is paired with the Goddess in radical feminist interpretation of the Genesis myth – the foundation myth of patriarchy. Eve is paired with Adam, as woman with man, in other interpretations of the Genesis myth, both traditional and alternative. Eve is also paired with Mary. This pairing works at two different levels: of sexual politics and theology. Thus, as we saw in chapter four, within the context of the Anglican ordination debate, it was clear to both Furlong and Harvey that male-generated Eve/Mary images act together as a means of male control to define, and so confine, women. Harvey attempts to reverse this dynamic, by urging women to redefine these images as empowering.

The Eve/Mary pair also acts at a theological level, in that it is implicated in Christian theology of sin and salvation: the divine Christ is depicted as second Adam, while the human Mary appears as second Eve. Finally, Eve is paired with Christ. This fourth pair is related to both Eve/Adam and Eve/Mary, as this fourth couple unambiguously includes Eve in the salvation of Christ. Eve thus stands in the same relation to Christ as Adam, so securing for woman an equivalent position in the economy of salvation, and challenging the gendered pairings of Adam with Christ and Eve with Mary. Our following discussion will reveal the significance of Eve's appearance in these four couples.

CWIRES Eve references fall into three groups. The first group comprises radical Christian critique, where the Eve/Mary pair is repudiated, and the second, writings from the boundary between the Christian women's movement and Womanspirit, where Eve is coupled with the Goddess. The third group comprises writings associated with the central Christian women's project, where Eve appears as a positive figure of women's rehabilitation within Christian theology, whether in the Eve/Mary pair, the Eve/Adam pair or the Eve/Christ pair. We begin with the first sitings of Eve, within pre-CWIRES radical Christian critique.

### *Eve in Pre-CWIRES Radical Christian Critique*

The earliest CWIRES Eve reference is Martha Lynne Nielson's 'Eve Got the First Bite!' where Nielson exhorts Churchmen, theologians and scions of Adam 'to restore to the daughters of Eve their rightful authority to speak up in church: to become Priestesses of the Divine' (1972). Though clearly linked to the issue of women's ordination, Nielson's tone is hardly rehabilitative. Her brief article implies the radical feminist view that women's lack of authority derives from male control, exerted through the image of Eve.

Likewise, Sheila Briggs criticises the 'Eve-Mary syndrome', in her contribution to *For The Banished Children of Eve* (1976:5). For Briggs, in formulating her critique of natural law as sanctioning women's inferiority and subjection, Eve symbolises woman as both 'submissive body in the order of nature and "revolting" body in the disorder of sin' (1976:2). Though Mary acts as a counter-balance to Eve, Briggs finds Mary wanting as a liberating symbol, as women cannot emulate the immaculately conceived Virgin Mother of God, and must therefore remain associated with Eve (1976:5). For Briggs, Catholic mariology is a conservative anti-feminist attempt to restrict women to motherhood (1976:5), while Eve is fixed by the traditional interpretation of the Genesis myth. Briggs' radical Catholic critique implies the alternative reading of the Genesis myth as foundation myth of patriarchy, and her argument runs directly counter to Harvey's proffering of Eve/Mary images as potentially empowering for women.

When Condren offered her introduction to feminist theology to 'the banished children of Eve' (1976b), the radical feminist interpretation of the Genesis myth is implied in her analysis also. Condren's radical critique seeks to expose the function of the myth in sexual politics, which banishes women, not only from the altar, but also from humankind and the world of thought (1976a). Condren fronts her pamphlet with a graphic portraying an enlarged woman's face barred, by an iron grille, from the altar, superimposed upon a picture of bishops, gathered to celebrate the mass. Condren's chosen title creates a new association with the familiar words of the Catholic prayer, *Salve Regina.*[4] It is clear from the cover image that 'the banished children of Eve' are her daughters, rather than her sons.

Condren's intention was, surely, to make a powerful representation of the continuing effects, upon women, of the traditional interpretation of the Genesis myth, with its culpable Eve. In tune with other radical feminists, Condren invites women to exercise a new constructive capacity – the former capacity of the Goddess as figure of women's sexuality and power being implied in her writings – rather than to engage in a 'rehabilitation of Eve'.

Neither alternative interpretations of Genesis, nor a reconfigured Eve, are relevant to the construction of her envisioned feminized 'beautitudinal community' (1978a). The nineteenth century 'vindication of the woman Eve' provides Condren's starting point, as – like Daly in *Beyond God the Father* (1973:69) – she cites, as epigraph, a passage from Elizabeth Cady Stanton's *The Women's Bible*, where Eve figures as the unnamed woman:

> Take the snake, the fruit-tree and the woman from the tableau, and we have no Fall, no frowning Judge, no Inferno, no everlasting punishment – hence no need of a Savior. Thus the bottom falls out of the whole Christian theology. Here is the reason why in all the Biblical researches and higher criticisms, the scholars never touch the position of women (cited in Condren, 1976a :21).

But, true to her radical feminist perspective, having exposed the function of this male-contrived Eve, Condren's attention turns elsewhere. Having identified notions of original sin [associated with Eve] and atoning sacrifice [of Christ] as the main elements in 'the theological underpinning of the social and ecclesiastical subjugation of women' (Condren, 1976a:21), Condren's trajectory contrasts markedly with that – to be encountered later in the chapter – in the third group of Christian women's writings, who likewise respond to this central insight.

As in Briggs, use of the unrealisable ideal of the Virgin Mother to facilitate male control of women, is crucial to Condren's critique of the Eve/Mary pair. Unlike Briggs, Condren is fascinated by the prior demise of the powerful Mother Goddess (1976a:22-23), leading her to analyse Eve/Mary in relation to the Goddess. Eve, the Goddess and Mary represent three ages in the religious history of Ireland in her Harvard doctoral thesis, published as *The Serpent and the Goddess: Women, Religion and Power in Celtic Ireland* (1989). Condren's radical feminist pairing of Eve and the Goddess focuses attention on the figure of the Goddess, submerged beneath patriarchal Christian religion, by identifying the serpent of the Genesis myth as representative of Goddess religion (1989:11), and the development of patriarchy in Ireland as the 'age of Eve' (1989:23-43). The Eve/Goddess pairing is superseded by the Eve/Mary pair. However, the demise of the Goddess is incomplete, as her female power lends an ambiguity to the imposed unrealisable Virgin Mother ideal.

There are echoes of Daly (1973: 81-96), in Condren's work. Daly's direct influence on Condren, as on Jenner, was atypical in the development of British Christian women's theology, given the mismatch between Daly's call to exodus from Christianity (Loades, 1990:186-7), and the rehabilitative ethos of the British movement. Also atypical of the movement was any serious engagement with the British Womanspirit movement, with its focus on the Goddess. But, as we saw in chapter three, members of the Quaker Women's Group (QWG), and the Unitarian Women's Group (UWG) participated in Womanspirit events and reflected on the figure of the Goddess, while Jen Duncan and Linda Hurcombe showed an openness to the Goddess. We now investigate sitings of Eve on the boundary between the Christian women's movement and Womanspirit.

*Eve on the Boundary Between the Christian Women's Movement and Womanspirit*

Moving to the second group of writings, British Womanspirit research – consistent with radical feminist alternative interpretation of the Genesis myth – focused on the Goddess, and ignored Eve. Concurrent with Condren's research, British Goddess traditions were recovered at sites such as Avebury, Silbury Hill and Glastonbury (Matriarchy Study Group *Politics of Matriarchy* 1978:40-4,55-57; *Arachne* 1 (May Eve 1983):4-10,11-13,19-26).

Asphodel embarked on research into the Goddess and the Hebrew and Christian Bible (Long, 1994:20). Though sharing Womanspirit disregard of Eve, she links Lilith to the Goddess (*Arachne,* 2 (Imbolc 1985):26-30). In her book, *In a Chariot Drawn by Lions* (Long, 1992), Asphodel discerns traces of Greek and Middle Eastern Wisdom Goddesses in the Hebrew bible, the apocryphal Book of the Wisdom of Solomon and – of significance for Christian feminists – in the New Testament equation of Jesus with Wisdom. Asphodel's focus on this Sophia theme was to be developed more fully in the post-1990 feminist theology of Fiorenza (1995) and Johnson (1996).

There is also a connection to be found between Asphodel's research and writings from the minority of Christian women who explored Womanspirit ideas and practices. The Swarthmore piece, 'Encountering Eve' (QWG, 1986:30-2), shows QWG openness to both Christianity and Womanspirit. Christian orientation is expressed in the positive figure of Eve. In this alternative interpretation, Eve has outgrown the garden and the parental God and, in reaching for the apple, chooses to partake in divine Wisdom (QWG, 1986:30-2). No mention is made of the Goddess, but in her sharing in divine Wisdom, the QWG Eve touches the Christian Sophia who, in Asphodel's work, draws from a recovered Goddess tradition. Attention given to the female divine within the Swarthmore text, in QWG openness to Womanspirit, and in portrayal of the serpent (Goddess) as a positive influence (QWG, 1986:30-2) expresses the liminal position of the QWG. In this pairing of Eve with the Goddess, the Christian women's positive Eve is affirmed, in contrast with the repudiation of Eve in radical feminism.

Similarly, both Eve and the Goddess feature in the life of the UWG. Thus, in a Unitarian sermon, Helen Campbell (1981) argues that Adam and Eve together made a free act in eating the apple, which contemporary men and women need to repeat. She contrasts the older creation story, 'male and female he created them', alike in the image of God, with the dominant portrayal of God as male and the longstanding denigration of women due to the portrayal of Eve as seductress and temptress. In contrast, in *Growing Together*, Ann Arthur parallels Asphodel's line of enquiry by locating the Goddess tradition submerged in the Old Testament record, then retrieving a neglected female imagery in the bible, medieval Christianity and the Unitarian tradition (Unitarian Working Party on Feminist Theology, 1985:3.1-3.4). Arthur thus demonstrates a Unitarian liminality between Christianity and Womanspirit, which is similar to that of the QWG.

However, there is a significant difference between Campbell's reference to Eve, and the Quaker 'Encountering Eve'. The QWG Eve is typical of her appearance in the third group of writings, associated with the central Christian women's movement. In 'Encountering Eve', the focus is upon Eve alone, who figures the 'second-wave' specificity of women's autonomy, mutuality and sexuality. In contrast, Campbell's assertion of Eve's equality with Adam is expressive of a continuing strand of Unitarian 'first-wave' Church feminism. Campbell and Arthur together demonstrate the juxtaposition of continuing 'first-wave' Church feminism with newer 'second-wave' feminist consciousness in UWG theological reflection.

In her editorial introduction to *Sex and God* (1987:1), Hurcombe effectively reiterates the radical feminist alternative interpretation of the Genesis creation myth as foundation myth of patriarchy. Despite the Eve theme in her first book (Dowell and Hurcombe, 1987), neither Hurcombe nor any of her contributors make any reference to Eve: the Christian women's Eve is absent from Hurcombe's 'exploration of the spiritual aspects of the erotic' (1987:6). This fact, together with a noticeable incongruity in contributions to the book between a timid Christian women's stance and a transgressive radical feminist style, suggests that the Anglican Eve does not function, like the Goddess, as figure of sexual power. Rather, Anglican women's declarations of a positive sexuality – whether in Collins' benign optimism or in the anti-misogynist trajectory that begins with Court – have the specific aim of redressing the traditional (exclusive) interpretation of the Genesis myth. By reconfiguring Eve and her sexuality, these positive declarations make an alternative interpretation, which is inclusive of women. The Anglican Eve is a symbol crafted to advance the Anglican ordination campaign: her symbolic power as figure of women's sexuality is muted in comparison with that of the Goddess.

Hurcombe's flirtation with Womanspirit reflects her attraction towards the female spiritual power promised in the rehabilitative strategy of the Womanspirit movement. However, with the exception of the Unitarian denomination, this expression of feminist spirituality sits uneasily with the central Christian women's project of the rehabilitation of woman within the institutional churches, to which Hurcombe remained committed. We now examine the third group of writings, which comprise the core of Christian women's theology, written from the mainstream of the movement.

### *Eve in the Central Rehabilitative Project of the Christian Women's Movement*

Eve figures large in these mainstream writings. Condren's evocative cover image to *For the Banished Children of Eve*, of woman – child of Eve – barred from the altar, invited identification with Eve on the part of contemporary women seeking women's access to the altar as priests. In the opening pages of chapter four, we examined evidence for the growth in this identification, first among Anglican women and then more widely. In addition, Condren's coining of the Catholic petition on behalf of 'the banished children of Eve' inaugurated – in contrast to her own project – a mainstream theological rehabilitation of Eve, as an aspect of the rehabilitation of Christian women within the churches.

Collins' assertion that 'the rehabilitation of Eve' is timely (1978:5) marks the beginning of Eve's theological rehabilitation as an aspect of the central Christian women's project. The Christian women's Eve appears paired, respectively, with Adam, Mary and Christ. We investigate, first, the minor CWIRES theme of the Eve/Mary pair, in which – contrasting with radical Christian critique – the positive potential, of both Eve and Mary, is explored.

This theme finds its strongest expression in writings by Ruth Windle and Susan Harvey. 'The Feminine in the Pattern of Redemption' (Windle, 1978) was published in the same year that Collins wrote 'The Rehabilitation of Eve'. Windle advances a parallel argument to that of Collins, when she portrays Eve as facilitating human maturity. Similarly, Harvey discovers a mythical Eve of Genesis who is 'a searching, thoughtful, openminded figure, willing to risk and ... to be accountable for her actions', an Eve who is silent in the remainder of the Old Testament (1981:4). Thus both Windle and Harvey contribute to the figuring of a positive British Christian women's Eve. Yet their pairing of Eve with Mary is atypical within Christian women's theology.

A further atypical feature is that both Windle and Harvey assert a redemptive role for Mary, in contrast to other (infrequent) mariological CWIRES references, where no mention is made of Eve and Mary appears as proponent of justice and representative of redeemed humanity, but not as a redemptive figure (*RCF NL* 15 (Feb 1980):2-3; Maitland, 1984:10; Robson, 1982f ,1984:134-7; Fedouloff, 1989 :24-6). Thus Harvey claims that in the doctrine of Mary as Virgin, Mother and Second Eve is found an image of equivalent power to that of Christ as Second Adam (1981:9-10), and Windle recommends Eve be recognised as sister of Mary, in the redemption of humanity (1978). Windle thus goes beyond Harvey in her rehabilitation of Eve, by restoring Eve to a redemptive role, equivalent to that of Mary. We will return to these British glimpses of Eve and Mary as female redemptive figures – atypical of the Christian women's movement – in the final chapter, where we locate British Christian women's theology on the wider stage of feminist theology.

At this point we return to the major CWIRES Eve theme in this core group of Christian women's writings. Collins makes an alternative interpretation of the Genesis myth, in which she portrays Eve as a positive figure of the unproblematic association of sexuality with spirituality (1978). However, the evident tension and misogyny concerning women's sexuality, which surfaced during the Anglican debate, revealed Collins' benign strategy for the rehabilitation of Eve as inadequate for the task in hand. The next Anglican appearance of Eve, while agreeing that Eve's rehabilitation is timely, shows an appreciation of the continuing power of the traditional interpretation and its effects within Christian churches and theology.

*Dispossessed Daughters of Eve* (Dowell and Hurcombe 1987) emphasises the importance of contemporary women's connection with Eve, as figured in the traditional interpretation, for their continuing 'dispossession'. Yet, while Dowell and Hurcombe reiterate Nielson's radical insight regarding women's status as daughters of Eve, and their lack of rightful authority, and while their chosen title echoes Condren's 'banished children of Eve', they contribute to the third, core group of writings, which support Christian women's rehabilitation within the churches.

Theologically, Dowell and Hurcombe perceive women's dispossession in terms of the contrast between the baptismal promise of sexual equality, in Galatians 3:28, and biblical portrayal of women's silence and subordination (1987:21-37). Their theological strategy, in support of the Christian women's rehabilitative project, is to claim women's rightful Christian heritage, already promised in the Christian baptismal statement. Christian women's rehabilitation is sought in their restoration to a former capacity of sexual equality, as pledged in this foundational Christian text.

Dowell and Hurcombe's claim thus provides an example of the 'whole theology' advocated in the second paragraph of Kroll's epigraph to this chapter, where the baptismal statement is also invoked. But Dowell and Hurcombe also begin the move beyond Kroll's terms of argument: a move, which is associated with the Anglican Eve. For they are clear that women's dispossession results from women's association with the traditional interpretation of Eve, and their book is a response to its outworking, as revealed within the Anglican ordination debate. Dowell and Hurcombe effectively declare that Eve, as well as Adam, is fully included in the salvation wrought in Christ, wherein the effects of the Fall are cancelled. Their case is tantamount to a claim that the rehabilitation of Eve is already achieved in Christ.

At first sight, Dowell and Hurcombe do not appear to follow Collins in reconfiguring the Eve of Genesis. Yet, when they argue that women's inclusion in the salvation of Christ necessarily challenges the longstanding exclusion of women in silence and subordination, they employ classical Christian orthodoxy to challenge the traditional interpretation of the Genesis myth. Though never stated, their argument implies the notion of a new Eve in Christ, in whom women's enforced exclusion in silence and subordination is contradicted. Implied also is a link between this new redeemed Eve and women's ordination: if Eve is included in the redemption of Christ, then women may be included in the priesthood.

Dowell and Hurcombe – like Collins – focus on Eve, with Adam as unnamed partner in the pair. Dowell and Hurcombe also implicitly pair Eve with Christ, just as Adam is paired in the notion of Christ as 'second Adam'. This pairing displaces Mary's role in redemption, and thus works counter to Mary as the female redemptive figure perceived by Windle and Harvey. Carol Smith and Kate Mertes, in papers given to the Oxford Women's Theology Seminar, develop the implications of these respective pairings of Eve with Adam and Christ. Thus Smith – as yet unaware of the work of the North American feminist theologian, Phyllis Trible (Smith, 1985:19) – makes an original scriptural exegesis of Priestly and

Yahwist versions of the Genesis myth. The aim of Smith's scholarly alternative reading is to subvert its citation in support of women's subordination (1985:3-6). For Smith, the Yahwist account enables exegesis capable of taking issue with traditional interpretations, which perceive the oppression of women as divinely ordained: she moves the onus of proof onto those who seek to perpetuate the subordination of women on the authority of the Genesis creation accounts (1985:18).

Smith's paper therefore lends support to Dowell and Hurcombe's arguments. But where Dowell and Hurcombe argue their case by prioritising the Galatians 3:28 baptismal formula over the primary reading of the Genesis myth, Smith reaches a similar conclusion, concerning biblical portrayal of women's silence and subordination, by exegesis of the Genesis texts alone. Though Smith's argument involves a reconfiguration of Eve which – like Campbell's – affirms Eve's equality with Adam, and contests imputations of Eve's weakness and inferiority (1985:10), the chosen title of her paper, 'On Eve', suggests the influence on Smith of Christian women's identification with the figure of Eve.

Mertes develops more fully Dowell and Hurcombe's embryonic argument concerning Eve's relationship with the salvation of Christ. In 'The Mask of Eve', Mertes takes issue with varied traditional readings of the Genesis myth – including that of Milton – which portray Eve as sexually corrupt sinner (1984a:1-2). Mertes defines the impact of interpretations influenced by these 'masks', when she argues that what people think of Eve, they think of women, so that a Church which accepts the masks of Eve will have difficulty over the full membership of women (1984a:9-10).

Mertes' theological argument is that these masks lead to Eve's exclusion from salvation history, as women's salvation following the Fall depends on her fulfilling her domestic role, rather than on the action of Christ (1984a:7). Elsewhere she describes women as being in the tradition of Eve, and thus in ambiguous relation to Christ (1984b:2), and defines feminist theology as emerging from 'a distinctive school of Christian feminism' which seeks to 'restructure traditional images of women in...Church and...world' according to their faith that women are fully included in the salvation of Christ (Mertes, 1984c:1).

Thus Mertes gives a fuller statement of Christian women's development of classical Christology, from the 'neither male nor female' of Kroll's 'whole theology', to an argument that Eve – and therefore contemporary Christian woman – is specifically included in the salvation of Christ. The orthodoxy of this position is well illustrated by Mary Hayter's, *The New Eve in Christ* (1987). As an Anglican deaconess, Hayter sets out to make a scholarly evaluation of, in the words of her subtitle, 'the use and abuse of the Bible in the debate about women in the Church'. Her stated aim is to steer a middle course between respective conservative and feminist 'misappropriations' of biblical material (Hayter, 1987:2). Hayter affirms the new Eve in Christ as in the image of God (1987:153), while her closing words attest her 'liberty' in Christ (1987:171). When Hayter concludes that New Testament teaching indicates that 'Christ is the pattern for all creatures (Col 1:15-

19), woman included, so that in Christ there is a new Eve as well as a new Adam' (1987:153), she speaks in terms of classical and orthodox Christology.

To sum up our explorations of this third, core group of Christian women's writings, arguments for the inclusion of Eve in the salvation of Christ lie at the heart of the theology emerging from the British Christian women's movement. This move represents a 'rehabilitation of Eve' in terms of the classical Christology expressed in Chalcedonian orthodoxy.

Our next task is to engage more fully with the legacy of 'second-wave' Christian feminist liturgy, in the exemplary writings of Janet Morley. Our particular concern here is with Morley's liturgical expression of the gender specificity of 'women as in the image of God'. Morley's approach contrasts with Kroll's commitment to sexual parity, which, as we saw in chapter three, is perpetuated in the work of Dowell and Hurcombe, Storkey and Mertes. In the previous chapter, we found that, during the second CWIRES phase, in the Catholic Women's Network and Women in Theology, 'second-wave' Christian feminist consciousness was held in tension with the central project of the rehabilitation of Christian women within the institutional churches. We now examine, in Morley's work, the theological fruits of 'second-wave' feminist consciousness as one aspect of Christian women's orthodox rehabilitative theology.

## Janet Morley: Theology in 'Second-Wave' Christian Feminist Liturgy

Ann Loades suggests that resetting the theological stage, by restoring 'lost coins' of feminine aspects of Christian tradition, will lead to changes in liturgy (1987:97). In contrast, for Janet Morley – as for numerous other women who created liturgical material which was later collected for publication – the creating and sharing of liturgy allowed new theological insights. Thus feminist liturgy was a meeting point between Christian women's consciousness, activity and theology.

There is a direct link between the Christian women's rehabilitation of Eve and Morley's theological writing. Mertes is clear that resistance to gender balance in imagery for God, or to interchangeable use of anthropomorphic images, is evidence of misogyny (1984c:7a). She perceives that the linked assertion, that women are less Christ-like than men, is used to justify attempted restriction of feminine activity within the Church (1984c:6). For Mertes, this assertion raises the serious question: 'are women truly, fundamentally, images of God?' (1984c:6-7).

We have seen that Christian women, Mertes among them, gave an affirmative answer to this question in their rehabilitation of Eve. Morley gives the same affirmative answer, which she takes as starting point for her theological construction. Though Eve is unnamed, the Genesis myth – and thus Eve – is implied in 'women in the image of God'. In this sense, Morley's theology is entirely congruent with the wider Christian women's rehabilitation of Eve. To affirm women as in the image of God is necessarily to confirm women as Christ-like, and to include Eve, with Adam, in the salvation of Christ.

Morley's work shows similarities to Hurcombe's project, in *Sex and God* (1987). Both explore sexuality and spirituality in 'second-wave' terms – in contrast to the lingering 'spiritualised sexuality' which we perceived in Robson's Hartlebury explorations – and both seek to escape the evident constraints on Anglican discussions of sexuality within the ordination debate.[5] Both Morley and Hurcombe manifest the 'declaration of a positive women's sexuality' urged by Court (1979:5). In the genre of 'second-wave' Christian feminist liturgy in general, and in Morley's work in particular, this positive declaration finds its strongest statement, celebrating women's autonomy, mutuality and sexuality in terms which are wholly compatible with Christian orthodoxy.

We will examine in more detail Morley's positive liturgical celebration of the feminine and of women as in the image of God (1984a:70), where she allows women's sexuality to be suggestive of language for addressing God (1988b, 1988c). While her unequivocal declaration affirms women's sexuality, and thus necessarily affirms women, it also generates new theological insight. Thus, in the preface to *All Desires Known*, Morley explains her rationale, for exploring neglected feminine biblical imagery, as enabling human experience of women's love to be taken up into imagery for God (1988a:5). Her collects include a prayer to 'God our lover, in whose arms we are held, and by whose passion we are known' (1988a:20). In contrast to Hurcombe's Womanspirit explorations, Morley locates her imaging of God in feminine terms, with its evocation of women's sexuality, within the tradition of Old Testament psalmists and medieval mystics (1988a:5).

Whereas much of the imagery appearing in Morley's liturgical writing is common currency among other liturgies collected for publication, her emphasis on darkness is distinctive. Morley stresses the importance of darkness having been excluded from God alongside the feminine (1988a:xii, 1988b:160, 1988c:30). She finds darkness and sexuality to be linked (Morley, 1988a:xii, 1988c:30), as illustrated in the following liturgical example:

> In darkness and in urgency
> I courted her insistently
> leaning towards the kisses of her mouth,
> yearning to know nothing…
>
> In darkness and security
> she came to me abundantly
> touching the speech and reluctant part of me
> needing to know nothing (Morley, 1988a:106).

As suggested by this selected passage, and by the titles, *All Desires Known* and 'I Desire Her With My Whole Heart' (1988a, 1988b), the notion of 'desire' is important in Morley's liturgical writing. The title of *All Desires Known* reiterates a phrase from a collect in the Book of Common Prayer (Morley, 1988a:1), but when Morley states that the Christian life concerns the integration of desire – personal, political and the longing for God – (1988a:5) her explorations are redolent of 'second-wave' feminist consciousness of sexuality, so bringing new associations into play with the seventeenth century Anglican text.

In addition, Morley argues that it is important to image the dark, difficult and frightening side of God in feminine terms intimate with women's experience, rather than women distancing these aspects as belonging to the 'male' God. In traditional interpretations of the Genesis myth, the danger and darkness of sin, associated with Eve, was to be remedied through the corrective patriarchal formula for the rehabilitation of woman through spiritual womanhood. In contrast, Morley associates danger and darkness with God and thus with woman made in God's image. Darkness is rehabilitated along with sexuality, particularly the long denigrated sexuality of women. Morley's theology thus makes a direct challenge to rehabilitative strategies, which impute superior moral qualities to women, whether in terms of lingering modified spiritual womanhood, or of radical feminist theorising of male violence versus female pacifism.

Thus through creating new liturgical language for speaking *to* God in the feminine, Morley also constructed new theological language for speaking *about* God in the feminine. Her work makes a direct challenge to the male God of exclusive language, a challenge which is avoided by strategies, which restrict exploration to God as Mother (Lewis, 1984) or those which attempt to move beyond gender (Maitland, 1990; Coakley (1988).[6]

For Morley, feminist theological challenge to the patriarchal God of exclusive language (British Council of Churches, 1984:7) recalls the Church to Christian orthodoxy (1983a:12). Her work is fully congruent with the demand for Christian women's inclusion within the institutional churches. Morley was widely involved in the consciousness-raising and activity of the Christian women's movement, in the development of 'second-wave' Christian feminist liturgy through Women in Theology and the St Hilda Community, and in the collection of representative liturgical writing for publication. The Christian women's movement provided the context in which her distinctive project took shape and reached fruition. Morley's blend of 'second-wave' Christian feminist consciousness with theological orthodoxy exemplifies the rehabilitative Christian women's project within the institutional churches.

Before concluding this chapter, we give due attention to the Catholic writings of Angela West who, like Morley, was a significant voice in Christian women's theology. However, where Morley's work was entirely in tune with the ethos of the Christian women's movement, to the extent that she exemplifies its hallmark fusion of 'second-wave' consciousness with the rehabilitative project, West's is an individual voice, which, as we shall see, is often raised over against the movement's ruling passions.

## Angela West: Preaching the Christian Gospel

West was less concerned with the central rehabilitative Christian women's project, than with women's participation in preaching the Gospel. As we discovered in chapter three, West linked preaching the gospel with working for justice, with particular emphasis on issues of world starvation and nuclear threat. In chapter four, we learnt that West's experience during the National Pastoral Congress (NPC) was a turning point, after which she moved away from engagement with the Catholic hierarchy, to write theology. Her work was informed by her involvement with the Oxford Women's Liturgy and the Greenham Vigil, also by her Blackfriars education in theology and her involvement with Pax Christi. Here we make a considered evaluation of West's contribution to Christian women's theology.

West's feminist theology is more a distinctive and individual woman's voice within Blackfriars theology[7] and Pax Christi, than a representative feminist theological expression of the Oxford Women's Liturgy or the Greenham Peace Vigil. Three stages are evident in her post-NPC theology, following her turn away from engagement with the Catholic hierarchy, to her theological writing on women's participation within the life and mission of the Church. Early writings stress the theological value of feminist critical consciousness acting from the margins upon Christianity. In the second stage, feminist consciousness moves from margin to centre through West's equation of the Oxford Women's Liturgy with the Body of Christ. Finally, in the third stage, West reverses the dynamic of her early writings, by using Christianity to critique 'second-wave' feminism.

There is also a noticeable shift of emphasis during the three stages of West's post-NPC writings. Her early stress – reflective of post-Vatican II categories appearing in NPC documents – is on the Church's vocation to work for justice in the world, associated by West with the particular issues of world starvation and the nuclear threat, and on women's involvement in the Church's mission. By the close of her second stage, her emphasis, expressed in terms of classical Christological orthodoxy, is on preaching the gospel of love in Christ.

We will examine each stage in more detail, beginning with West's exploration of a creative role for women's critical consciousness. In her article, 'Genesis and Patriarchy' (1981a ,1981c), West emphasises the theological potential of women's cultural marginalisation, which enables women to perceive and subvert patriarchal distortions to Christian theology. Two (linked) points are significant. First, West reasserts the Judaeo-Christian myth of origins over against the psychoanalytic alternative offered by Juliet Mitchell, in *Psychoanalysis and Feminism* (1974). Second, where Mitchell ignores the Genesis myth and Eve, West makes a specific contribution to the CWIRES Eve theme in her reconfiguration of the Eve of Genesis.

In contrast to Mitchell's alternative Marxist/psychoanalytic account of the origins of patriarchy, West returns to the Judaeo-Christian myth and detects patriarchal origins in the post-Lapsarian assignment to Eve of responsibility for reproduction, so placing her on the boundary of patriarchal culture (1981a:21-2). Despite sharing the concerns of common humanity, contemporary women – like Eve – are marginalised (1981a:21). The twist in West's argument appears when she asserts the potential of the 'radical ambiguity' of women's marginality to patriarchal culture: thus marginalised, women are 'well placed to become [culture's] critics' (1981a:2). For West, Christian theology, rather than women themselves, will be the principal beneficiary of women's critical consciousness. The essential integrity of theology requires feminist subversion of patriarchal misappropriation of the Word – the object of theological discourse – so revealing the [undistorted] Word (1981a:19).

West also perceives an 'eschatological mode of thinking' in Mitchell's vision of a future beyond the apparently 'eternal' forms of patriarchy (1981c:422), with women as central to its construction (1981c:424). West then parallels the eschatological message of Jesus – the focus of political and liberation theology – with Mitchell's vision: she finds the language of apocalypse and of Genesis in Jesus' language of salvation history (1981c:431). West's reconfigured Eve is thus linked with this feminist work, in which a return to origins allows the [eschatologically indicated] correction of patriarchal misappropriation of the gospel. West concludes by citing Trible's 'Eve and Adam' (1981c:431), to assert the possibility of return to pre-Lapsarian sexual equality.

In contrast with the Anglican Eve, or with Morley's women in the image of God, West is little interested in Eve's specific identity over against Adam, nor does she argue for the inclusion of woman as new Eve in Christ. Eve's subversive work results in her reinstatement as equal to Adam – but this equality is within the vocational marginality of discipleship: West urges women to transform women's structural marginality into such vocational marginality (1981c:429). When she states, in 'Bodiliness and the Good News', that 'It is only as Christians that women can be authoritative because the foundation of Christian truth is not patriarchy; it is a truth that originates ... with God' (West, 1982b:15), she speaks of an authority associated with 'discipleship' rather than of women assuming authoritative roles within the institutional church. West's recommendation of vocational marginality may well have the same implications for women in the churches as Hebblethwaite's eschewal of power.

West's prime concern is always with the rehabilitation of Christian theology, and Eve features as a tool for this project, rather than as a positive figure of the rehabilitation of Eve within the institutional churches. Thus, although in her early work West perceives the rehabilitation of Christian theology as dependent upon the corrective potential of the Christian women's movement – symbolised in Eve – her view changes by the end of the CWIRES period.

In the second stage in her theology, West locates women as central within, rather than as marginal to, the Church's mission to the world, at first emphasising the Church's vocation of social justice, and later preaching the gospel of love in Christ. Her article, 'Sex and Salvation: a Christian Feminist Bible Study on I Corinthians 6:12-7:39' (West, 1984a), is representative of a central strand of her thinking during this second stage.[8] We clarify this shift by drawing on a number of preceding texts.

An early sermon, preached by West at the Oxford Women's Liturgy, affirms women's participation in the Church's vocation to preach the gospel and work for justice, in a world context of mass starvation and nuclear threat (West, 1981b:4-5). Thus the gospel imperative towards justice – now revealed through feminist subversion of its patriarchal misappropriation – is preached in sermons at the

Women's Liturgy and expressed in West's theological perception of the Oxford Women's Liturgy as eucharistic community and as the Body of Christ.

For West, liturgy acts as foundation for theology and ministry, in the Oxford Women's Liturgy as in the baptismal and eucharistic communities of the Pauline churches (1981d:3-4).[9] West uses the method followed in 'Genesis and Patriarchy', when she refers to both biblical and feminist texts to advance her argument, drawing parallels between issues facing the Oxford Women's Liturgy, the Corinthian Church, and the wider women's movement (1983b:1; 1984a:1).[10] Her discussion centres around three common issues.

First, Corinthian Christians believed they were living in the end times, while contemporary feminists fear a nuclear holocaust (West, 1981b:1; 1984a:10-11). Here West's emphasis upon justice is at its strongest. The solidarity shown by the Oxford Women's Liturgy with the wider women's movement through the Greenham Peace Vigil is inferred, while the imminent end focuses attention on issues of justice within the life of both Corinthian and contemporary communities (West, 1981b:4-5).

Second, the contemporary women's movement faces issues of race, class and gender, which were also present in 'the politics of sex and food' within the Corinthian Church (West, 1983b:1), being worked out within the wider imperative of building up the body of Christ, despite fractures of class, race and gender (West, 1983a:3-15). In 'Sex and Salvation' (1984a), West narrows her focus to the politics of sex alone. Her prime concern throughout these writings is with the unity of the body of Christ, rather than with the implications of intra-feminist conflicts. This focus signals the shift away from social justice as primary concern, towards classical Christology.

Third, West parallels Paul's love for the Body of Christ with Susan Griffin's passionate feminist critique of pornography, which Griffin portrays as a degradation of the human body and spirit deriving from the body-hating Christian ascetic tradition (1983b:3, 1984a:74). West also identifies Gayle Rubin's contrasting libertarian feminist position regarding pornography, with the 'libertarian' Corinthian faction (West, 1983b:7-80). West agrees with Griffin that libertine and ascetic factions share an anti-carnal mentality, which contrasts with Paul's attempt to protect the Body of Christ from fissure by mediation between the Corinthian factions (West, 1983b:15). Her conclusion to 'Sex and Salvation' (Loades, 1990:80) exalts the Christian calling to preach the gospel, over alignment with any particular sexual practices [and thus over alignment with conflicting positions indicated by either Griffin or Rubin].

Writings in this second stage, as epitomised in 'Sex and Salvation', effectively rehabilitate Pauline writings from their patriarchal misappropriation, with West speaking from her grounding within the Oxford Women's Liturgy, as one manifestation of the Body of Christ. West is able to engage with Paul's 'good news' in I Corinthians, so enabling her to critique patriarchal Christian interpretation of Paul (Loades, 1990:74-5): West hears the Pauline good news and, as a member 'in Christ', preaches the 'love of Christ' (Loades, 1990:80).

West also asserts, in her conclusion to 'Sex and Salvation', that the Pauline good news enables her to critique 'recent experiences within the women's liberation movement' (Loades, 1990:80). In West's third stage, this latter critique takes precedence. West's Christian critique of feminism was an element within her earlier writings. When, in 'Genesis and Patriarchy' (1981a, 1981c), West interprets Mitchell's *Psychoanalysis and Feminism*, in terms of a move from Genesis to apocalypse, she intends her argument to have wider implications than the subversion of patriarchal Christian theology. And when she claims that feminist theology seeks to reclaim the [theological] cultural myths which belong to the collectivity, from their misappropriation by class and patriarchy (1981a:20), West's 'collectivity' extends beyond Christianity. Thus when West states, 'The task of Feminist Theology ... [is] to relocate these psychoanalytic myths [as identified by Mitchell] back in the particular historical-ideological framework – which for our culture means the Judaeo-Christian tradition' (N.d.:7), she asserts her – suitably corrected – Christian theology, grounded in the authority of the gospel, as foundational for contemporary Western culture. West makes a similar claim in her criticism of the Womanspirit movement, 'A Faith for Feminists', where she rejects the feminist turn to the Goddess on the grounds that feminists necessarily belong within the Judaeo-Christian Western tradition, which superseded ahistorical matriarchal Goddess religion (West, 1982a:13).

'A Faith for Feminists' illustrates well the implications of West's Christian foundationalism. She criticises the turn to the Goddess as a misguided attempt to replace the incarnational Christian tradition with 'a new mythology based on women's experience', reflective of women's new spiritual consciousness (1982a:4). West's claim, in this article, that traditional women's experience is subverted in the Oxford Christian feminists (1982a:15) by the correctives, to members' liberal bourgeois conditioning, of *Marxism and Christianity* (1982a:5-6) [my emphasis] supports the view that West's is primarily a distinctive voice of Blackfriars theology, rather than of the Christian women's movement: for most women in the Christian women's movement, involved in emergent 'second-wave' Christian feminist consciousness and activity, the major corrective was feminism, rather than 'Marxism and Christianity'.

During the latter part of the CWIRES period, critique of the women's movement predominates in West's writings. Thus, in a conference paper for a joint CWN and Pax Christi study day, *The Widow's Mite: Good News For Women?*, West urges her listeners to concentrate on being disciples, asserting this is more important than contemporary feminist preoccupation with issues of race (1986). Similarly, in a paper entitled 'Wisdom in the Faith of our First Century Sisters', given during the Wisdom of Christian Feminism lecture series, she warns that the new wisdom of feminism does not necessarily coincide with the wisdom of God (1988:15).

In sum, despite the depth of her involvement with the Oxford Christian Feminists and at Greenham, West's theological exploration of issues concerning women and Christianity takes place within the context of an existing Blackfriars theology. Room is made in this Blackfriars genre for West's feminist theology, just as physical space was offered at Blackfriars to house the CWIRES project. Within this theological context, Marxism acts as a critical discourse, capable of releasing the Word from its various theological distortions. West uses feminism as a critical tool in a parallel way to the Dominican use of Marxism within *New Blackfriars* theology.

West was always more interested in theology, than in the position of women in the churches. Her relationship to the Christian women's movement, and her particular 'second-wave' Christian feminist consciousness, are thus distinct from the central rehabilitative project and ethos of the wider Christian women's movement. West's contribution is also distinct from the radical Christian variants within the movement, represented in differing forms in Jenner, Condren and Field-Bibb. We have already encountered West's differences with Jenner over the nature of 'feminist theology'. Where Condren and Field-Bibb sharpened their feminist critical consciousness, using tools of sociological analysis, West's arguments are entirely theological: once feminism has done its work in correcting patriarchal distortions, it is discarded, having no further role. For West, theology – suitably corrected – is foundational and all sufficient.

Yet, paradoxically, West's theology is entirely congruent with the 1976 quote from Una Kroll, standing as epigraph to this chapter. West's writing, during her first two stages, embodies the challenge of feminist theology, as set out in Kroll's first paragraph, while West's assertion of women as preachers of the gospel 'in Christ' coheres with the 'whole theology', envisioned in her second paragraph. Neither Kroll nor West seek to move beyond classical Christological formulations, as West shares Kroll's view that gender differences are already transcended in Christ.

Kroll's definition of feminist theology is both perpetuated and developed in Christian women's central theological theme of 'the new Eve in Christ'. Morley's exploration of feminine imagery for God lends further definition to Eve, as distinct to Adam, in Christ. In contrast, West sees no need to accommodate women's specificity, and thus to develop Kroll's theme.

## Conclusion

Theology was not the overriding concern of the British Christian women's movement, given its central preoccupation with change in the position of women in the institutional churches. For many women, 'second-wave' Christian feminist consciousness-raising was best expressed in reformist activity, which required no new theological justification. Nevertheless, the movement generated new theological insight, which was both expressive and supportive of Christian women's consciousness and activity.

Given the rehabilitative ethos of the movement, it is unsurprising that Christian women's theology was widely perceived as corrective to the patriarchal theology underpinning women's exclusion from a full role within the institutional churches. My discussion has also identified the minority genre of writings, which went beyond the central rehabilitative and corrective project. These range from the open-ended consciousness-raising of the Feminist Theology Project under Judith Jenner's guidance, and of the Quaker Women's Group, and the confidence shown by members of the Unitarian Women's Group in the scope offered by their denominational tradition, where apparently no prior rehabilitation of Eve was necessary.

We have seen that Jacqueline Field-Bibb's *Women Towards Priesthood* (1991) looks to deinstitutionalisation of Christianity, rather than to reform of the institutional churches: the rehabilitative project is not Field-Bibb's principal concern. Yet, Field-Bibb's analysis of woman in Christianity as 'other', the differentiator of a male divine, touches on a similar awareness emerging among Anglican women. Field-Bibb's recommendation that feminist theology, based on feminist theory, provides superior symbols to traditional Catholicism is realised in a different form in 'second-wave' Christian feminist liturgical exploration. This realisation also informs Morley's theology, where Field-Bibb's suggested development of symbols is found in Morley's feminine imagery for God, though remaining within the parameters of traditional Anglicanism. Similarly, Catholic liturgical experimentation within the Catholic Women's Network developed in relation to traditional Catholicism, rather than at Field-Bibb's recommended distance.

Condren, like Field-Bibb, makes a sociological critique of the oppressive effects of institutionalised religion, recommending the creation of feminized 'beautitudinal community', rather than the reform of institutional religion. Her interest in Christian religion leads her to start from the radical feminist alternative interpretation of the Genesis myth as foundation myth of patriarchy, thus revealing the Goddess suppressed beneath patriarchal Christianity, but also to include the oppressive function of the Eve/Mary pair in her analysis. This double movement connects her with the Goddess of Womanspirit – there are parallels between *The Serpent and the Goddess* (Condren, 1989) and Asphodels's *In a Chariot Drawn By Lions* (Long, 1992) – and the hinterland explorations by the Quaker Women's Group, Unitarian Women's Group and Linda Hurcombe in *Sex and God*.

Condren also provides the Christian women's movement with its central organising motif: Christian women, who sought change in the position of women in the churches, were struck by Condren's evocative image of themselves as 'banished children of Eve'. As Eve's 'dispossessed daughters' they campaigned for their own rehabilitation within the churches. Diana Collins' phrase, 'the rehabilitation of Eve', epitomised Eve as emblem for their project.

We have seen the importance of Eve and her rehabilitation within the core of Christian women's theology, associated with the central rehabilitative project. The theme of the redemptive potential of Eve and Mary, though touched upon by both Windle and Harvey, was little developed. Rather, the classical Christological formulation, evident in Kroll's epigraph to this chapter, provides the touchstone for Christianity after correction of its patriarchal distortions. We found a significant theological development of the Christian women's Eve theme, in the shift from Kroll's assertion of the Galatians 3:28 baptismal promise – in Christ there is neither male nor female – to the positive assertion of a 'new Eve in Christ'. This latter assertion claims an unambiguous place for women, in their specificity, within the salvation of Christ.

This thoroughly orthodox position is entirely congruent with the central Christian women's project of women's rehabilitation within the institutional churches. The specificity of Eve, distinguishing mark of the British Christian women's movement, is related to the theological creativity of liturgical experiment infused with 'second-wave' Christian feminist consciousness, which finds its strongest expression in Morley's writing. Exploration of the potential of women in the image of God, in developing feminine imagery for God, opened up a different direction to a mere assertion of Eve's equality with Adam.

Catholic Christian women's writings are represented in the radical critiques of Field-Bibb and Condren, but writings from the rehabilitative Catholic core of the movement are absent from my discussion – though we encountered the widespread renewed critique of the position of women in the Catholic Church in chapter four. The dearth of theological writing from the centre Catholic ground – represented in women such as Pat Pinsent, Ianthe Pratt and Alexina Murphy – is reflected in its absence within this chapter.

We have discovered, in Angela West, a significant Catholic voice, whose theological writings belong neither with radical critique of Christianity, nor with the rehabilitative project of the Christian women's movement. Despite West's lively engagement with feminist theory, and her notion of feminist theology as corrective to patriarchal theology, she eventually parts company with the wider Christian women's movement in her Christian critique of feminism.

We have also seen that West's theology is entirely congruent with Kroll's early definition of feminist theology. West shares with Kroll an indifference to the expression of the specificity of women's autonomy, mutuality and sexuality, which characterises both Morley's work, and the notion of a new Eve in Christ. Whereas Kroll envisioned her whole theology as accompanying eventual sexual parity within the institutional churches, West writes Christian theology irrespective of women's position in the institutional church. Though West's involvement with the Christian women's movement was important while feminism acted as corrective to Christian theology, it became less so as she applied Christian theology as corrective to feminism. Thus where Morley is both an individual voice, and a voice of the wider movement in its various manifestations, West is an individual voice who – despite the scale of her involvement with the Oxford Christian feminists and Greenham – was more grounded in Blackfriars theology than in the Christian women's movement.

We are now in a position to return to the question raised, in chapter three, as to the rehabilitative strategy adopted by Christian women, who embraced 'second-wave' Christian feminist consciousness, so repudiating the strategy of women's restoration to good repute. We have seen that secular socialist feminists and religious Womanspirit feminists alike sought to restore women to a new constructive capacity. While socialist feminists were sufficiently secure in their secularism to have left behind notions of rehabilitation, Womanspirit was clearly rehabilitative in its concern to counter the continuing oppressive effects of Christianity upon women. The minority genre of radical Christian critique shared the strategy of restoration of women to a new constructive capacity with the wider women's movement.

In contrast, Christian women's central rehabilitative strategy was the restoration of women to a former capacity: one obscured by patriarchal misappropriation, but now to be restored through the corrective effect of feminist theology upon patriarchal distortions. Christian women's readings of the Genesis myth, which portrayed Eve as a positive figure, together with privileging of the Galatians 3:28 baptismal formula, defined this former capacity, which the movement sought to restore. The effects of harnessing 'second-wave' consciousness, to Christian women's rehabilitative project, is seen in this opting for restoration to a former capacity – already defined in (properly interpreted) Christian orthodoxy – rather than to a new constructive capacity, as favoured in the wider women's' movement and in radical Christian women's theology.

This chapter completes our threefold analysis of the CWIRES material in terms of Christian women's consciousness, activity and theology, using Eve and her rehabilitation as heuristic device. We have noted occasional reference to the influence of North American feminist theology: Grailville upon Jenner and the Feminist Theology Project; Fiorenza on Field-Bibb; Daly on Condren; *Womanspirit Rising* on British Womanspirit and Ruether's consistent presence on the CWN. But Christian women's theology is an indigenous expression of the concerns of the British Christian women's movement: it is not a response to the stimulus of North American feminist theology.

However, during the 1970s and 1980s, feminist theology was developing, first in North America, later in Europe and postcolonial contexts, emerging also within the British academy by the end of the CWIRES period. In the final chapter, we investigate the relation between this wider body of feminist theology, and the Christian women's rehabilitation of Eve, with its central project of the inclusion of Eve in the salvation of Christ. We locate Eve and her rehabilitation on the wider stage of feminist theology.

## Notes

1 Jenner produced a book-length manuscript describing the process of doing theology from the experience of women within the FTP (interview with Judith Jenner, 9 May 1996). It is a loss to British feminist theology that this book was never published, due to the demise of the Methodist Publishing House, Epworth Press.

2 See Field-Bibb (1989:40) for a succinct summary of her thesis, which emphasises the centrality of this insight to her conclusions.

3 West only attended the first two meetings of the FTP and, when later invited to participate in the publication of *Our Stories*, her letter (cited in my text and in *Our Stories*) declined the invitation, expressing her reservations about the FTP process.

[4] A clue to this origin of her phrase appears when Condren quotes the words of *Salve Regina* in subsequent writings (1997:38).

[5] Thus *Sex and God* includes substantial North American academic contributions on the Christian tradition and, respectively, women's sexuality (Ruether, 1987), and lesbian sexuality (Briggs, 1987; Hunt, 1987).

[6] Cf Maitland's attempts to counter the tradition of masochistic practice, wherein female saints identified with the crucified body of Christ (1987:130-1), by recommending Hildegard of Bingen, as historical precedent and contemporary model of women's positive identification with the divine figure of Sophia (1987:138-9). Implicit, though undeveloped, in this article is recovery of feminine imagery for the divine, which is congruent with Morley's explorations, but adopts a contrasting strategy to Maitland (1990).

[7] 'Blackfriars theology': theological debate stimulated by the Dominican community at Blackfriars, Oxford – the hosts of the CWIRES project – and reflected in articles published in the journal, *New Blackfriars*.

[8] The reference refers to the unpublished text, present in CWIRES, though the full bibliographic reference gives details of subsequent publication, first in *MC* and subsequently in Loades (1990:72-80). Comparison of the earlier CWIRES text with the version in Loades (1990) demonstrates the shift in emphasis from earlier reference to justice and nuclear threat, to the later text, which refers to the gospel of love in Christ. Reference is made to West (1984a [CW D28]) or to Loades (1990) as appropriate.

[9] West here uses the term featuring in NPC documents, 'eucharistic community', while in subsequent writings (1982b, 1983a, 1983b) she refers to the Oxford Women's Liturgy as the Body of Christ.

[10] However, in the later published version of 'Sex and Salvation', (Loades, 1990:72-80) West confines her analysis to issues facing the Corinthian Church and the contemporary women's movement, without reference to the Oxford Women's Liturgy.

## Chapter 6

# The Rehabilitation of Eve on a Wider Stage: Eve and Feminist Theology

In this final chapter, our horizon broadens beyond the perspective of the British Christian women's movement of the 1970s and 1980s. We find that, in these same two decades, in the feminist theology taking shape outside Britain, a paradigm shift occurred in christ*oa*logical[1] revisioning, away from the classical paradigm of salvation in Christ, to a claim that women's struggle for justice in the contemporary world is redemptive. In contrast, British Christian women's theology, with its emphasis upon the rehabilitation of Eve and its commitment to women's rehabilitation within the institutional churches, remained within the classical paradigm of redemption.

Our focus here is on developments led by North American writers. Although the diversification of feminist theology, by inclusion of additional voices to those of its white, middle-class, North American pioneers, was of enormous importance during the 1980s, the paradigm shift was navigated by those same pioneers, who thus remain central to our explorations. True to the theme of this book, we begin with Eve. We soon discover that she is largely absent from North American feminist theology, which has no need to repeat the nineteenth century 'vindication of the woman Eve'. Rather, sexual equality before the Fall is taken as premise for a new line of theological development.

We trace this new line of development, after establishing that it emerges from the christological agenda set by Mary Daly, an agenda which is addressed through two related feminist strategies. In the first strategy, Christ is figured as liberator, and this equation of salvation with liberation allows the related emergence of female liberative figures – Mary, Christa (and the Goddess) – thus providing alternative redemptive figures to the male Christ. The second strategy involves a christ*oa*logical shift, which begins in the early work of Carter Heyward. In this shift, a move is made from any single liberative/redemptive *figure* to liberative/redemptive *community*, communal redemption being characterised by 'our passion for justice'.

Our next task is to investigate British academic feminist theology, emergent in the latter 1980s, enquiring of its relation to, respectively, the christ*oa*logical paradigm shift of North American feminist theology, and the classical salvation paradigm of Christian women's theology. We find that the concerns of the British Christian women's movement appear to have the greater influence upon emergent

British academic writing, unearthing traces of Eve which serve to strengthen this impression. Towards the end of the CWIRES period, we find evidence of serious engagement with North American feminist theology, in the work of Julie Hopkins, Mary Grey and, to a lesser extent, Daphne Hampson: Hopkins alone is alert to the North American christ*oa*logical paradigm shift. By the end of the CWIRES period, there are slight signs of an emergent academic British feminist theology, which is both independent of the concerns of the Christian women's movement, and broadly congruent with, though not reliant upon, North American feminist theology.

We begin by demonstrating the absence of Eve, as significant figure, from North American feminist theology.

## Eve

The radical feminist interpretation of the Genesis myth, as foundation myth of patriarchy, originates in North American feminist theology. In chapter three, we encountered, in brief, the part played by Mary Daly and Merlin Stone in the dissemination of this alternative reading. We will examine their work in more detail here.

Daly makes her radical feminist interpretation after her post-Christian turn. Prior to this shift, in her first book, *The Church and the Second Sex* (1985 [1968]), she criticises the effects of traditional interpretations of the myth, offering her own alternative reading, where Eve is reconfigured as equal to Adam. Her interpretation thus affirms women's equality with men. Daly's feminist suspicion of the traditional interpretation, with its patriarchal figure of Eve, was raised by Simone de Beauvoir's observation that: 'In the legends of Eve and Pandora men have taken up arms against women' (cited in Daly, 1985:62).

Daly documents the oppressive effects, for women, of 'uncritical acceptance of the androcentric myth of Eve's creation' (1985:86). She cites evidence from modern biblical scholarship, which contradicts the longstanding implication of women's subordination (1985:78), so attempting to correct this 'misunderstanding' on the part of 'preachers and theologians' (1985:77): such a turn would lead them to forsake the misconceived traditional interpretation, in favour of Daly's recommended alternative. Daly's alternative rendering is similar to that of the biblical scholar, Phyllis Trible, in her attempt to 'depatriarchalise' the Bible (1973, 1979, 1990:26-7). Thus Trible asserts the 'intended equality [of man and woman] with each other; their solidarity in sin and suffering; and their shared need of redemption' (1973:48). Her alternative interpretation allows her forcefully to assert that the myth of the Fall does not legitimate the oppression of women (1973:47).

Following her post-Christian turn, Daly makes her distinctive interpretation of the Genesis myth: as foundation myth of patriarchy. In *Beyond God the Father*, she repudiates Trible's efforts (1973:206). Reflecting anew on her former reasoning, Daly asserts that, within the patriarchal Christian tradition, 'it will always be too late [for women], that mere reform and modernized scholarship [such as Trible's] will allow millions more to live and die ...[convinced] of their divinely ordained inferiority' (1985:22).

Eve plays a key role in Daly's new argument. Daly develops Elizabeth Cady Stanton's insight, first expressed in *The Women's Bible* (1985 [1895]), that the myth of the Fall is a 'myth of feminine evil' which provides the foundation of Christianity (cited in Daly, 1973:47). 'Women as a caste', Daly writes, 'are "Eve" and are punished by a cohesive set of laws, customs and social arrangements that enforce an all-pervasive double standard' (1973:62). True to her radical feminist alternative reading of the myth, Daly attempts no 'vindication of the woman Eve'. Rather, her response is 'to tear... the image of the Fall from its context in patriarchal religion,' by replacing the patriarchal Fall *from* the sacred with the 'positive and healing' Fall initiated by women *into* the sacred which is freedom (1973:67).

Crucially, Daly's reinterpretation of the Fall challenges the 'christolatrous' assertion that salvation comes only through the male, while women are identified with Eve and evil, even in their imitation of the sacrificial love of Christ (1973:77). Once again, Daly develops the earlier insight of Cady Stanton's, that 'the bottom falls out of Christian theology' if the patriarchal Genesis myth – a myth of feminine evil – is challenged (cited in Daly, 1973:69). From this point on, Daly parts company with alternative interpretations, where Eve is reconfigured, instead affirming female sexuality and power as the means of women's rehabilitation from the ongoing, and entwined, effects of the foundation myth of patriarchy, and Christolatry.

Daly replaces patriarchal notions of sin and salvation – where Eve is responsible for original sin, and consequently woman is in need of a male redeemer – with her concept of the original sin of sexism, in which women are cast as 'primordial scapegoats' (1973:47). For Daly, active repudiation of the myth of feminine evil 'will require a corporate redemptive action by women' of the women's movement (1973:55), which 'drives beyond Christolatry' (1973:96). As we will see, following Daly's devastating critique, women's 'corporate redemptive action' was to be similarly privileged in the paradigm shift represented in feminist christ*oa*logies, wherein women figure as both redeemer and redeemed.

Merlin Stone's version of the Genesis myth as foundation myth of patriarchy, in *The Paradise Papers: the Suppression of Women's Rites* (1976), emphasises the function of the attribution of guilt to Eve and woman, as the destruction of Goddess religion, wherein woman was deified (1976:214,24). Stone argues that the myth justified the suppression of the Goddess, the subordination of women, the association of sexuality with evil and the appropriation of female procreative power by a male creator (1976:236-40). Stone contends that the serpent, fruit-tree and 'sexually-tempting women who took advice from serpents' – the three elements in Stanton's tableau also – symbolised the presence of the female deity (Stone, 1976:215-234). Thus there is a sense in which the Goddess, suppressed by patriarchal religion, is present in Eve. However, the focus in the North American Womanspirit movement – as in British Womanspirit, as we saw in chapter three – is upon the suppressed Goddess herself, rather than on Eve. For Womanspirit, the

Goddess, implied and subjected in the patriarchal myth, has a greater potential than the overlaying figure of Eve.

In the introduction to this book, we encountered Stone's assessment that, for nineteenth century feminists, 'the vindication of the rights of women was in a sense a vindication of the woman Eve' (1976:246). The thesis argued in this book is that the British Christian women's movement, of the 1970s and 1980s, constituted a renewed 'vindication of the woman Eve' within Christian churches and theology, though the moment for such a vindication had passed in the wider British women's movement. In the previous chapter, we discovered the British Christian women's vindication and rehabilitation of the woman Eve in different guises, its strongest manifestation being the 'new Eve in Christ'.

The moment for such a vindication of Eve had passed also in North American feminist theology. After Trible's alternative interpretation of the Genesis creation story, and Daly and Stone's powerful naming of the foundation myth of patriarchy, Eve fades away.[2] This is illustrated by the extract selected from *The Paradise Papers* for inclusion in the – now classic – collection, *Womanspirit Rising* (Christ and Plaskow, 1979:120-30), where no mention of Eve is made.[3] The figure of Eve neither invites identification on the part of 'second-wave' North American Christian feminist theologians, nor does she appear in their work.[4]

This absence of Eve is well illustrated in the alternative interpretation of the Genesis myth, in Rosemary Ruether's *Sexism and God-Talk*. Ruether differentiates the 'essence' of humanity – the potential and authentic humanity made *in imago Dei* – from the 'existence' of humanity as 'fallen Adam' (*sic*), distorted and sinful (1992 [1983]:93). Although Ruether critiques the correlation of *imago Dei*/sin with maleness/femaleness, and although her discussion of Christian anthropologies includes reference to Eve (1992:94-9), her starting point is common humanity, or authentic essence, which applies equally to women and men. Ruether makes no particular appeal on behalf of Eve, in advancing her critical principle of feminist theology: the promotion of the full humanity of women (1992:18).

Further, in contrast to Morley's reflections on women in the image of God – arising in the British context with its prominent Eve theme – Ruether does not explore women's specificity *in imago Dei*. Ruether exemplifies the implied premise of North American twentieth century feminist theology – given its prime statement by Trible – that an alternative interpretation of Genesis, where Eve is equal to Adam and consequently women's equality with men is affirmed, has already replaced the longstanding traditional interpretation.[5]

This alternative interpretation has thus displaced the figuration of Eve, as '"revolting" body in the disorder of sin' (Briggs, 1976:2), in the traditional interpretation of the Genesis myth. North American Christian feminist theology turns its attention directly to women in the order of salvation, without recourse to Eve. Whereas British Christian women's theology culminated in the rehabilitative inclusion of Eve in the salvation of Christ, Daly's critique of 'Christolatry' set the agenda for the feminist theology which emerged in North America, then diversified elsewhere. We now turn our attention to feminist Christ*oa*logy, and to the feminist christ*oa*logical revisioning which was of central importance in the development of

North American Christian feminist theology, during the 1970s and 1980s. Here we discern the paradigm shift from classical Chalcedonian orthodoxy to women's redemptive community.

## Women and Redemption

We take as our starting point a paradigm shift identified by the British researcher, Julie Hopkins, clarifying that feminist Christ*oa*logy is central to the shift she detects – though this christ*oa*logical focus remains implicit in Hopkins' own analysis. We then discriminate the discrete steps in christ*oa*logical revisioning, through which this paradigm shift is effected. Two distinct, albeit linked, strategies are discernible.

The first strategy posits a liberative/redemptive Christ, being extended in the female liberative/redemptive figures of Mary and the Christa.[6] The second strategy, which begins with Carter Heyward, makes a gradual shift in emphasis from a single salvific figure to a focus upon women's redemptive community. In the course of our investigations, the ambiguity of Christa – a figure of women's suffering, rather than of women's redemptive qualities – is thrown into relief. We find this shortcoming addressed, within this second strategy, by Brock's redemptive Christa/Community. Our discussion of women and redemption concludes with a brief discussion of feminist christ*oa*logical revisioning in relation to the christological orthodoxy of the British Christian women's movement.

Hopkins' perceptive analysis appears in her doctoral thesis, 'The Understanding of History in English-Speaking Western Christian Feminist Theology' (1988). As indicated by her title, Hopkins' principal concern is with theological understandings of history. Thus she argues that the Augustinian model of dialectical theology – that salvation is initiated by God beyond history as an eschatological event – is rejected by feminist theology as untenable (1988:11). But when she identifies, in feminist theology, 'a profound paradigm shift in epistemology and theology' (Hopkins, 1988: abstract), Christology provides the key to her thesis, being the organising focus of her ensuing collection of essays, *Towards a Feminist Christology* (Hopkins, 1995).

Hopkins' argument for a paradigm shift is congruent with our privileging of christ*oa*logical revisioning within pre-1990 feminist theology. We now examine, in more detail, the development of the two christ*oa*logical strategies, which together amount to a christ*oa*logical revisioning. We begin with strategies reliant on a single liberative figure.

### *Redemptive Figures*

Three distinct christ*oa*logical approaches make up the first strategy. The first approach occurs in Ruether's counter to Daly's critique, by positing Christ as liberator: liberation and redemption are conjoined, following the precedent set by liberation theology. Thus Ruether makes the first decisive move in asking 'Can a Male Savior Save Women?' (1992:116). Her answer is to locate Jesus as liberator, central to the biblical prophetic tradition, (1992:135-7), so correlating her feminist critical principle – the promotion of the full humanity of women – with biblical critical principles of the prophetic, messianic tradition (1985a), wherein Christ as both liberator and redeemer is grounded. Ruether's christological strategy is a key aspect of her feminist liberation theology (1972b,1975a,1979,1985a,1985b,1988, 1992).[7]

Ruether's strategy is reiterated in the christological focus within postcolonial women's theology. Here Christ as liberator is identified with the suffering of the poor, especially women, and with the redemptive struggle for liberation and justice (Tamez, 1989:81-95; Oduyoye, 1989; Chung Hyun Kyung, 1990:53-73; Kwok Pui-Lan, 1984; Fabella and Oduyoye, 1988:22-46,108-117).

The second approach is found in liberation mariology, where Mary emerges as a liberative, and thus redemptive, figure. Once more, postcolonial women's theology contributes to this development. Liberation mariology begins with critique of Mary, as male-created ideal of the eternal feminine, and re-envisages her as a sister to contemporary women, who seek justice and their own liberation (Ruether, 1979,1992:152-8). Latin American and Asian women theologians develop this theme by identifying Mary with women, the poorest of the poor. Thus Ivone Gebara and María Clara Bingemar, in *Mary – Mother of God, Mother of the Poor* (1989; King, 1994:275-281), elaborate new Marian configurations arising from the poor.

A 'Summary Statement on Feminist Mariology' (King, 1994:270-4), written by an ecumenical group of Asian Christian women in 1987, declares, 'We see feminist Mariology as a liberation theology that gives hope of humanization to all the world' (King, 1994:274). Chung Hyung Kyung, in *Struggle to be the Sun Again*, synthesises Asian women's mariology, identifying two distinct understandings of Mary as 'co-redeemer for human salvation' (Chung, 1990:83-4). As 'co-redemptrix', Mary chooses to co-operate in the history of redemption, so providing a model encouraging contemporary women to co-operate in their own redemption.[8] A contrasting Filipino understanding of Mary sees her as co-redeemer with Jesus, the liberative figures of Jesus and Mary achieving equal stature in this matriarchal indigenous culture.[9] In these various feminist mariologies, Mary becomes a liberative, and therefore redemptive, figure alongside Jesus.

For Western women – as is clear in British Christian women's critique – mariology has reinforced a long tradition which condones women's patient endurance of suffering. Perhaps it is significant that it is within the liberative activity of Asian women, whose heritage is outside that of Western Christian culture, that Mary is most powerfully reconfigured.

The third approach emerges in the ambiguous figure of the Christa. As an image of a female Christ, the Christa is a female redemptive figure. But the power of this image is compromised by its identification of women with the suffering, as opposed to salvific, Christ. Daly's critique of Christolatry highlights the damage done to women by their identification with Christ's suffering, and questions the notion that suffering is redemptive. Brown and Parker (1989) attribute women's 'acculturation to abuse' (1989:1) primarily to Christianity, with its 'central image of Christ on the cross as savior of the world' (1989:2). Like Stanton and Daly before them, they question the notion of original sin, without which there is no need of a saviour (1989:2), and thus reject classical theologies of atonement and contemporary theologies of the suffering God. Christian theology, they argue, is necessarily abusive in insisting that the crucifixion – which they portray as divinely sanctioned child-abuse – is salvific (Brown and Parker, 1989:26,23).

Nonetheless, the abuse, and consequent suffering, of women continues. In Susan Thistlethwaite's *Sex, Race and God*, Christa appears as a figure of the woman survivor of violent abuse (1990:93-107), and Thistlethwaite gives testimony to the power of the Christa figure in bringing women's experiences of violent abuse out of silence into speech (1990:93).

Further, she states that, '"Christa" is not experienced by many women as legitimating violence against them but as identifying with their pain and freeing them from the guilt that somehow, because of the original sin of being female, they deserved what they got' (Thistlethwaite, 1990:93). Thus Christa evokes healing in women survivors of abuse, and is therefore a redemptive figure. However, as Brown and Parker's critique suggests, the Christa appears to be implicated in the continuing effects of the 'myth of feminine evil', and her redemptive scope seems more limited than that of the liberative figures of the male Christ, or even the female Mary.

In spite of these reservations, the appearance within feminist Christology of the female, christ*a*logical redemptive figures, Mary and Christa, is significant. However, the power of both – like that of the British Christian women's Eve – is muted in comparison to the acclaimed power of the Goddess, as female figure of the divine. It is important to locate the Goddess as a post-Christian response to Daly's critique of Christolatry, and in this sense as an alternative female liberative figure. The Goddess is also linked with the uncovering of a Christian female divine, in which the muting effect is reversed. Thus attention given to the suppressed matriarchal tradition by Christian feminist theologians (Collins, 1974; Christ and Plaskow, 1979:149-58; Ruether, 1992:47-61; Moltmann-Wendel, 1986:43-59) is significant for the post-1990 development of Christian feminist sophiaology (Fiorenza, 1995; Johnson 1996). We have already noted the importance of the work of the British Womanspirit researcher, Asphodel, in this regard.

We now turn to the second strategy for countering Daly's critique of Christolatry. The second christ*oa*logical strategy, which shifts the focus from a single liberative figure to redemptive community, opens up new possibilities in women's relation to redemption. Our next task is to explore the potential of such corporate redemption.

### *Redemptive Community*

Carter Heyward pioneered the move from redemptive figure to redemptive community. However, Heyward's initiative was already implicit in Ruether's work, where she identifies Christ with contemporary liberative and redemptive humanity, rather than as 'encapsulated "once-for-all" in the [single redemptive figure of] the historical Jesus' (Ruether, 1992:138).[10] We will make two contrasting approaches to this strategy, beginning by investigating the strong theme of women's liberative community within feminist theology, then examining the christ*oa*logical claiming of women's community as redemptive. Clearly this claim perpetuates the linkage between liberation and redemption, which appears in the first christ*oa*logical strategy.

The identity of feminist theology, as a liberation theology, discloses a new potential for contemporary communities of faith: liberative communities are therefore redemptive, offering different possibilities to the action of any single redemptive figure. Women's liberative community is important in the work of Elisabeth Schussler Fiorenza, Mary Hunt and Sharon Welch. The contemporary *ekklesia* of women, or 'women-church, the movement of self-identified women and women-identified men in biblical religion' (Fiorenza, 1985:126), is key to Fiorenza's liberation theology (1975,1984b,1995). *Ekklesia/* women-church is the site for reconstruction of a 'discipleship of equals' modelled on egalitarian Christian origins (1984a:97): *ekklesia/*women-church informs and resources Fiorenza's commitment to transform gender relations.[11]

Women-Church is significant also for Ruether (1988) – as we saw in chapter five – and for Mary Hunt (1989:50,159-60). Women's liberative community takes the form of 'communities of resistance and solidarity', rather than feminist *ekklesia* or Women-Church, in Sharon Welch's feminist theology of liberation (1985) and feminist ethic of risk (1990). But Welch's work, no less than that of Fiorenza, Ruether and Hunt, lends depth to the conceptualisation of women's communities, which resources the growing understanding of such communities as redemptive.

Carter Heyward's doctoral thesis, *The Redemption of God* (1982), and her collection of essays, *Our Passion for Justice* (1984), articulate this understanding. Heyward makes explicit the christ*oa*logical claim that women's liberative community is redemptive. With Heyward, the emphasis shifts from theology of liberation – Ruether's Christ as liberator – to theology of relation – Heyward's co-creative power in relation, present in women's work infused with 'our passion for justice' (1984).[12] For Heyward 'Re-imaging Jesus [as power in relation] becomes the first step in re-imaging Christ or Christology' (1982:35). The importance of Daly's critique of Christolatry, for Heyward, is clear when she pays tribute to the 'vision of theological possibility' (1984:10) arising from Daly's willingness to challenge 'the assumption behind the givenness of Jesus Christ as authority' (1984:9). Heyward's own pursuit of this theological possibility is evident in her christological shift. Not only is Christ now identified with 'our passion for justice', but christological action in the contemporary world depends upon our willingness to participate in this project. For Heyward, the moral question is 'whether or not we will choose to claim our shared power ... that is good, creative, and redemptive when it is ours together' (1984:122). The importance of liberative community, to Heyward, is clear when she states that our shared power is 'nothing less than evil when we "possess it" as ours and ours alone' (1984:122). Her essays make clear that all are included, that the justice sought through power in relation involves issues of race, postcolonialism, gender, sexuality and economic privilege or disadvantage.

Jacqueline Grant, in *White Women's Christ and Black Women's Jesus* (1989), her womanist response to white feminist Christology, makes a Christalogical move, which contributes to christ*oa*logical revisioning in terms of redemptive community, while resisting the universalising terms of white women's experience. Thus Grant identifies Christ specifically with the community of poor, black women, emphasising black women's strengths, as well as their sufferings (1989:217,230). For Grant, women's redemptive community is epitomised in the communal life shared by poor black women.

Heyward engages directly with the issue of women's suffering and redemption. She emphatically refuses the notion of suffering as redemptive, by portraying Jesus as rejecting a sadistic God who requires sacrifice, and claiming that Jesus' crucifixion was an evil human act, in consequence of his struggle against injustice (Heyward, 1982:54-8) – an analysis which Brown and Parker commend (1989:25-6). For Heyward, it is our co-creative, co-redemptive passion for justice – the appropriate response to suffering – which is divinely sanctioned, not human suffering in itself.

However, despite Heyward's radical christological revisioning, given the close relation between suffering and redemption in classical Christology, an ambiguity remains, exacerbated by the ready explanation of women's suffering in terms of 'the myth of feminine evil'. This ambiguity is addressed by Rita Nakishman Brock, who gives the survivor of abuse a central position, when she further develops Heyward's relational Christology, in her *Journeys by Heart: a Christology of Erotic Power* (Brock, 1989). Brock expands the single suffering/redemptive Christa figure by revisioning Christa in terms of women's redemptive community, which she names Christa/Community.

For Brock, Christa/Community is the site of erotic power within connectedness, wherein the broken heart of patriarchy is healed (1988:87-8). Brock's Christa/Community is to be found wherever this healing occurs. Within her feminised Christa/Community, the strength of communal erotic and redemptive power counters the effects of women's suffering. Brock's affirmation of the constructive capacity of erotic power is a potent counter to the 'myth of feminine evil'. Her Christa/Community manifests Daly's 'positive and healing' Fall into the sacred which is freedom (Daly, 1973:67), and Daly's recommended 'corporate redemptive action' which actively repudiates the myth of feminine evil (1973:55), and so 'drives beyond Christolatry' (1973:96). Brock's Christa/Community thus goes some way towards overcoming the ambiguity of the singular, suffering Christa figure.[13]

At this point we will revisit the theme of women's liberative community in the (pre-1990) work of Fiorenza, Ruether, Hunt and Welch. It is possible to tease out the strong overlap in themes of mutuality, relationality and justice-seeking community between the christ*oa*logical writing of Heyward and Brock, and the work of Mary Hunt, where no explicit christ*oa*logical theme is developed. In *Fierce Tenderness: a Feminist Theology of Friendship* (1989), Hunt suggests women's friendships as a useful paradigm for right relation for the whole of creation (1989:2). However, although she argues that women's experience of mutuality in the struggle for justice is generative of new imagery for the divine (Hunt, 1989:68-9), is revelatory (1989:84-5) and worthy of sacramentalisation (1989:116-8), Hunt neither uses christological categories nor speaks of redemption. Her work is theological in that she 'attends to the divine-human nexus in all its diversity and complexity' (1989:9). It is more significant, for Hunt, that women's friendships are inspirational towards justice-seeking action, than to name this action as redemptive.

However, given their common themes of mutuality, relationality and justice-seeking community, Hunt's feminist theology of friendship can be read as enriching the christ*oa*logical revisioning as redemptive community, developed by Heyward and Brock. Thus Women-Church as an explicit referent for Hunt's theology, becomes a referent for the christoalogical redemptive communities envisioned by Heyward and Brock. In similar vein, Welch's 'communities of resistance and solidarity' lend depth to explicit christ*oa*logical revisioning in Heyward, Grant and Brock. This observation does not impose christ*oa*logical categories upon Hunt and Welch, but demonstrates how their work coheres with the christ*oa*logical revisoning, which emerges during the 1980s. Hopkins' suggestion, that the Christ emergent within feminist theology is a communal symbol for group activity towards liberation, 'the transpersonal power released through creative and emancipatory solidarity' (1988:276), lends further weight to this christ*oa*logical interpretation. And Welch and Hunt feature large among the feminist theologians featured by Hopkins.

Examination of post-1990 texts also supports this argument for a christ*oa*logical paradigm shift during the 1970s and 1980s. Thus Fiorenza, in *Jesus,* questions classical formulations (1995:162), in her turn to Chokmah-Sophia-Wisdom traditions 'to find appropriate language about the Divine' (1995:132). Her intention is to counter dominant 'christological dogmas' (1995:26) by constructing a 'different christological rhetoric' (Fiorenza, 1995:60). *Jesus* is spoken from the 'ekklesia of wo/men', committed to the struggle for justice. Thus the second strategy, of a christ*oa*logical revisioning, as redemptive community engaged in the struggle for justice, is made manifest.

Similarly, Ruether, in *Women and Redemption*, names a 'paradigm shift', completed in twentieth century feminist theology (1998:273), in terms which provide further evidence of christ*oa*logical revisioning:

> Feminists reject the classical notion that the human soul is radically fallen ... therefore needing an outside mediator who does the work of reconciliation for us. ... [A]n external redeemer is not necessary ... [b]ut 'grace events' ... set us on the path of struggle for just and loving relations.
>
> [The story of Jesus] is a root story for the redemptive process in which we must all be engaged, but he does not and cannot do it for us. ... His story can model what we need to do, but it happens only when all of us do it for ourselves and with one another (1998:275).

It is clear that Ruether's notions of 'redemptive humanity' (1992:138) and 'redemptive community' (1988:61) are a form of christ*oa*logical revisioning, which moves beyond the limitations imposed by her feminist appropriation of liberation theology's Christ, the liberator. Her explicit christ*oa*logical focus demonstrates her move from the first christ*oa*logical strategy, emphasising a single liberative/redemptive figure, to the second, where redemptive humanity and community engaged in the redemptive process do what is modelled in the Jesus story, but which cannot be done for us. Thus Ruether's post-1990 work, like Fiorenza's, confirms the importance of post-Daly christ*oa*logical revisioning within feminist theology.

In sum, we find constructed in the writings of this group of North American feminist theologians, a Christian version of Daly's envisaged 'corporate redemptive action by women' (1973:55), which is often – though not always – analysed in christ*oa*logical categories. The paradigm shift embodied in this work gains sharper definition in significant post-1990 texts.

It will be instructive to revisit British Christian women's theology in the light of our analysis of this paradigm shift. We now return to British Christian women's theology, seeking to clarify further its relationship with North American feminist theology.

### *British Christian Women's Theology and Feminist Christoalogical Revisioning*

We consider three aspects: the status of Eve, the contrast between Heyward's theology and Christian women's theology emerging from the British Anglican women's ordination debate, and Ruether's theological influence within the British Christian women's movement.

*The Status of Eve* In contrast to the female liberative/redemptive figures of wider feminist theology – Mary, Christa and the Goddess – Eve does not function as a female redemptive figure in British Christian women's theology. Despite Windle's urging that Eve be recognised as sister in redemption to Mary (1978), neither Eve nor Mary assume redemptive roles. Across the spectrum of British Christian women's theological writing, from Kroll to West, salvation is 'in Christ', while Eve represents the explicit inclusion of woman among the redeemed.

*Heyward and British Christian women's theology* Heyward throws light on one significant factor at work in the divergent development of British Christian women's christological orthodoxy, and North American feminist christ*oa*logical revisioning. She describes an 'early task' of North American feminist theology, which set out to prove that women, like men, are created in the image of God, and that the Galatians 3:28 formula takes precedence over texts which recommend the subordination of women (1984:7). Heyward thus draws attention to a North American debate over the position of women in the churches. Sexually egalitarian readings of bible and tradition were advanced (L.Swidler, 1971,1979; Patrick, 1975; Church, 1975; Phipps, 1976,1979,1988; Tavard, 1975; Tracy, 1978), feminist reassessment was made of Paul's position regarding women in the Church (Scroggs, 1972,1974; Hall, 1974 and Pagels, 1974) and women's sexual equality within the churches was affirmed (A.Swidler, 1967,1976,1978; L.and A.Swidler, 1970,1977; Scroggs, 1978; Bergant, 1983). The feminist theology which developed in North America, concurrent with the British Christian women's movement, takes as read this 'early task', before embarking on the christ*oa*logical revisioning, which is its principal achievement.[14] Although Heyward's 'early task' was begun well before the impact of Daly's agenda-setting *Beyond God the Father* (1973), it continued alongside the christ*oa*logical revisioning examined in this chapter.

There is a marked similarity between this North American debate, and the British debate associated with rehabilitation of Christian women within the institutional churches. Both concern the inclusion of women within Christian Church and theology. There is also a notable difference, as I have already argued, in the North American stress upon the sexual equality of Eve and Adam, in contrast to the prominence of the British Eve theme, with its stress upon women's specificity.

In chapter four, we noted the impact of Kroll's encouragement of liturgical experimentation inclusive of women, and the effectiveness of her passionate stand resisting the precedent set by the North American Episcopal Church, in the illegal ordination of women. It is surely of significance that Heyward was among the fourteen women illegally ordained in Philadelphia, in 1974. Her christological revisioning, and her participation in the Philadelphia ordinations, indicate that Heyward adopts the transgressive 'vision of theological possibility', which she perceives in Daly. In contrast, the British Christian women's movement, even in its strongest expression of 'second-wave' Christian feminist consciousness, as epitomised in Morley's liturgical writing, takes a rehabilitative rather than transgressive stance, remaining within the parameters of the classical paradigm of salvation, rather than participating in North American christ*oa*logical revisioning.

*Ruether and British Christian Women's Theology* We have already seen, in chapter five, the close connection between Ruether and the British Christian women's movement. In the context of the current discussion, it will be helpful to say more about the relationship between Ruether's feminist theology and British Christian women's theology. We have already discovered that, Condren and Jenner apart, there was little response to Daly's writings within the British Christian women's movement. Despite Condren's drawing upon Daly's critique of Christolatry, in 'For the Banished Children of Eve' (1976a), that critique failed to set an agenda for the women of the British movement. In contrast, Ruether's critical principle, the promotion of the full humanity of women, dovetailed with the ethos of the British Christian women's movement. Thus, for example, Ruether's critical principle sat well with Kate Mertes' assertion of the full humanity of women (1982:5, 1984c:2), and also supported Mertes' British argument for the full humanity of Eve (1984a:10).

We have seen that the second christ*oa*logical strategy was already implicit in Ruether's notion of redemptive humanity, in *Sexism and God-Talk*, and that it was thus compatible with her conception of Women-Church as redemptive community. However, Ruether's explicit christological position was articulated in terms of the liberative Christ, prior to her clear statement of the paradigm shift within feminist theology, in *Women and Redemption*. Thus, during the CWIRES period, Ruether's Christology remained centred on the redemptive figure of the male Jesus. More significantly, given that Daly's critique had not set a christological agenda for British Christian women, Ruether's promotion of the full humanity of women had a greater resonance, with the Christian women's project, than her Christology, with its already-negotiated first step beyond the classical paradigm of salvation.

Ruether's debate with Daphne Hampson (Hampson and Ruether, 1987) illustrates how her Christology remained obscured. Ruether – somewhat unexpectedly – argued her case for the compatibility of Christianity and feminism on eschatological grounds, reliant upon Bultmann. Hopkins adjudicates that Ruether lost the argument, but that she could have argued her case successfully – in terms consistent with her own work – on the historical ground of verifiable Christian emancipatory praxis (1988:81-2). Yet Christ as liberator, rather than redemptive humanity, predominated within Ruether's emancipatory praxis, until her explicit valorisation of redemptive community in *Women and Redemption* (1998): certainly, Ruether's British audience would receive no hint of christ*oa*logical revisioning from listening to this debate.

Though some British Christian women may have been aware of Ruether's liberative Christ, it is apparent that there was no general appreciation of the significance of North American christ*oa*logical revisioning. Hopkins' (academic) insight, concerning the significance of the paradigm shift within North American feminist theology, was not current within the Christian women's movement.

In sum – with the few exceptions already highlighted – North American feminist theology, even that of Ruether, had little direct influence upon the development of British Christian women's theology. Rather, British writers addressed their own issues. The Christian women's movement, with its rehabilitative project of change in the position of women in the institutional churches, determined the agenda for Christian women's theology. This agenda is similar to the body of North American writing addressing feminist theology's 'early task', but different to the predominant concerns of academic North American feminist theology, during the late 1970s and 1980s.

Our enquiry so far has concerned theology arising from the British women's movement, and from academic North American feminist theology. There is a third element in the equation: the feminist theology emerging in the British academy during the latter CWIRES period. Our final task is to evaluate this late arrival on the scene, and to establish the respective influence of the Christian women's movement, and of North American feminist theology, upon it.

We will discover that feminist theology emergent in the British academy prior to 1990 – with the notable exception of Julie Hopkins – reflected concerns, of the British Christian women's movement, more strongly than the preoccupations of North American feminist theology. Thus early British academic writings in feminist theology were concerned with the rehabilitation of women within classic salvation history, while the christ*oa*logical revisioning evident in North American work was absent.

## Feminist Theology in the British Academy

### *The Influence of the British Christian Women's Movement*

The Christian women's movement preceded the emergence of British academic feminist theology by a decade. Against the background of the growing movement, professional British women theologians became spokeswomen on the position of women in the churches. The first three currents within the churches – post-Vatican II Catholic renewal, the World Council of Churches Community of Women and Men in the Church dialogue and the Anglican ordination debate – provided the context for their public contribution.

Thus, within post-Vatican II Catholic renewal, Ursula King, Janet Soskice and Mary Grey showed an awareness of the Christian women's movement in their work. Ursula King – a member of the St Joan's International Alliance – developed feminist perspectives in the study of world religions, demonstrating a knowledge of British Womanspirit,[15] as well as the Christian women's movement (1981a, 1981b,1984,1993 [1989]). She also addressed general audiences. Janet Martin Soskice spoke at a joint Catholic and Anglican conference on women's ordination, (*CWN NL* 10 (Mar 1987):8) and supported the organisation of open lectures on feminist theology in Cambridge, later published as *Women's Voices* (Elwes, 1992). Mary Grey was involved with the Catholic Women's Network and other Catholic groups (The Grail, 1985; *CWN NL* 9 (Dec 1986):18, 14 (Mar 1988):7,23).

Ann Loades made an academic contribution to the dialogue between the churches and the women's movement, inspired by the World Council of Churches (WCC). In her Scott-Holland lectures, on Theology and the Significance of Gender, later published as *Searching for Lost Coins* (1987), Loades speaks as a feminist theologian. Her description of feminist theology as creating an 'imaginative, moral and theological shift' (1990:10) is reminiscent of Maude Royden's claim of the 'profound morality' of the ['first-wave'] women's movement: there is a neat link in the fact that Scott-Holland had been supportive of Royden. Loades' approach reflects the reiteration of 'first-wave' Church feminism within the WCC current, while her biblical metaphor of searching for lost coins is congruent with the notion of women bearing gifts to the church, which we encountered in chapter four.

The Anglican ordination debate was significant in the genesis of the – radically different – feminist theologies of Sarah Coakley and Daphne Hampson. As contributor to *Mirror to the Church*, and subsequently, Coakley shows a subtle appreciation of the role of Christian doctrine in underpinning patriarchal societal norms (1988,1990). The impact of the Christian women's rehabilitative project is visible in her stress on the practical outworkings of relations between the sexes within the church as more significant than doctrinal adjustments (1990:353), and in her reference to 'repressive patriarchal structures in [the] Church' (1990:345).

Coakley's elegant erudition sets her apart from the women who wrote from the Christian women's movement. She makes no appeal to Eve, or to the foundational texts from which women's full inclusion is argued – the re-envisaged Genesis myth or Galatians 3. Yet her project of achieving 'a more equitable representation of male and female creatureliness before God' (1990:353) is close to the project of the British movement among Christian women: the rehabilitation of Eve within Christianity. Further, Coakley's chosen starting point of creaturely dependence upon God contrasts with the priority given to the active commitment of 'our passion for justice' within North American redemptive women's communities. In short, Coakley's concerns are closer to those of the British Christian women's movement than to the emerging paradigm shift within North American feminist theology.

We are already aware, from chapter three, that the Anglican ordination debate was formative in shaping Hampson's post-Christian feminist theology (1985,1988), which finds its most systematic expression in *Theology and Feminism* (Hampson, 1990). Hampson's profile within the British Christian women's movement was raised by her debate with Ruether, 'Is There a Place for Feminists in the Christian Church?'. Hampson argues that Christianity and feminism are incompatible, as Christianity inevitably brings the patriarchal past into the present (Hampson and Ruether, 1987:1), and because Christianity is neither true nor moral (1990:1). She offers an alternative Schleiermacherian notion of a relational God, accessible through religious experience, in whom the male symbolism of Christianity is replaced (Hampson and Ruether, 1987:2).

Hampson thus constructs an ethical post-Christian religious alternative. In looking to feminist theories of relationship to supply ethical alternatives (1986a, 1990:116-26), she draws on sources which inform Heyward, Brock and Hunt also. Though critical of the foundational place of women's (as opposed to human) experience in feminist theology (1990:170), Hampson looks to women's relationality and connectedness, as facilitating new ways to perceive and conceive the presence of God in our world (1990:173).

Hampson's critique of Christianity as untrue relies upon her assertion of traditional salvation history, as the irreducible core of Christianity. Yet it is precisely this assertion of Christian truth which is challenged in the paradigm shift effected by feminist theology (Hopkins, 1988:242; Ruether, 1998:275). For Hampson, Christology means the portrayal of Jesus Christ (1990:50) and it must, she asserts, 'inescapably' grapple with divine and human natures in hypostatic union (1990:59). However, such 'grappling' is left behind in the christ*oa*logical revisioning which constitutes the feminist theological paradigm shift: as Hopkins says (1988:273), such dualistic vertical imagery is best avoided. The paradigm shift challenges Hampson's definition of the irreducible core of Christianity, and thus challenges the rationale of her post-Christian turn.

The British Christian women's movement was intransigent in the face of Hampson's carefully constructed criticism of Christianity. Her rejection of every feminist strategy, which seeks to accommodate feminism with Christianity, is based on her assertion that it is better for women to replace the patriarchal myth of

Christianity with new feminist myths (Hampson, 1990:41-6). In contrast, women within the Christian women's movement were seeking the rehabilitation of women within the institutional churches, and women's inclusion within the salvation of Christ.

Yet Hampson shared with the British Christian women's movement the formative influence of the Anglican ordination debate, and attachment to the classical paradigm of salvation history. Her turn to feminist theories of relation created common ground, not only with North American feminist theology, but also with the 'second-wave' Christian feminism of the Christian women's movement. This is well illustrated by Hampson's portrayal of a group 'of mostly Christian women', happy to share in feminist liturgy focused on symbols of 'light... life and... connectedness' (1990:112) as manifesting her envisaged ethical post-Christian religious practice. Despite these similarities, Hampson's post-Christian position sets her against the central rehabilitative ethos of the British Christian women's movement, and of those British academic theologians who share and support this rehabilitative aim.

Further evidence of the influence of the movement, upon emergent academic feminist theology, is found in occasional glimpses of the Christian women's Eve. We will make brief investigation of these.

### *Eve in British Academic Writing*

The Christian women's Eve theme surfaces in British academic writing. Thus Janet Martin Soskice made the final reference to Eve during the CWIRES period, in her reiteration of the 1981 MOW drama production, *After Eve* (1990), as title for her edited collection of theologians' responses to feminism. Introducing the book, Soskice asked a question which resonates with Christian women's concerns: 'What then does it mean to be a woman in the Jewish or Christian tradition, a woman "after Eve"?' (1990:xi).

There is a second glimpse of Eve in Mary Grey's rationale for her doctoral research into feminism and Christian redemption: 'the continuing punishment of Eve' accounts for the social injustice done to women (1989:12), thus there is a need to '[speak] specifically about the redemption of *women*' (1989:11). Grey's starting point thus contrasts with that of North American feminist theologians who, as we have seen, make no reference to Eve in their christ*oa*logical revisioning.

Finally, Julie Hopkins turns to the Genesis myth in search of an alternative understanding of the Incarnation. In proffering Trible's Genesis account of male and female as born in *imago Dei* (Hopkins, 1988:273), Hopkins repeats Trible's statement of the premise of twentieth century North American feminist theology, which we discovered earlier in this chapter. But when Hopkins emphasises male and female as sharing the *ruach* of God/ess, and then features Eve as participating in the desire of God/ess to create (1988:273), she reiterates both the British Eve theme, and Morley's explorations of women in the image of God. In writing of the suffering God/ess, women in labour, and the cosmos in travail, as co-operating in the birth of the future matrix (1988:273), Hopkins identifies Eve with God/ess, who suffers as she creates. Hopkins' Eve is reminiscent of the Quaker Women's Group encounter, with an Eve who is close to the female divine (QWG, 1986:30-2). In Hopkins, Eve appears as the redemptive figure envisaged by Windle (1978), though never realised in British Christian women's theology.

Thus both Soskice and Grey repeat the commonplace Christian women's insight that the predicament of contemporary Christian women is linked to the legacy of Eve. Likewise Hopkins, in exceeding Trible's assertion of sexual equality between Eve and Adam by featuring women's specificity in Eve, reiterates the British Christian women's Eve theme. Yet Hopkins, being alert to the North American christ*oa*logical paradigm shift, is interested in exploring Eve as a redemptive figure. Where Morley's exploration of women in the image of God remains within the classical paradigm of salvation, Hopkins' Eve belongs within the christ*oa*logical revisioning of the new paradigm.

Like Hopkins, Mary Grey engaged seriously with North American feminist theology in her doctoral research. But Grey stays closer to the classical paradigm of salvation than to the North American authors with whom she engages, thus remaining closer to British Christian women's concerns than does Hopkins. We will assess more fully the influence of North American feminist theology on Grey's theology.

## *Mary Grey and the Influence of North American Feminist Theology*

In *Redeeming the Dream* (1989), Grey makes a distinctive and original contribution to feminist christ*oa*logical revisioning. But, as we will see, in significant ways, her work is distinct from North American feminist christ*oa*logy. Like Heyward, Grey 'understands creation and redemption as a unified process' (1989:4), though Grey emphasises the reclaiming of subjugated knowledge, so allowing the 're-membering' (Daly), or re-connection 'of a lost sense of wholeness' (1989:10). Drawing upon process theology to envision divine-human co-operation, Grey states: 'By preserving the "different voice", by remaining close to a more profound relational scene, women are forming part of the divine redeeming task for the world' (1989:36). Finding Heyward's work 'inspirational' (1989:89), Grey envisions 'the very being of God [as] a passion both for justice-making and deeper forms of mutuality' (1989:89).

However, despite the theological creativity of Grey's 'inclusive and process Christology' (1989:172), her work is distinctively British in its concern with the rehabilitation of women within the institutional churches, and her christ*oa*logical revisioning is different in kind from the North American paradigm shift. Thus, in contrast to Heyward and the wider christ*oa*logical revisioning stimulated by Heyward's work, Grey wishes to retain the uniqueness of incarnation and resurrection. She therefore attempts to reclaim the cross and atonement for feminist theology (1989:107-8), in contrast to their repudiation in North American work, given the association of both cross and atonement with 'the myth of feminine evil'.

Grey sees Christa as having 'expressed the vulnerability and victim role of women' (1989:13), which she works to overcome by re-imaging atonement as atone-ment, 'a fundamental drive to unity and wholeness, which itself sparks off the creative-redemptive process' (Grey, 1989:126). Disowning 'lingering aspects of guilt and expiation' (1989:126), Grey's approach re-members a hidden strand of mutuality-in-relation, which – significantly – she claims to be already present within Christian tradition (1989:127). Grey's creative strategy is to contradict the prominent death motif, expressed in the 'Christus Victor', High Priest and Victim symbols of Christ the Redeemer, (1989:150) with the reclaimed subjugated 'different voice' of women associated with birthing. She retains the cross as central symbol among new symbols of creative birth-giving, connectedness and mutuality 'to keep alive the memory of the redemptive, relational power at the heart of existence' (1989:151), the crucified and risen Jesus symbolising 'the empowering hope that "crucified woman" may yet be "redemptive woman"' (1989:152). Grey also advocates the raising up of 'counter-symbols of women as redemptive (1989:173).

Yet, Grey's synthesis of Heyward's Christology with process thought leads her work in a different direction to the second step, towards corporate redemption, in North American christ*oa*logical revisioning. Grey's reliance upon process theology, in her creative fusion of creation and redemption, leaves the primacy of God as creator and redeemer intact. For Grey, women are redemptive when empowered by the life, death and resurrection of Jesus (1989:172), and Christ points to God, 'the whole source of redemption' (1989:173). Thus women's redemptive qualities are derivative, in contrast to their co-creator, co-redeemer status in Heyward's redemption of God, and to the redemptive 'passion for justice' of liberative communities. Grey's God as 'whole source of redemption' plays the major part, rather than redemptive woman. In contrast, when Ruether speaks of Jesus, 'who does not and cannot do it for us', as 'root metaphor' for the redemptive process (1998:275), women's redemptive community assumes a larger responsibility.

In short, Grey's reliance upon the God as source, of process theology, her insistence that mutuality-in-relation is already present, though subjugated, in Christian tradition, and her feminist revision of atonement are closer to classical salvation history, than to the paradigm shift which moves beyond it. When Grey lays out the implications of her Christology for the Church, her reflections are congruent with Catholic concerns and praxis within the British Christian women's movement, in the liturgy and wider life of the Oxford Christian feminists and the Catholic Women's Network. Thus she outlines a prophetic role for feminist spirituality of mutuality, in 'denouncing injustice in ecclesial structures, in androcentric and misogynist texts [and] exclusive language in the liturgy' (1989:172).

Further, when Grey suggests that the connectedness of the feminist relational self adds 'fresh understanding to the enfleshed nature of the Body of Christ' (Grey, 1989:151), she weaves 'the divine creative power of just and redemptive relationality' incarnate in Jesus (1989:172) into the theme of the 'Body of Christ', already developed by Angela West (1983a,1983b). And when Grey states, 'The women who belong to … "Women-Church" groups in many instances are feeding back into the wider church structures the fruits of their insights and experiences' (1989:173), she expresses the ethos of the British Christian women's movement, rather than that of North American Women-Church.

Thus, though expressed in scholarly form and in theological language, Grey's work coheres with the ethos of the Catholic Women's Network (CWN). She reflects British Christian women's perceptions, of women as bearers of gifts to the church, and of CWN and Women in Theology (WIT) as models of a renewed church, always locating themselves within the institutional churches, rather than as autonomous bases outside it. Where Hopkins is the first to perceive the paradigm shift in North American feminist theology, Grey – envisaging the models of reformed church embodied in CWN and WIT – entreats the Church to 'repent the wrongs done to women' (Grey, 1989:172) and to build mutual relations.

Grey's project goes well beyond the 'early task' of feminist theology, as described by Heyward, and constructively breaks new theological ground. However, reading her work in the context of the British Christian women's movement lends further confirmation to our earlier evaluation that the movement sought the rehabilitation of women within Christianity, without making Heyward's transgressive move. Despite her indebtedness to Heyward, Grey resists this step. Thus her closing statement, that in God's redemption 'all human efforts at self-liberation become taken up and unified with the redeeming forces of life itself' (Grey, 1989:173), is a different conception of divine-human relations to Heyward's 'co-creators and co-redeemers', to Brock's Christa/Community and to Hunt's community of justice-seeking friends. The difference in conception reflects the difference between the rehabilitative project of the British Christian women's movement, and North American christ*oa*logical revisioning.

However, by the end of the CWIRES period, it is possible to glimpse an emergent new direction in British academic feminist theology. This new impetus is independent of the concerns of the British Christian women's movement and, though congruent with the paradigm shift of North American feminist theology, forges a different path. Grace Jantzen leads the way.

### *A New Impetus in the British Academy*

In the final year of the CWIRES period, Jantzen wrote an editorial, 'Who Needs Feminism?' (1990), to an edition of the journal *Theology* devoted to feminist theology. Her editorial signals a new impetus, which was to develop during the 1990s. Jantzen sets out her claim:

> What is central to feminist theology … and what makes it crucial for everybody and for all forms of theological scholarship, is that feminists argue that Christian theology has for centuries been in the grip of a series of interlocking and destructive dualisms. Because Christianity has strongly affected the shape of western culture, these dualisms are pervasive in the thought structures throughout parts of the world historically dominated by that culture (1990:339-40).

Once more, Hopkins is our guide, as she is alert to a relevant link between Jantzen's doctoral thesis (1984) and a key component of Ruether's feminist theology, which appears in the citation above: the critique of dualisms (Hopkins, 1988: 212). We will make a brief digression here as, given our focus on christ*oa*logical revisoning, this critique has not yet featured in our explorations. Ruether's critique of dualisms is a lynchpin of her early work, appearing, for example, in 'Mother Earth and the Megamachine' (Ruether, 1972a), though playing no part in her consolidating analysis in *Women and Redemption* (1998).

Critique of dualisms thus provides a point of contact between the new impetus in Jantzen's work, and North American feminist theology. In *God's World, God's Body* (1984), Jantzen investigates a move from the cosmic dualism of the traditional picture, which conceives of God as spiritual and the world as material, to holism, where God and the world are conceived to be a single reality. The motivation of her earlier work – to respond to a widespread contemporary view that cosmic dualism is no longer tenable (Jantzen, 1984:155) – develops into a feminist commitment to transform dualism, because of its past legacy and continuing outworking of devastating harm.

In her sharper analysis, in 'Who Needs Feminism?', Jantzen argues that God-world, mind-body and male-female dualisms lead to 'the identification of the male with the mental and with God' (1990:342), reflected in western male mastery of the earth, subordination of women, and imperialist and racist mastery of non-white races and non-Christian cultures (1990:340-2). Further, 'Christianity has colluded with this oppressive structuring not only by providing its ideological underpinnings but also in some structural dualisms of its own', notably the clerical-lay division, and the (unsurprising) refusal of women's ordination (Jantzen, 1990:342-3). 'It becomes clear that ... [feminism is about] a fundamental change in [existing structures] and a whole revisioning of the Church, humankind, and the whole world, along holistic rather than dualistic lines' (1990:343).

In Jantzen's editorial, a critical consciousness – similar to that of Condren and Field-Bibb – finds expression, though Jantzen is informed by philosophy, rather than sociology. Jantzen makes fleeting reference to women's ordination (1990:343) within a wider perspective on both women's subordination within Christianity, and the dynamics of male domination revealed in women's exclusion from ordination. This wider perspective was already expressed by Condren (1976a,1978b,1989) and soon to reach fruition in Field-Bibb (1991). As we have seen, neither Condren, nor Field-Bibb, reflect the central rehabilitative ethos of the British Christian women's movement. No more does Jantzen.

Ruether uses the biblical *imago Dei* to contradict and resist dualistic legitimation of sexual hierarchy (1992:93-4). In contrast, Jantzen finds the roots of dualism in Platonic thought (1990:340), while Eve and the Genesis myth appear only in her (secondary) analysis of Augustinian 'theological justification for the misogynism pervading western culture' (1990:341). Jantzen simply documents the injustice wrought by dualism as incontrovertible evidence against its perpetuation. Her philosophical project thus exceeds the terms of the christ*oa*logical revisioning of North American feminist theology, while sharing the defining feature of the redemptive communities associated with the new paradigm: commitment to the struggle for justice.

## Conclusion

Christ*oa*logical revisioning was central to the paradigm shift made in North American feminist theology, being identified first by Hopkins, and then confirmed in Ruether's consolidating evaluation of feminist theology, *Women and Redemption* (1998). The contrast between North American feminist theology and British Christian women's theology becomes clear: the former makes a christ*oa*logical paradigm shift, while the latter remains within the classical paradigm of salvation.

The organising themes of British Christian women's theology – the rehabilitation of Eve, and the inclusion of woman in the salvation of Christ – served to highlight the interpretation of (mainly) North American feminist theology offered here. Our findings, in this chapter, confirm the contrast between British concern with the specificity of the woman, Eve, and North American emphasis on sexual equality between Eve and Adam. Thus Ruether uses *imago Dei* to assert sexual equality as foundational, whereas Morley uses women in the image of God as her starting point for exploration of God in the feminine.

We have clarified that Heyward's 'early task' of feminist theology was represented in a North American debate where women's equality was asserted in terms of alternative interpretations of the Genesis creation myth, and by arguing the primacy of Galatians 3:28 over subordinationist texts. This North American discussion paralleled British Christian women's call for women's inclusion within Christian churches and theology, based on the same texts – though British attention to Eve and to woman's specificity again marks a British/North American difference.

However, this 'early task' has not been our principal concern. Rather, we have found the development of christ*oa*logical revisioning to be directly related to the absence of the Eve theme in North America work, following the alternative interpretation of the Genesis myth, as foundation myth of patriarchy, by Daly and Stone. Daly's work is crucial, because of her linking of 'Christolatry' with the 'myth of feminine evil' (Stanton), centred on Eve. Where British Christian women's theology attempts to vindicate Eve, by arguing for her inclusion among the redeemed 'in Christ', twentieth century North American Christian feminist theology assumes the vindication of the woman, Eve, and sets about addressing the agenda set by Daly, in her critique of Christolatry.

We have seen that christ*oa*logical revisioning in the form of redemptive community creates a form of 'corporate redemptive action', which 'drives beyond Christolatry' (Daly). Daly was clear that such corporate action actively repudiates the myth of feminine evil. In the shift from redemptive figure to redemptive community, the ambiguity of the redemptive Mary, given mariological stress on longsuffering obedience, and of the Christa, given her identification of woman with the suffering Christ, is overcome in affirming women as redemptive, as well as redeemed.

After establishing the contrast between North American academic feminist theology, and British Christian women's theology, we have located feminist theology in the British academy during the 1980s, between these divergent influences. We found that the concerns of the Christian women's movement were a stronger influence in the early 1980s, though both Julie Hopkins and Mary Grey engage seriously with North American feminist theology, in their respective doctoral research projects, in the latter 1980s. By the end of the CWIRES period, Hopkins had left Britain to work in Europe, and her research conclusion – recognition of the paradigm shift – was not widely disseminated. Grey makes a distinctive contribution to the christ*oa*logical revisioning begun in Heyward, but we have seen that her arguments are also expressive of the British Christian women's ethos, remaining closer to the classical paradigm of salvation than to the shift inherent in North American work. In the final year of the CWIRES period, we glimpsed, in Grace Jantzen, the appearance of a critical consciousness in British academic feminist theology, which goes beyond the rehabilitative terms of the Christian women's movement.

We found traces of the Christian women's' Eve in British academic writings. With the exception of Hopkins (and Jantzen, who makes no mention of Christology) we find the classical paradigm of salvation is assumed, even by Daphne Hampson in her post-Christian critique of Christianity. Thus our conclusion must be that the rehabilitative concerns of the British Christian women's movement were the stronger influence upon British academic feminist theology, prior to 1990. Yet Jantzen's editorial of the final CWIRES year, promises new directions for British academic feminist theology during the approaching 1990s.

---

## Notes

1 Christ*oa*logy and christ*oa*logical are used here to denote explicit attention to sexual difference, in contrast with the implicit male gender, and/or the minimalising of gender, in the traditional term, 'christology'. The terms are generic: they include differing feminist strategies for taking sexual difference into account. However, references to 'feminist christology', 'Christology' and 'christological' also appear in the text, reflecting the usage of the feminist theologians cited.

2 Ruether, in *New Woman, New Earth* states that misogynistic texts attribute the origins of evil to Eve (1975a:15): 'woman becomes "Eve", an unnatural creation of a male ruling class' (1975a:10). She also criticises the Freudian theory of femininity as 'the psychoanalytic analogue of the religious myth of Eve as Adam's rib' (1975a:146). Ruether gives far more attention to the sublimation of the Mother Goddess than to the male myth of Eve. In short, Eve is not a positive figure for women.

3 Though the editors add a brief comment on the difference of the archetypal woman in Goddess-worshipping religions from our image of femaleness derived from the myth of

Eve (Christ and Plaskow, 1979:123). Eve also makes a minor appearance in Christ's essay on the Goddess, in Christ's statement that the [male] myth of Eve symbolises 'the misogynist antibody tradition in Western thought' (Christ, 1979;279). As in Ruether, this male-derived Eve is not ascribed any positive potential for women.

4 There is an apparent contradiction of my statement in Carol Meyers' *Discovering Eve* (1988). However, Meyers' project is to 'recover the pristine Eve' of the Genesis narrative beneath the expositions of Jewish and Christian antiquity (1988:77). She explores Eve as Everywoman, (1988:4) but this apparent similarity with British Christian women's theology breaks down in that Meyers wishes to retrieve the Everywoman of ancient Israel (1988:4), rather than to relate Eve to contemporary woman.

Elaine Pagels' fascinating study, *Adam, Eve and the Serpent* (1988), also sets out to trace the influence of exegesis of the Genesis myth upon Christian doctrine and teaching on sexuality during the first four centuries of Christianity. Eve is explored alongside Adam and the serpent, just as Trible explores Eve alongside Adam, in contrast with British interest in the specificity of Eve.

However, Meyers hints at a theological refiguring of Eve, when she locates Genesis 3 within the genre of biblical Wisdom literature with its close connection between woman and wisdom (1988:90). The serpent confers wisdom and 'it is the woman, and not the man, who perceives the desirability of procuring wisdom' (1988:91), thus providing the first instance of a relationship which reaches its climax in the Proverbs personification of Wisdom as woman. Meyers suggests the mythic background, for the association of the female and the qualities of wisdom, is found in a Semitic wisdom goddess (1988:91). This refiguring of Eve remains implicit.

5 As we will see, there was a North American debate on this question, beginning in the 1960s, where the primacy of Galatians 3:28 over subordinationist texts – the central argument made by Kroll (1976) and Dowell and Hurcombe (1987) – was also addressed.

6 The Christa is a figure of a crucified woman (Thistlethwaite, 1990:92-3).

7 Letty Russell also develops a liberation theology, stressing human liberation and partnership between women and men (1972,1974,1976,1979,1982a,1982b,1985), with the Bible as source of her expectation of justice and liberation (1985:138-43). Russell writes from a Protestant perspective, influenced by the WCC Community of Women and Men in the Church programmes (Russell, 1972:3,5,12), wherein she is reluctant to differentiate women's liberation from wider human liberation. A male Saviour is thus unproblematic for Russell, and her work does not contribute to the christ*oa*logical expansion, which is the subject of my analysis. See Hopkins, (1988:97-110) for a critical assessment of Russell's work as an attempted fusion of Moltmann's theology of hope with liberation and feminist theology. Hopkins argues this project must fail, as human liberation remains subsumed under androcentric, dogmatic theology (1988:110).

8 Chung derives this view from Emily Mei Ling Chen, who contributed to the 1987 conference.

9 Here Chung draws upon the work of Loretto-Eugenia Mapa.

10 The dual structure of Ruether's Christology (Hopkins, 1988:230-40) juxtaposes a messianic element with a sophiaological/cosmological element, wherein Sophia is equated with Christ (1988:237-8). The christ*oa*logical shift, discerned in this book, from Christ as liberator to women's redemptive community, takes place in Ruether's work between *Sexism and God-Talk* (1992 [1983]) and *Women and Redemption* (1998). Hopkins' dual analysis bridges Ruether's articulation of women's redemptive

community, in *Women and Redemption*, and the evident sophiaology of Fiorenza and Johnson.

[11] Egalitarian, inclusive relations between Jesus and his followers as model for the contemporary church is a well-worked theme (Ruether, 1992:136-8; Moltmann-Wendel 1982, 1986:79-82, 121-32,139-45; Heyward 1982:35-47). This line of enquiry owes much to Leonard Swidler's much-quoted thesis, that 'Jesus Was a Feminist' (Thistlethwaite, 1990:94). However, where these authors rely on readings of (patriarchal) gospel texts, Fiorenza's hermeneutic of suspicion allows a reconstructive challenge to silences within the texts.

[12] Heyward develops her thesis amid a variety of writings, where themes of mutuality, 'connectedness' and the self-in-relation are privileged within theologies of relation (Farley, 1975,1976; Heyward, 1982,1984; Brock, 1988; Hunt, 1989; Grey, 1989; Plaskow and Christ, 1989:171-266). These themes are also worked in feminist ethics (Haney, 1980; Andolson, 1981; Harrison, 1985; Robb, 1981, 1985; C.Keller, 1989). Although Heyward writes as a feminist liberation theologian, the sources informing this body of work describe a different concept of social transformation to the Marxist perspectives infusing earlier liberation theologies, and perceptible in Ruether's work. Thus Heyward's intervention marks the effect of 'theology of relation' upon feminist christ*oa*logy which relied, in its first stage, on feminist liberation theology. Post-1990, Johnson (1996) makes a skilful synthesis of these two components.

[13] Thistlethwaite criticises Brock as, like Heyward and Wilson-Kastner, perpetuating theologies of connectedness which give insufficient weight to the struggles and conflicts which arise from differences, including differences between feminists (1990:107). While endorsing her criticism, our concern here is the shift from christologies depending upon a single salvific figure, whether Christ, Christa or Mary, to redemptive community. Thistlethwaite's privileging of survivors of abuse as the site of 'resurrection' [*sic* cf redemption] (1990:107-8) is somewhat reductive, given the scale of suffering in the experience of women and men. Brock, in contrast, places survivors of abuse in a central position within her analysis of the wider broken-heartedness wrought by patriarchy.

[14] As the above references show, though Heyward's 'early task' was begun well before the agenda-setting impact of Daly's *Beyond God the Father* (1973), it continued alongside the christ*oa*logical revisioning discussed here.

[15] King was in contact with Asphodel, through the European Society of Women in Theological Research. Asphodel spoke of King's interest in Womanspirit research (Interview with Asphodel 20 August, 1995).

# Conclusion

Our journey into the past is now complete, and it is time to return to our immediate context, to face our contemporary conundrums and challenges. It is time also that I relinquish the first person plural 'we', with which I have attempted to guide my reader, encouraging you to adopt my vantage point, and to see what I have seen. I return to the 'I' of my Introduction – and you to your preferred critical stance.

My concluding discussion will appraise issues raised by this initial study of that remarkable outburst of activity during the 1970s and 1980s, which I have named as the British Christian women's movement. I will depict the key elements of the movement, as a prelude to estimating its impact on Christian theology, on institutional change within the churches, and on women's consciousness.

The key elements of the British Christian women's movement of the 1970s and 1980s may be drawn together around four broad axes. First, the movement was forged in the crucible of the post-1960s cultural shift, which set in motion four broad currents within the churches. The four currents were: post-Vatican II Catholic renewal; the World Council of Churches Community of Women and Men in the Church programme; the reinvigoration of the debate over women's ordination in the Catholic, Anglican and Methodist churches; and a post-1960s radical Christianity. Each of these currents gave rise to a new urgency concerning the position of women in the churches. These church-based currents intersected with the 'second-wave' women's movement. The British Christian women's movement was generated amid these five currents.

Second, the specific outworking of the Anglican women's ordination debate, within the Church of England, was of critical significance for the ethos of the British Christian women's movement. The delay in the synod decision to ordain women into the 1990s – in comparison with progress made elsewhere, such as in New Zealand but particularly in the North American Episcopal Church – shaped the British context within which the four currents followed their peculiar British course. The ongoing campaign in support of women's ordination, conducted by the CPG, alongside AGOW, during the 1970s, to be superseded by the longstanding MOW campaign, active throughout the CWIRES period, was the factor of greatest significance in the shaping of a coherent Christian women's movement, with a distinctive rehabilitative ethos. Solidarity with the Anglican campaign provided the glue holding disparate elements together in a single movement. The Anglican debate lent impetus to the creation of a British Christian women's theology, and provided the most significant stimulus towards theological writing.

Third, the Christian women's Eve – the symbol of the movement – emerged in the Anglican context. Her significance is that she highlights the absence of a 'first-wave' vindication of the woman Eve in the British context. I have argued that the reliance of 'first-wave' feminism, including Church feminism, upon spiritual womanhood as vehicle, meant that 'first-wave' feminists effectively threw in their lot with Mary, and settled for the pedestal of ascribed moral superiority. The 'second-wave' Christian women's movement opted, instead, for Eve, and in so doing exposed the root of male Christian justification of misogyny, with its continuing implications for women. The Christian women's Eve symbolised their demand for full acceptance of modern 'second-wave' woman, in all her commitment to women's autonomy, mutuality and sexuality, within the institutional churches. Further, Eve symbolised the infusion of this 'second-wave' consciousness within reinvigorated Church feminist goals: the vehicle of spiritual womanhood may have been rejected but, none the less, the embers of the 'first-wave' project were rekindled.

Many factors shaped Eve as the Christian women's symbolic. There was the absence of any British equivalent of Cady Stanton's *The Women's Bible*, and thus, in the age of the Angel, a failure to see the work of 'first-wave' feminism as 'a vindication of the woman Eve'. There was the confidence of British secularism, which obviated the need for freethinking interpretations of the Genesis myth outside the Christian arena. There was the continuing legacy of spiritual womanhood, with its good repute linked to the absent Eve, whose monstrous tendencies – of such concern to Milton – are domesticated in the tame Angel at home. There was that showcase of Christian misogyny and distrust of women's sexuality: the seemingly unending Anglican ordination debate. There was the cultural shift of the 1960s, expressed in the four currents in the churches, and in particular in the rise of 'second-wave' feminism. Together these factors created the conditions in which Eve was forged as a figure of women's autonomy, mutuality and sexuality, symbolising the desire of post-1960s woman to achieve the unrealised goal of 'first-wave' 'Church feminism': the full inclusion of women in the life of the institutional churches.

Fourth, I am not claiming that the British Christian women's movement was monolithic. On the contrary, diverse elements demonstrated their allegiance to the wider movement. In the 1970s, prior to the launch of CWIRES, radical Christian publications voiced Mary Condren's (Catholic) and Judith Jenner's (Methodist) radical perspectives, alongside the more moderate Anglican voices of Una Kroll and Diana Collins, and the Catholic 'Church feminist' research of Joan Morris. (Janet Morley was poised somewhere between these two integrities). After the early 1980s, Methodist contributions became less marked and Anglican and Catholic groups – CWN and WIT – gave the main shape to the movement, with a significant few feminist women from the Free Church denominations locating themselves within WIT. But Quaker and Unitarian women's groups were also important, choosing from their inception to align themselves with the wider movement. Catholic and Anglican women had major issues with their denominations, giving rise to both critique, and the conceptions of Christian women's groups as offering gifts to their church, and constituting models of a reformed church. Both 'gift' and 'model' were infused with 'second-wave' consciousness of the identity, which contemporary women were in the business of constructing – with women's autonomy, mutuality and sexuality as focal points. This 'second-wave' identity explains the link with Quaker and Unitarian women's groups. The traditions of Old Dissent also created the conditions for a Quaker and Unitarian engagement with the British Womanspirit network. I also found traces of the Christian women's Eve in the life of both the QWG and the UWG.

In short, I have documented the life of a movement, both unified around the Anglican women's ordination campaign, and diverse, showing the vibrant spread of 'second-wave' feminist consciousness, the upsurge of Christian women's denominational activity and the theological expression of this outburst. My analysis has valorised the Anglican attempt to rehabilitate Eve, by claiming an unambiguous place for contemporary woman in 'salvation in Christ'. I have also acknowledged writings, which transcended the aim of the rehabilitation of women within the institutional churches – principally those of Condren, Jenner, Field-Bibb and West. However, I have argued, emphatically, that the rehabilitative ethos predominated, so that, for example, even McEwan's 'document of alienation' (1991) is shaped by the reformism of the CWN.

I move on to the theological legacy of the British Christian women's movement. Three achievements stand out. Lingering expectations of spiritual womanhood, as setting the standard expected of women, were decisively challenged. The issue of women's ambiguous place in the scheme of salvation, and the link between this ambiguity and resistance to women's ordination, was exposed and a theological resolution offered in Hayter's 'new Eve in Christ'.

The movement has left a legacy of Christian women's liturgy, informed by 'second-wave' consciousness and alert to the theological significance of women's specificity. This legacy is resistant to the unacknowledged dominance of male specificity as the norm. In the different place of today, arguments about gender equality, with their corollary of equal access and the full inclusion of women, are largely won – though much remains to be done in this regard. Our attention is now drawn to the conundrums of difference, in which gender, ethnicity and sexuality constitute the giant categories. The complexities of women's specificity demand our engagement. Morley's liturgical exploration of God in the feminine retains its resonance.

Furthermore, the British Christian women's strategy of claiming a rehabilitation of Eve in terms of Chalcedonian orthodoxy, rather than in terms of the christ*oa*logical paradigm shift of North American feminist theology, may be more enduring in the face of the post-1990 swing towards neo-orthodoxy. Feminist theology finds itself in a new predicament. An impasse has been reached between those, such as Linda Woodhead, in 'Spiritualising the Sacred' (1997), and Angela West, in *Deadly Innocence* (1995), who seek to reinstate the classical paradigm of salvation history, and those who traverse the paradigm shift wrought in North American christ*oa*logical revisioning.

In both Woodhead and West, the paradigm shift is reversed as the classical redeemed community is reinstated, in place of the redemptive community, committed to the global struggle for justice. Woodhead's refusal of language about God in female images, which Elizabeth Johnson, in *She Who Is*, so gently urges upon the whole faith community (Johnson, 1996:6), epitomises the refusal of the new paradigm in terms of the old. It is noticeable that the gospel of justice, so prominent in West's early writings, has become the 'gospel of liberation from guilt' (West, 1995:xviii). Justice is left to the judgement of God, rather than to the work of the people. Christians participate in the redeemed – but not redemptive – community of the Church. Feminists are welcome – as long as they maintain allegiance to classical formulations, which set the standard by which the paradigm shift of feminist theology is judged and rejected. By the end of West's book, the 'theological edifice', under temporary threat of demolition during the previous thirty years of feminist theology (1995:xviii), is once again shored up.

It is interesting, given the centrality of Eve in this book, to note that West reasserts classical salvation history over against the 'moralistic version of the spare rib story' (1995:87), wherein, in West's view, feminist theology follows radical feminism in declaring women innocent. West thus reads radical feminism as reversing the verdict concerning Eve's guilt, meted out in the traditional interpretation of the Genesis myth. In contrast, West reinstates this reading, with disobedient Eve as emblem of women's capacity for sin (West 1995:208).

Although she claims this capacity confirms women's spiritual equality with men (1995:208), West restores the Eve/Mary pair as models for women: together, Eve's disobedience and Mary's fiat demonstrate our freedom to reject or choose God (West, 1995:210). Thus West recommends Mary – suitably liberated from both feminine and feminist idealisations – as 'model for obedient faith and discipleship', for feminists wishing to 'rediscover and represent the redeemed community within the church that we inherit' (1995:213). Where, in 'Genesis and Patriarchy' (West, 1981a), Eve's marginality allows her to subvert patriarchal distortion of the Word of God, in *Deadly Innocence* Eve reverts to her familiar role as figure of women's disobedience. In reconstructing the theological edifice in this way, even 'the new Eve in Christ' reverts to the second Eve: the obedient Mary.

West's implication of feminist theology in the myth of female innocence is severely criticised by Ruether, as an inaccurate falsification. For Ruether, the point of feminist theology is not women's innocence or guilt, but that women, like men, are responsible for making an active choice to resist evil (Ruether, 1997). In *Women and Redemption*, Ruether speaks appreciatively of the work of the Latin American feminist theologian, Yvonne Gebara:

> We must, as Gebara puts it, "take the side of the serpent" ... refusing the orders of the patriarchal God that keep us in a state of childish dependency. We can then recognise that the fragile fruit of the tree of life is indeed lovely and good for discernment, and eat the fruit with relish... This is the possible redemption of life on earth (Ruether, 1998:254).

Gebara's interpretation is reminiscent of that of Eliza Sharples: the Owenite Eve with whom this book opened.

I have argued for the distinctiveness of the British Christian women's Eve. And the Christian women's Eve is poised between the paradigm shift of North American feminist theology, and its neo-orthodox critics. Which has greater potential for the redemption of humankind: West's reinstated disobedient Eve, and Mary as ikon of the redeemed community, or Gebara's vision of the redemption of life on earth? In the third millenium, will Christian faith be passed on as belief in a 'particular and unrepeatable drama of redemption' (West, 1995:212) expressed through 'foundational beliefs ... fixed in formulation (Woodhead, 1993:173)? Or is the paradigm shift which destabilizes 'the dogmatic authoritarian stance of patriarchal religion' (Fiorenza, 1995:10), 'connect[s] feminist and classical wisdom' (Johnson, 1996:8) and calls the people of the church to a new understanding of redemption (Ruether, 1998:277) a necessary revisioning for our time? If neo-orthodoxy succeeds in rolling back feminist theology, will British women's humbler insights remain?

Having posed these questions over the theological legacy of the British Christian women's movement, I turn to its legacy within the institutional churches. I make three comments. The Christian women's movement contributed to the raising of consciousness concerning inclusive liturgical language. However, the interpretation made in this book, about the limits of Church of Scotland explorations of God as Mother, has wider significance. There is a continuing reluctance to follow Morley in moving beyond this divine image of spiritual womanhood: the only acceptable face of God in the feminine.

Second, the Roman Catholic hierarchical opposition to women's ordination has hardened, and women ordained as Anglican priests face indignities arising from the 'two integrities' compromise, which safeguards the position of opponents to women in the priesthood. Ordained women with episcopal potential are in the same miserable position of exclusion, as their sisters in the British Christian women's movement of the 1970s and 1980s, during the CPG/AGOW and MOW campaigns.

Third, there is evidence of increased participation of women in the governing structures of the denominations since the 1980s. I suspect that the WCC-inspired dialogue between the churches and the women's movement was a significant factor in this change. The difficulties in monitoring the dialogue from CWIRES evidence, as discussed in chapter four, do not enable a sound judgement to be made on the basis of this research, and even less allow an exact assessment of the influence of the Christian women's movement. However, I suggest that its existence was an important contextual factor.

My final assessment concerns the legacy of the Christian women's movement in women's consciousness. I discuss two aspects. First, there is the direct effect of the movement on those involved, at the centre or on the periphery of the movement. As with all social movements, the rise of the wave lifts up those it embraces; after its fall, the next generation has no clear grasp of its effect. Burning issues for one generation leave the next unmoved. However, the influence of those involved in the movement continues through their presence within their churches.

Second, Eve maintains a distinctive place in British women's consciousness. In 1995, the BBC broadcast a series of five fifteen minute television programmes under the title, 'Discovering Eve' (Hossick, 1995). A programme flyer explains that 'Discovering Eve' concerns 'the spiritual in women's lives ... the roots of feminine spirituality, and ... the effect a female vision of God might have on traditional religion'. Further, Angela Tilby (1998) names her review of Ruether's *Women and Redemption*, 'Eve's Changing Status'. In both cases, Eve stands for contemporary Christian woman, and the usage can be claimed as a reflection of the Christian women's Eve in Christian circles, in the years following the movement.

However, Eve also has a resonance in British women's consciousness beyond the denominational churches. I suggest that this is more attributable to Eve as Everywoman in the free thought tradition, represented in this book by Eliza Sharples, than to wider effects of the Christian women's Eve – who is herself a Christian re-appropriation of this Everywoman figure. One prominent example is Helena Kennedy's choice, in naming her study of women and the British system of justice, *Eve Was Framed* (1992). In her attempt to preserve the 'historic victories' (1992:26) of the Married Women's Property Acts under current conditions, Kennedy argues that the legacy of Eve is still evident in the prevalent discriminatory view that women should behave better than men. Clearly the said victories relied upon women adopting the strategy of protecting their good repute. But as Kennedy puts it, 'Why should women be considered the moral cornerstones of society? ... Poor old Eve' (1992:18).

Pamela Norris, in her *The Story of Eve* (Norris, 1998), also suggests that there is yet life in Eve. According to the text within the dustjacket: '*The Story of Eve* is the history of Everywoman'. Norris – a British literary author – documents the traditional myth in its various literary revisionings, while her afterword anticipates future alternative readings (1998:402). However, Julie Burchill (1999) makes an outspoken repudiation of Eve in her review of the book. With characteristic verve, Burchill pronounces that Eve 'is a male fantasy figure, and as such a bore' and 'We don't need myths; we need more of the truth ...Eve, of course, is the mother of all myths'. Further, women who refer to themselves as Daughters of Eve are guilty of perpetuating the Eternal Feminine. Norris' book, in Burchill's view is 'profoundly and embarassingly conservative'. Burchill is as assured in her secularism as I found socialist feminism to be, in my discussion of Eve in relation to the 'second-wave' women's movement.

Yet, despite Burchill, British feminist secularism and the fact that Judaeo-Christianity can no longer claim to provide a common Western cultural tradition, the Judaeo-Christian Genesis myth continues to invite alternative readings. Feminist readings invite identification with Eve on the part of contemporary women, in similar fashion to the British Christian women's Eve of the 1970s and 1980s. Two examples will suffice.

There is an embryonic Eve in postcolonial African women's theology. Eve as 'Mother of the Race' is posed as challenge to the implication of motherhood in white supremacist eugenics. Thus Teresa Okure discusses the 'constitutive significance of Eve' (1988:48), who as '"the mother of all the living"' plays a role akin to that of God, the source and giver of life (1988:51). Similarly, Brigalia Bam identifies Mother Eve – 'Mitochondrial Eve' (1998:347) – with the black women of Africa, as common mother of the human race.

Then Andrea Nye (1992) makes philosophical investigation of women's specificity. This book closes with Nye's question, evocative of the Mother Goddess suppressed beneath the Genesis myth, yet resonant with the tension between Gebara's christ*oa*logical revisioning and the British Christian women's 'new Eve in Christ':

> Can the serpent, whispering to Eve in the sweet sinuous words of desire, succeed in communicating a meaning outside Jahweh's orders? (Nye, 1992:233).

## Appendix 1

# Christian Women's Information and Resources (CWIRES) Leaflet

**C.W.I.R.S.[1] Christian Women's Information and Resource Service (incorporating the Ecumenical Feminist Trust)**

April 1979
In the last year there has been a great increase in the number of people working for change in the position of women in the church. New groups are active locally and nationally, and the amount of material being produced is increasing. A greater exchange of material, experience and expertise is taking place internationally and between denominations, and the number of women studying and training is growing. This is also the year of the WCC study THE COMMUNITY OF WOMEN AND MEN IN THE CHURCH, and next year the major conference emerging from the study will be held in this country. It is now essential that these increases in activity and resources be matched with an increased effectiveness of distribution.

The CHRISTIAN WOMEN'S INFORMATION AND RESOURCE SERVICE is being set up to meet this need, by a group of trustees and a working party drawn from the many groups active in the development of churchwomanship in this country. We are engaged in:

- compiling a comprehensive list of groups working to develop and change the present position of women in the church
- distributing 'funny money' which was first used in America in the campaign for the ordination of Episcopalian women
- drawing up a list of relevant resources available in Britain – books, pamphlets, studypacks, articles, liturgies
- developing a resources bank of material on models of ministry, theology and liturgy, and collections of material produced by various groups

Our aim is to keep people across the country in touch with Christian feminist developments and activities.

We need your support to expand this work. Individuals are asked to subscribe £2 a year, groups and organisations £5. We also need your views for the future development of CWIRS, and a Council will be elected later this year from the member groups and individual members.

CWIRS is not a strong, centralised organisation. It is a network, dependent on the willingness of all to share resources. We welcome details of your own publications and activities, and of any resources you have found or would like to obtain. We hope that you are interested in this new initiative and that you will support it - and find support from it.

Trish Marsh (Secretary)
For CWIRS trustees and working group

(Source: unlisted CWIRES papers)

---

## Note

[1] The acronym CWIRS was later changed to CWIRES.

# Appendix 2
## Groups Concerned with the Position of Women in the Church

**Table 1 Groups Founded pre-1960**

| *Name* | *Acronym* | *Date* | *Details* | *Newsletter* |
|---|---|---|---|---|
| St Joan's International Alliance | SJIA | (1911) | Origins in Catholic Women's Suffrage Society (CWSS) | *Catholic Citizen (CC)* |
| Society for the Ministry of Women in the Church | SMWC | 1930 | Founded on disbandment of the League of the Church Militant | *SMWC NL* |
| Anglican Group for the Ordination of Women | AGOW | 1930 | Founded on disbandment of the League of the Church Militant; merged with MOW in 1979 | |

**Table 2 Pre-CWIRES Groups, 1972-1978**

| *Name* | *Acronym* | *Date* | *Details* | *Newsletter* |
|---|---|---|---|---|
| Christian Parity Group | CPG | 1972 | Founded by Una Kroll | *CPG NL* |
| Student Christian Movement of Britain and Ireland Women's Project | SCM WP | 1976 | Origins in World Student Christian Federation Women's Project; founded at the 1975 WSCF conference in Lillehammer | |
| Roman Catholic Feminists | RCFs | 1977 | Founded by Jackie Field (Bibb) | *RCF NL* |
| Oxford Catholic Women's Group And Oxford Christian Feminists | | mid 1970s | Catholic group grew from Catholic renewal activity; Jo Garcia founded the Oxford Christian Feminists | |

**Table 3 New Initiatives in 1978**

| *Name* | *Acronym* | *Date* | *Details* | *Newsletter* |
|---|---|---|---|---|
| Christian Women's Information and Resources Project | CWIRES | 1978 | Founded by members of London Christian feminists, Oxford Christian Feminists etc | *CWIRES NL* |
| Ecumenical Feminist Trust | EFT | 1978 | Soon merged with CWIRES | |
| Movement for the Ordination of Women | MOW | 1978/9 | Founded after 1978 vote in Church of England Synod against the immediate ordination of women | *MOW NL*, *Chrysalis* |
| The *Christian Feminist Newsletter* | *CF NL* | 1978 | Founded by Sheila Robinson as ecumenical version of the *RCF NL* | *CF NL* |
| Quaker Women's Group | QWG | 1978 | Founded at Yearly Meeting | *QWG NL* |

**Table 4 CWIRES Period Phase One: 1978-1983**

| *Name* | *Acronym* | *Date* | *Details* | *Newsletter* |
|---|---|---|---|---|
| Variety of new Christian Feminist groups formed across the country, eg the East London Christian Feminists, the Plymouth Women's Theology Group | | 1979-1983 | Network of groups based on the *CF NL* | *CF NL* |
| Feminist Theology Project | FTP | 1980-1982 | Founded by Judith Jenner; fixed term | *Our Stories* |
| Quaker Women's Group | QWG | 1978 | Founded at Yearly Meeting | *QWG NL* |
| Unitarian Women's Group | UWG | 1981 | Founded at General Assembly | *UWG NL* |

**Table 5 CWIRES Period Phase Two: 1983-1990**

| *Name* | *Acronym* | *Date* | *Details* | *Newsletter* |
|---|---|---|---|---|
| Women in Theology | WIT | 1983/4 | Origin in Women's Training for Ordination Project | *WIT Mailing* |
| Catholic Women's Network | CWN | 1984 | Founded at conference held at Strawberry Hill, Called to Full Humanity | *CWN NL* |

# Appendix 3

# Women in Theology: a Feminist Reconsideration of Christian Theology

**1. Self-Definition.**

An analysis of where we stand as women: -

as persons – an exploration of psychological and biological factors

in society – an exploration of cultural roles, sex and gender

in the Church – an analysis of women's position in the Church today.

**2. The 'Patriarchal System' and women's critique of it.**

The history of the women's movement, women's literature, art, poetry etc. sexual politics, the patriarchal family etc.

**3. What is theology and how can we do it?**

Basic literacy in theology – finding out our own assumptions and understanding faith.

**4. The way the Bible has been used.**

The critical approach to the Bible: textual criticism, historical criticism, grammatical criticism, literary criticism, form criticism, redaction criticism.

**5. Wherein lies the Bible's authority?**

The nature of revelation and inspiration.

**6. Women's approach to the text.**

A consideration of feminist methods. "The hermenuetics of suspicion" – attempts to construct adequate interpretation.

**7. How can we use God language today?**

What language can we find as women to voice our experience of God today?

**8. God in the past.**

*God as Creator*

primitive religion
Greek and Egyptian religion
Goddess cults.

*God as Liberator*

Exodus.

*God-language in the Old Testament*

– female imagery.

*God-language in the New Testament*

– female imagery
– the question of 'fatherhood'.

*God-language in the history of doctrine*

*God-language in other religions*

**9. Women's participation in the history and literature of the people of Israel.**

**10. Women's participation in New Testament times.**

*Women and the life and teaching of Jesus.*

*Women and the person and work of Christ.*

*Early Christian communities and women's role.*

**11. The discipleship and priesthood of women today.**

**12. The community of the Church and feminist community.**

**13. Mariology.**

**14. Women's spirituality.**

(Source: *WIT* (Dec 1984): enclosure)

## Appendix 4

# Roman Catholic Feminists Manifesto and Catholic Women's Network Founding Aims and Position Paper

**RCF Manifesto**

The six-point manifesto expressed critical concern with:

1. The exodus of women from the RC Church to the woman's movement.
2. The polarisation of female sexuality in the Church valuing nuns over ordinary women who are only recognised as wife/mother.
3. Restriction of women's talents to 'the flower-arranging syndrome'.
4. Inappropriate Church teaching based on natural law about contraception and abortion.
5. The effects of Marian piety in producing feelings of inferiority, anxiety and breakdown in ordinary women.
6. 'Masculine' symbolism and language in liturgy and patriarchal resistance to female celebrants at the Eucharist.

(Source: *RCF NL* 3 (Oct 1977):1)

**CWN Founding Aims**

A flyer for the 1984 conference, Called to Full Humanity, described the purpose of the inaugural conference as to:

> meet; share experience of the Church; worship together; articulate a vision of Church free from sexism, classism and racism and plan priorities and action for change in the Catholic Church in Britain.

(Source: CWN, 1984b)

**Founding aims defined:**

1. to form local groups and a newsletter as means of communication between women seeking change in their position in the Church.
2. liturgical development, by promotion of inclusive language in Church liturgy and inclusion of women as eucharistic ministers, readers, servers and preachers, and also by liturgical experiment outside the mainstream.
3. women's theological education, and funding and organisation of conferences.

(Source: *CWN NL* 1 (Dec 1984):2)

**CWN Position Paper (summary with excerpts)**

1. ***Church*** - Full participation of all members is to be encouraged, together with development of base communities outside official Church structures.

2. ***Language*** - Inclusive liturgical language is necessary to represent God adequately, and to heal the schizophrenic effects of denigration of women by the Church Fathers combined with exaltation of the Virgin Mary.

3. ***Priesthood and Laity*** - Critique is made of: the hierarchical clergy-lay relationship; compulsory celibacy; inadequate training of priests which fails to equip them for appropriate relations with women, and of the relegation of laywomen, as opposed to laymen, to the laity.

4. ***Ordination and Ministry*** - CWN wishes to see women taking their rightful place in liturgy in the celebration of the Eucharist: 'Women should preach, be altar-servers, eucharistic ministers, catechists, leaders of prayer', within a Church which has shifted from clericalisation to 'an egalitarian ministry of all the baptised'. CWN supports women's ordination in the Anglican Church and while some members support Catholic women's ordination as a means of change, others give priority to a renewed, non-hierarchical ministry.

5. ***Social Justice*** - The Vatican II commitment to social justice must lead to Church support for self-determination of women and all marginalised groups, and the Church must examine and remedy its own oppressive practices: 'the equality of women within the Church is a justice issue'.

6. ***Strategy and Vision*** - CWN is committed to:- promoting lay involvement and witness in the Church; encouraging women's leadership in the Church; healing the pain of alienation.

(Source: CWN, 1987:2-8)

# Bibliography


Andolson, Barbara Hilkert (1981), 'Agape in Feminist Ethics'. In *Journal of Religious Ethics* 9 1 (1981): 69-83.

Asphodel [P. Long] (1994), 'The Goddess Movement in Britain Today'. In *Feminist Theology* 5 (Jan 1994): 11-39.

Bacchi, Carol Lee (1990), *Same Difference: Feminism and Sexual Difference*. Sydney: Allen.

Bam, Brigalia (1998), 'All About Eve: Woman of Africa'. In *Anglicanism: A Global Communion.* (Eds) Andrew Wingate, Kevin Ward, Carrie Pemberton and Wilson Sitshebo. London: Mowbray Cassell: 347-53.

Bass, Dorothy C. (1979), '"Their Prodigious Influence": Women, Religion and Reform in Antebellum America'. In *Women of Spirit*. (Eds) Rosemary Radford Ruether and Eleanor McLaughlin. New York: Simon and Schuster: 279-300.

Battiscombe, Georgina and Marghanita Laski (eds) (1965), *A Chaplet for Charlotte Yonge*. London: Cresset.

Beasley-Murray, G.R. (1983), *Man and Woman in the Church.* London: The Baptist Union.

Bergant, Dianne (1983), 'A Roman Catholic Paradigm'. In *Journal of Ecumenical Studies* 20 4 (1983): 549-57.

Bland, Lucy (1995), *Banishing the Beast: English Feminism and Sexual Morality, 1885-1914.* Harmondsworth: Penguin.

Bliss, Kathleen (1952), *The Service and Status of Women in the Churches*. London: SCM.

Borrowdale, Ann (1989), *A Woman's Work: Changing Christian Attitudes*. London: SPCK.

Briggs, Sheila (1987), 'Sexual Justice and the "Righteousness of God"'. In *Sex and God: Some Varieties of Women's Religious Experience.* (Ed) Linda Hurcombe. London: Routledge: 251-77.

Brock, Rita Nakishma (1988), *Journeys By Heart: a Christology of Erotic Power*. New York: Crossroad.

Brontë, Charlotte (1974) [1849]), *Shirley*. (Eds) Andrew and Judith Hook. Harmondsworth: Penguin.

Brown, Joanne Carlson and Rebecca Parker (1989), 'For God So Loved the World?'. In *Christianity, Patriarchy and Abuse: a Feminist Critique.* (Eds) Joanne Carlson Brown and Carole R. Bohn. New York: Pilgrim.

Burchill, Julie (1999), 'All About Eve All Over Again'. Review of *The Story of Eve* by Pamela Norris. In the *Guardian* 16 Jan 1999.

Buxton, Pia (1988), 'The Way Things Change'. In *Women Priest? Is the Ordination of Women Contrary to Christian Faith?* Ed. Alyson Peberdy. Women in Religion Series. Basingstoke: Marshall Pickering-Collins: 61-9.

Byrne, Lavinia (1988), *Women Before God*. London: SPCK.

Casteras, Susan P. (1986), 'Virgin Vows: The Early Victorian Artists' Portrayal of Nuns and Novices'. In *Religion in the Lives of English Women, 1760-1930*. (Ed) Gail Malmgreen. London: Croom Helm: 129-54.

Christ, Carol P. (1979), 'Why Women Need the Goddess: Phenomenological, Psychological, and Political Reflections'. In *Womanspirit Rising: a Feminist Reader in Religion*. (Eds). Carol P. Christ and Judith Plaskow. New York: Harper: 273-87.

Christ, Carol P. and Judith Plaskow (eds) (1979),*Womanspirit Rising: a Feminist Reader in Religion*. New York: Harper.

Chung, Hyun Kyung (1990), *Struggle to be the Sun Again: Introducing Asian Women's Theology*. London: SCM.

Church, F. Forrester (1975), 'Sex and Salvation in Tertullian'. In *Harvard Theological Review* 68 (1975): 83-101.

Coakley, Sarah (1988), '"Femininity" and the Holy Spirit?'. In *Mirror to the Church.* (Ed) Monica Furlong. London: SPCK: 124-35.

Coakley, Sarah (1990), 'Creaturehood before God: Male and Female'. In *Theology* XCIII (Sep/Oct 1990): 343-54.

Collins, Sheila D. (1974), *A Different Heaven and Earth: a Feminist Perspective on Religion*. Valley Forge: Judson.

Condren, Mary T. (1989), *The Serpent and the Goddess: Women, Religion and Power in Celtic Ireland*. New York: Harper.

Condren, Mary T. (1992), Review of *Women Towards Priesthood: Ministerial Politics and Feminist Praxis* by Jacqueline Field-Bibb. In *The Furrow* (Feb 1992) 43 2: 116-9.

Condren, Mary T. (1997), 'Mercy Not Sacrifice: Toward a Celtic Theology'. *Feminist Theology* 15 (May 1997): 31-54.

Coote, Anna and Campbell, Beatrix (1987), *Sweet Freedom*. Second edition. Oxford: Basil Blackwell.

Court, Gillian (1980), 'What Kind of Peace Is It?'. In *Theology* 83 694 (1980): 243-9.

Crawford, Janet and Michael Kinnamon (eds) (1983), *In God's Image: Reflections on Identity, Human Wholeness and the Authority of Scripture*. Geneva: WCC.

Daggers, Jenny (2000), 'The Origins and Development of Feminist Theology in Britain, 1960-1990'. University of Manchester. Unpublished PhD thesis.

Dale, Jennifer and Peggy Foster (1986), *Feminists and State Welfare*. London: Routledge.

Daly, Mary (1973), *Beyond God the Father: Towards a Philosophy of Women's Liberation*. Boston: Beacon.

Daly, Mary (1985 [1968]), *The Church and the Second Sex*. Third edition. Boston: Beacon.

Dowell, Susan (1991), 'One Holy and Divided Trinity'. In *Women Experiencing Church: a Document of Alienation.* (Ed) Dorothea McEwan. Leominster: Gracewing: 153-60.

Dowell, Susan and Linda Hurcombe (1987 [1981]), *Dispossessed Daughters of Eve: Faith and Feminism*. Second edition. London: SPCK.

Dyson, Anthony (1984), 'Dr Leonard on the Ordination of Women: a Response'. In *Theology* 87 716: 87-95.

Eliot, George (1962 [1871]), *Middlemarch*. Introduction Quentin Anderson. London: Collier-Macmillan.

Elwes, Teresa (ed) (1992), *Women's Voices: Essays in Contemporary Feminist Theology*. Women in Religion Series. London: Marshall Pickering-Collins.

Fabella, Virginia and Mercy Amba Oduyoye (eds) (1988),*With Passion and Compassion: Third World Women Doing Theology*. Maryknoll: Orbis.

Farley, Margaret A. (1975), 'New Patterns of Relationship: Beginnings of a Moral Revolution'. In *Theological Studies* 36 4 (1975): 627-46.

Farley, Margaret A. (1976), 'Sources of Sexual Inequality in the History of Christian Thought'. In *Journal of Religion* 56 2 (1976): 162-76.

Field-Bibb, Jacqueline (1989), 'From "The Church to Wickedary": The Theology and Philosophy of Mary Daly'. In *MC* N.S. xxx 4 (1989): 35-41.

Field-Bibb, Jacqueline (1991), *Women Towards Priesthood: Ministerial Politics and Feminist Praxis*. Cambridge: Cambridge UP.

Fiorenza, Elisabeth Schussler (1975), 'Feminist Theology as a Critical Theology of Liberation'. In *Theological Studies* 36 (1975): 605-26.

Fiorenza, Elisabeth Schussler (1979), 'Towards a Liberating and Liberated Theology: Women Theologians and Feminist Theology in the USA'. *Concilium* 15 (1979): 22-32.

Fiorenza, Elisabeth Schussler (1984a), *In Memory of Her: a Feminist Theological Reconstruction of Christian Origins*. London: SCM.

Fiorenza, Elisabeth Schussler (1984b), *Bread Not Stone: the Challenge of Feminist Biblical Interpretation*. Boston: Beacon.

Fiorenza, Elisabeth Schussler (1985), 'The Will to Choose or to Reject: Continuing our Critical Work'. In *Feminist Interpretation of the Bible*. (Ed) Letty M. Russell. Oxford: Blackwell: 125-36.

Fiorenza, Elisabeth Schussler (1995), *Jesus Miriam's Child, Sophia's Prophet: Critical Issues in Feminist Christology*. London: SCM.

Fletcher, Sheila (1989), *Maude Royden: A Life*. Oxford: Blackwell.

Forster, Margaret (1986), *Significant Sisters: the Grassroots of Active Feminism, 1839-1939*. Harmondsworth: Penguin.

Furlong, Monica (ed) (1984), *Feminine in the Church*. London: SPCK.

Furlong, Monica (ed) (1988a), *Mirror to the Church*. London: SPCK.

Furlong, Monica (1991a), 'Introduction: a "Non-Sexist" Community'. In *Women Included: a Book of Services and Prayers*. St Hilda Community. London: SPCK: 5-15.

Furlong, Monica (1991b), *A Dangerous Delight: Women and Power in the Church*, London: SPCK.

Garcia, Jo and Sara Maitland (eds) (1983), *Walking on the Water: Women Talk About Spirituality*. London: Virago.

Gebara, Ivone and Maria Clara Bingemer (1989), *Mary, Mother of God, Mother of the Poor*. Maryknoll: Orbis.

Gee, Peter (1982), 'Fifty Issues: Ten Years of Movement'. In *Movement* 50 (1982): 13-15+.

Gilbert, Sandra M. and Susan Gubar (1979), *The Madwoman in the Attic*. Newhaven: Yale UP.

Gill, Sean (1994), *Women in the Church of England: From the Eighteenth Century to the Present*. London: SPCK.

Gillespie, Joanna Bowen (1987), 'Gasping for Larger Measures: Joanna Turner, Eighteenth Century Activist'. In *Journal of Feminist Studies in Religion* 3 (1987): 31-55.

Gössman, Elisabeth (1998), 'Women's Ordination and the Vatican'. In *Feminist Theology* 18 (1998): 67-86.

Grant, Jacqueline (1989), *White Women's Christ and Black Women's Jesus: White Feminist Christology and Womanist Response*. Atlanta: Scholars.

Grey, Mary (1989), *Redeeming the Dream: Feminism, Redemption and the Christian Tradition*. London: SPCK.

Hall, Barbara (1974), 'Paul and Women'. In *Theology Today* 31 1 (1974): 50-55.

Hampson, Daphne (1988), 'On Power and Gender'. In *Modern Theology* 4, 3 (1988): 234-50.

Hampson, Daphne (1990), *Theology and Feminism*. Oxford: Blackwell.

Haney, Eleanor Humes (1980), 'What is Feminist Ethics? A Proposal for Continuing Discussion'. In *Journal of Religious Ethics* 8 (1980): 115-24.

Harrison, Beverley Wildung (1985), 'The Power of Anger in the Work of Love'. In *Making the Connections: Essays in Feminist Social Ethics*. (Ed) Carol S. Robb Boston: Beacon: 5-19.

Hayter, Mary (1987), *The New Eve in Christ: the Use and Abuse of the Bible in the Debate about Women in the Church*. London: SPCK.

Hebblethwaite, Margaret (1984b), *Motherhood and God.*. London: Chapman.
Heeney, Brian (1988), *The Women's Movement in the Church of England, 1850-1930*. Oxford: Clarendon.
Herzel, Susannah (1981), *A Voice for Women: The Women's Department of the World Council of Churches*. Geneva: WCC.
Heyward, Carter (1982), *The Redemption of God: a Theology of Mutual Relation*. Washington: UP of America.
Heyward, Carter (1984), *Our Passion for Justice*. New York: Pilgrim.
Hoad, Ann (1984), 'Crumbs from the Table: Towards a Whole Priesthood'. In *Feminine in the Church*. (Ed) Monica Furlong. London: SPCK: 100-18
Hopkins, Julie Marina (1988), 'The Understanding of History in English-Speaking Western Christian Feminist Theology'. University of Bristol. Unpublished PhD thesis.
Hopkins, Julie Marina (1995), *Towards a Feminist Christology: Jesus of Nazareth, European Women and the Christological Crisis*. London: SPCK.
Hossick, Pamela (1995), 'Discovering Eve'. Press Release. Oct 1995. Manchester: BBC 1.
Howard, Christian (1977), 'Ordination of Women in the Anglican Communion and the Ecumenical Debate'. In *Ecumenical Review* 29 (1977): 234-53.
Hunt, Mary (1987), 'Friends in Deed'. In *Sex and God: Some Varieties of Women's Religious Experience*. (Ed) Linda Hurcombe. London: Routledge: 46-54.
Hunt, Mary (1989), *Fierce Tenderness: A Feminist Theology of Friendship*. New York: Crossroad.
Hurcombe, Linda (ed) (1987), *Sex and God: Some Varieties of Women's Religious Experience*. London: Routledge.
Inkpin, Jonathan David Francis (1996), 'Combating the "Sin of Self-Sacrifice?": Christian Feminism in the Women's Suffrage Struggle, 1903-1918'. University of Durham. Unpublished PhD thesis.
Jackson, Stevi (ed) (1993), *Women's Studies: a Reader*. London: Harvester.
Jackson, Stevi and Sue Scott (eds) (1996), *Feminism and Sexuality: a Reader*. Edinburgh: Edinburgh University Press.
Jantzen, Grace M. (1984), *God's World, God's Body*. London: DLT.
Jantzen, Grace M. (1990), 'Who Needs Feminism?'. In *Theology* XCIII 755 (Sep/Oct 1990): 339-43.
Jeffreys, Sheila (1985), *The Spinster and Her Enemies: Feminism and Sexuality, 1860-1930*. London: Pandora.
Johnson, Elizabeth A. (1996), *She Who Is: The Mystery of God in Feminist Theological Discourse*. New York: Crossroad.
Keay, Kathy (ed) (1987), *Men, Women and God: Evangelicals on Feminism*. Basingstoke: Marshall.
Keller, Catherine (1989), 'Feminism and the Ethic of Inseparability'. In *Weaving the Visions: New Patterns in Feminist Spirituality*. (Eds) Judith Plaskow and Carol P. Christ. New York: Harper: 256-65.
Kennedy, Helena (1992), *Eve Was Framed*. London: Chatto and Windus.
King, Ursula (1984), 'Voices of Protest: Voices of Promise, Exploring Spirituality for a New Age'. The 1984 Hibbert Lecture. London: Hibbert Trust.
King, Ursula (1985), 'Women in Dialogue: A New Vision of Ecumenism', Seventh Cardinal Heenan Memorial Lecture. In *Heythrop Journal* 26 (1985): 125-42. Reprint in *Feminist Theology: a Reader*. (Ed) Anne Loades. London: SPCK, 1990: 275-9.
King, Ursula (1993 [1989]), *Women and Spirituality: Voices of Protest and Promise*. Second edition. Basingstoke: Macmillan.

King, Ursula (ed) (1994), *Feminist Theology from the Third World: a Reader*. London: SPCK.

Kroll, Una (1975), *Flesh of My Flesh*. London: DLT.

Kroll, Una (1987), 'A Womb-Centred Life'. In *Sex and God: Some Varieties of Religious Experience*. (Ed) Linda Hurcombe. London: Routledge: 90-103.

Kwok, Pui-Lan (1984), 'God Weeps with our Pain'. In *The East Asia Journal of Theology* 2 2 (1984): 228-32.

Langley, Myrtle (1983), *Equal Woman: a Christian Feminist Perspective*. Basingstoke: Marshall.

Lassetter, Vivienne M. (1994), 'Faith and Favour: Religion and Social Commentary in the Lives of Victorian Women'. University of Manchester. Unpublished MA thesis.

Lewis, Alan E. (ed) (1984), *The Motherhood of God: a Report by a Study Group Appointed by the Woman's Guild and the Panel of Doctrine on the Invitation of the General Assembly of the Church of Scotland*. Edinburgh: St Andrew.

Loades, Ann (1987), *Searching For Lost Coins: Explorations in Christianity and Feminism*. London: SPCK.

Loades, Ann (ed) (1990), *Feminist Theology: a Reader*. London: SPCK.

Long, Asphodel P. (1992), *In a Chariot Drawn By Lions: the Search for the Female in Deity*. London: Women's Press.

Long, Asphodel P. (1994), 'The Goddess Movement in Britain Today'. In *Feminist Theology* 5 (Jan 1994): 11-39.

Maison, Margaret (1986), '"Thine, Only Thine!" Women Hymn Writers in Britain, 1760-1835'. In *Religion in the Lives of English Women, 1760-1930*. (Ed.) Gail Malmgreen. London: Croom Helm.

Maitland, Sara (1983), *Map of the New Country: Women and Christianity*. London: Routledge Press.

Maitland, Sara (1987), 'Passionate Prayer: Masochistic Images in Women's Experience'. In *Sex and God: Some Varieties of Women's Religious Experience*. (Ed) Linda Hurcombe. London: Routledge: 125-40.

Maitland, Sara (1988), *Very Heaven: Looking Back at the 1960s*. London: Virago.

Maitland, Sara (1990), 'Ways of Relating'. In *Feminist Theology: a Reader*. (Ed) Ann Loades. London: SPCK: 148-57.

Malmgreen, Gail (ed.) (1986), *Religion in the Lives of English Women, 1760-1930*. London: Croom Helm.

Marcuse, Herbert (1969 [1965]), 'Repressive Tolerance'. In *A Critique of Pure Tolerance*. Robert Paul Wolff, Barrington Moore Jr and Herbert Marcuse. London: Jonathan Cape: 93-137.

Marwick, Arthur (1998), *The Sixties: Cultural Revolution in Britain, France, Italy and the United States c1958-c1974*. Oxford: OUP.

Matriarchy Study Group (1977), *Goddess Shrew*. London: Matriarchy Study Group.

Matriarchy Study Group (1978), *Politics of Matriarchy*. London: Matriarchy Study Group.

Mayor, Stephen (1969), 'The Ministry of Women: a Report on the Argument'. In *MC* N.S. xii 3 (1969): 222-9.

McEwan, Dorothea (ed) (1991), *Women Experiencing Church: a Document of Alienation*. Leominster: Gracewing.

Meyers, Carol (1988), *Discovering Eve: Ancient Israelite Women in Context*. Oxford: OUP.

Milbank, Alison (1987), 'Josephine Butler: Christianity, Feminism and Social Action'. In *Disciplines of Faith: Studies in Religion, Politics and Patriarchy*. (Eds) Jim Obelkevich, Lyndal Roper and Raphael Samuel. History Workshop. London: Routledge.

Mill, John Stuart (1870) [1869]), *The Subjection of Women.* Third Edition. London: Longman, Green, Reader and Dyer.
Mitchell, Juliet (1974), *Psychoanalysis and Feminism.* Harmondsworth: Penguin.
Moltmann-Wendel, Elisabeth (1982), *The Women Around Jesus.* London: SCM.
Moltmann-Wendel, Elisabeth (1986), *A Land Flowing with Milk and Honey: Perspectives on Feminist Theology.* London: SCM.
Moore, P.L. (ed) (1978), *Man, Woman and the Priesthood of Christ.* London: SPCK.
Morley, Janet (1984a), '"The Faltering Words of Men": Exclusive Language in the Liturgy'. In *Feminine in the Church.* (Ed) Monica Furlong. London: SPCK: 56-70.
Morley, Janet (1988a), *All Desires Known.* London: WIT and MOW.
Morley, Janet (1988b), 'I Desire Her with My Whole Heart'. In *Feminist Theology: a Reader.* (Ed) Ann Loades. London: SPCK, 1990: 158-163. Reprint. From *The Month* 21:2 (1988b): 541-4.
Morley, Janet (1988c), 'Liturgy and Danger'. In *Mirror to the Church.* (Ed) Monica Furlong. London: SPCK: 24-38.
Morris, Joan (1973), *Against Nature, Against God: the History of Women with Clerical Ordination and the Jurisdiction of Bishops.* London: Mowbrays. Also published as *The Lady Was A Bishop: the Hidden History of Women with Clerical Ordination and the Jurisdiction of Bishops.* New York: Macmillan.
Morris, Joan (1985), *Pope John VIII – an English Woman: Alias Pope Joan.* London: Vrai.
Murphy, Alexina (1992), 'New Catholic Women in England'. In *The Voice of the Turtledove: New Catholic Women in Europe.* Ed. Anne Brotherton. New York: Paulist: 39-60.
Nash, Elizabeth J. (1979), 'The Church and Women's Rights'. In *Theology* 82 686 (1979): 118-22.
Norris, Pamela (1998), *The Story of Eve.* London: Picador Macmillan.
Nye, Andrea (1992), 'The Voice of the Serpent: French Feminism and Philosophy of Language'. In *Women, Knowledge and Reality: Explorations in Feminist Philosophy.* (Eds) Ann Garry and Marilyn Pearsall. New York: Routledge: 233-49.
Obelkevich, Jim, Lyndal Roper and Raphael Samuel (eds) (1987), *Disciplines of Faith: Studies in Religion, Politics and Patriarchy.* History Workshop. London: Routledge.
Oduyoye, Mercy Amba (1989), 'Alive to What God is Doing'. *Ecumenical Review* 41 1989: 194-200.
Offen, Karen (1988), 'Defining Feminism: a Comparative Historical Approach'. In *Signs* 14 (1988): 119-57.
Okure, Teresa (1988), 'Women in the Bible'. In *With Passion and Compassion: Third World Women Doing Theology.* (Eds) Virginia Fabella and Mercy Amba Oduyoye. New York: Orbis: 47-59.
Pagels, Elaine H. (1974), 'Paul and Women: a Response to Recent Discussion'. In *Journal of the American Academy of Religion* 42 3 (1974): 538-49.
Pagels, Elaine H. (1988), *Adam, Eve and the Serpent.* London: Weidenfield and Nicholson.
Parvey, Constance F. (ed) (1983), *The Community of Women and Men in the Church: the Sheffield Report.* Geneva: WCC.
Patrick, Anne E. (1975), 'Women and Religion: a Survey of Significant Literature, 1965-1974'. In *Theological Studies* 36 4 (1975): 737-65.
Peberdy, Alyson (ed) (1988), *Women Priest? Is the Ordination of Women Contrary to Christian Faith?.* Women in Religion Series. Basingstoke: Marshall Pickering-Collins.
Phipps, William E. (1976), 'Adam's Rib: Bone of Contention'. In *Theology Today* 33 3 (1976): 263-73.

Phipps, William E. (1979), 'The Sex of God'. In *Journal of Ecumenical Studies* 16 (1979): 515-17.

Phipps, William E. (1988), 'Eve and Pandora Contrasted'. In *Theology Today* 45 1 (1988): 34-48.

Pinsent, Pat (1992), 'Christian Feminism in the Seventeenth Century'. In *Feminist Theology* 1 (Sep 1992): 58-73.

Plaskow, Judith and Carol P. Christ (eds) (1989), *Weaving the Visions: New Patterns in Feminist Spirituality*. New York: Harper.

Pratt, Ianthe (1994), 'Interview with Ianthe Pratt'. In *Feminist Theology* 7 (1994): 15-28. By Dorothea McEwan.

Quaker Women's Group (1986), *Bringing the Invisible into the Light: Some Quaker Feminists Speak of their Experience*. Ashford: Headley.

Rehmann-Sutter, Christoph (1996), '"Frankensteinian Knowledge"?'. In *The Monist* 79 2 (1996): 264-79.

Rendall, Jane (ed) (1987a), *Equal or Different: Women's Politics, 1800-1914*. Oxford: Blackwell: 1-27.

Rendall, Jane (1987b), 'A Moral Engine? Feminism, Liberalism and the Englishwoman's Journal'. *Equal or Different: Women's Politics, 1800-1914*. (Ed) Jane Rendall. Oxford: Blackwell: 112-37.

Rich, Adrienne (1980), 'Compulsory Heterosexuality and Lesbian Existence'. In *Signs* 3 (1980): 631-60.

Robb, Carol S. (1981), 'A Framework for Feminist Ethics'. In *Journal of Religious Ethics* 9 1 (1981): 48-68.

Robb, Carol S. (1985), *Making the Connections: Essays in Feminist Social Ethics*. Boston: Beacon.

Robson, Jill (1984), 'Mary: My Sister'. In *Feminine in the Church*. (Ed) Monica Furlong. London: SPCK: 119-38.

Rose, Judith (1992), 'Stereotype and Shadow in the Work of Christina Rossetti and Gwen John'. In *Feminist Theology* 1 (Sep 1992): 97-106.

Roszak, Theodore (1970 [1968]), *The Making of a Counter Culture: Reflections on the Technocratic Society and Its Youthful Opposition*. London: Faber and Faber.

Rowbotham, Sheila (1973), *Hidden from History: 300 Years of Women's Oppression and the Fight Against It*. London: Pluto.

Rowbotham, Sheila (1983), 'When Adam Delved and Eve Span'. In *Dreams and Dilemmas: Collected Writings*. Sheila Rowbotham. London: Virago: 199-207.

Rowbotham, Sheila (1989), *The Past is Before Us: Feminism in Action Since the 1960s*. London: Pandora.

Ruether, Rosemary Radford (1972b), *Liberation Theology: Human Hope Confronts Christian History and American Power*. New York: Paulist.

Ruether, Rosemary Radford (ed) (1974), *Religion and Sexism: Images of Women in the Jewish and Christian Traditions*. New York: Simon.

Ruether, Rosemary Radford (1975), *New Woman New Earth: Sexist Ideologies and Human Liberation*. New York: Seabury.

Ruether, Rosemary Radford (1979), *Mary – The Feminine Face of the Church*. London: SCM.

Ruether, Rosemary Radford (1985a), 'Feminist Interpretation: a Method of Correlation.' In *Feminist Interpretation of the Bible*. (Ed) Letty M. Russell. Oxford: Blackwell: 111-24.

Ruether, Rosemary Radford (1985b), 'Theology as Critique of and Emancipation from Sexism.' In *The Vocation of the Theologian*. (Ed) T.W. Jennings Jnr. Philadelphia: Fortress: 25-36.

Ruether, Rosemary Radford (1987), 'Ascetism and Feminism: Strange Bedmates?' In *Sex and God: Some Varieties of Religious Experience.* (Ed) Linda Hurcombe. London: Routledge: 229-48.

Ruether, Rosemary Radford (1988), *Women-Church: Theology and Practice of Feminist Liturgical Communities.* San Francisco: Harper.

Ruether, Rosemary Radford (1992 [1983]), *Sexism and God-Talk.* Second edition. London: SCM.

Ruether, Rosemary Radford (1997), Review of *Deadly Innocence: Feminism and the Mythology of Sin* by Angela West. In *Feminist Theology* 14 (Jan 1997): 126-8.

Ruether, Rosemary Radford (1998), *Women and Redemption: A Theological History.* London: SCM.

Ruether, Rosemary Radford and Eleanor M. McLaughlin, (eds) (1979), *Women of Spirit: Female Leadership in the Jewish and Christian Traditions.* New York: Simon.

Ruskin, John (1905 [1864]), *Sesame and Lilies.* London: George Allen.

Russell, Letty M. (1972), 'Human Liberation in a Feminine Perspective: a Working Paper for the New York Task Force on Women in Changing Institutions.' In *Study Encounter* World Council of Churches 81 (1972) SE/20.

Russell, Letty M. (1974), *Human Liberation in a Feminist Perspective: a Theology.* Philadelphia: Westminster.

Russell, Letty M. (ed) (1976), *The Liberating Word.* Philadelphia: Westminster.

Russell, Letty M. (1979), *The Future of Partnership.* Philadelphia: Westminster Press.

Russell, Letty M. (1982a), *Becoming Human.* Philadelphia: Westminster.

Russell, Letty M. (1982b), 'Feminist Critique: Opportunity for Co-operation'. In *Journal for the Study of the Old Testament* 22 (1982): 67-71.

Russell, Letty M. (ed) (1985), *Feminist Interpretation of the Bible.* Oxford: Blackwell.

Saiving, Valerie C. (1979), 'The Human Situation: a Feminine View'. In *Womanspirit Rising: a Feminist Reader in Religion.* (Eds) Carol P. Christ and Judith Plaskow. New York: Harper: 25-42.

Schreiner, Olive (1911), *Woman and Labour.* London: Fisher Unwin.

Scroggs, Robin (1972), 'Paul and the Eschatological Woman'. In *Journal of the American Academy of Religion* 40 3 (1972): 283-303.

Scroggs, Robin (1974), 'Paul and the Eschatological Woman Revisited'. *Journal of the American Academy of Religion* 42 3 (1974): 532-37.

Scroggs, Robin (1978), 'The Next Step: A Common Humanity'. In *Theology Today* 34 4 (1978): 395-401.

Segal, Lynne (1987), *Is the Future Female? Troubled Thoughts on Contemporary Feminism.* London: Virago.

Snitow, Ann, Christine Stansell and Sharon Thompson (eds) (1984), *Desire: The Politics of Sexuality.* London: Virago.

Soper, Kate (1983), 'New Introduction'. In *Enfranchisement of Women* Harriet Taylor Mill and *The Subjection of Women* John Stuart Mill. London: Virago: i-xiv.

Soskice, Janet Martin (ed) (1990), *After Eve: Women, Theology and the Christian Tradition.* Women in Religion Series. London: Marshall Pickering-Collins.

Spretnak, Charlene (ed) (1982), *The Politics of Women's Spirituality: Essays on the Rise of Spiritual Power Within the Feminist Movement.* New York: Anchor-Doubleday.

St Hilda Community (1991), *Women Included: A Book of Services and Prayers.* London: SPCK.

Stanton, Elizabeth Cady (1985), *The Women's Bible: The Original Feminist Attack on the Bible.* Reprint. Edinburgh: Polygon.

Stone, Merlin (1976), *The Paradise Papers: the Suppression of Women's Rites* London: Virago Quartet.

Storkey, Elaine (1985), *What's Right With Feminism?*. London: SPCK.

Storkey, Elaine (1988), 'Sex and Sexuality in the Church'. In *Mirror to the Church.* (Ed) Monica Furlong. London: SPCK: 47-61.

Sturrock, June (1995), *"Heaven and Home": Charlotte M. Yonge's Domestic Fiction and the Victorian Debate over Women*. English Literary Studies. Monograph 66. Victoria, Canada: University of Victoria.

Swidler, Leonard (1979), *Biblical Affirmations of Women*. Philadelphia: Westminster Press.

Swidler, Leonard and Arlene (eds) (1970), *Bishops and People.* Philadelphia: Westminster.

Swidler, Leonard and Arlene (1977), *Women Priests: A Catholic Commentary on the Vatican Declaration*. New York: Paulist.

Tamez, Elsa (ed) (1989), *Through Her Eyes: Women's Theology from Latin America.* Maryknoll: Orbis.

Tanner, Mary (1983), 'A Chance to Change'. In *MC* N.S. xxv 3 (1983): 22-9.

Tanner, Mary (1984), 'Called to Priesthood: Interpreting Women's Experience'. *Feminine in the Church.* (Ed) Monica Furlong. London: SPCK: 150-62.

Tavard, George H. (1975), 'Sexist Language in Theology?'. *Theological Studies* 36 4 (1975): 700-24.

Taylor, Barbara (1983), *Eve and the New Jerusalem: Socialism and Feminism in the Nineteenth Century*. London: Virago.

Thistlethwaite, Susan B. (1990), *Sex, Race and God.* London: Chapman.

Thomas, Ronwyn Goodsir (1992), 'Authority in the Church: Fraudulent Fabrication - Larceny from the Laity'. In *Feminist Theology* 1 (Sep 1992): 27-57.

Thompson, E.P. (1968 [1963]), *The Making of the English Working Class.* Second edition. Harmondsworth: Penguin.

Tilby, Angela (1998), 'Eve's Changing Status'. Review of Rosemary Radford Ruether *Women and Redemption: a Theological History.* SCM. In *Church Times* 30 October 1998: 16.

Tracy, David (1978), 'Christian Faith and Radical Equality'. In *Theology Today* 34 4 (1978): 370-7.

Trible, Phyllis (1973), 'Depatriarchalising in Biblical Interpretation'. In *Journal of the American Academy of Religion* 41 1 (1973): 30-48.

Trible, Phyllis (1979), 'Eve and Adam: Genesis 2-3 Reread'. In *Womanspirit Rising: a Feminist Reader in Religion.* (Eds) Carol P. Christ and Judith Plaskow. New York: Harper: 74-83.

Trible, Phyllis (1990), 'Feminist Hermeneutics and Biblical Studies'. In *Feminist Theology: a Reader*. (Ed) Ann Loades. London: SPCK: 23-9.

Vance, Carol (ed) (1992), *Pleasure and Danger: Exploring Female Sexuality.* London: Pandora. Harper Collins imprint.

Vicinus, Martha (1985), *Independent Women: Work and Community for Single Women, 1850-1920*. London: Virago.

Walkowitz Judith R (1983), 'Male Vice and Female Virtue: Feminism and the Politics of Prostitution in Nineteenth-Century Britain'. In *Desire: The Politics of Sexuality.* (Eds) Ann Snitow, Christine Stansell and Sharon Thompson. London: Virago.

Weaver, Mary Jo (1989), 'Who Is the Goddess and Where Does She Get Us?'. In *Journal of Feminist Studies in Religion* 5 1 (1989): 49-64.

Webb, Pauline (1979), *Where Are the Women? for the People in the Pew.* London: Epworth.

Webster, Margaret (1994), *A New Strength, A New Song: the Journey to Women's Priesthood*. London: Mowbray.
Weeks, Jeffrey (1981), *Sex, Politics and Society: the Regulation of Sexuality Since 1800*. Themes in British Social History series. (Ed) J. Stevenson. London: Longmans.
Welch, Sharon D. (1985), *Communities of Resistance and Solidarity: A Feminist Theology of Liberation*. Maryknoll: Orbis.
Welch, Sharon D. (1990), *A Feminist Ethic of Risk*. Minneapolis: Fortress.
West, Angela (1995), *Deadly Innocence: Feminism and the Mythology of Sin*. London: Mowbray.
Willis, Elaine (1987), 'Nothing is Sacred, All is Profane'. In *Sex and God: Some Varieties of Women's Religious Experience*. (Ed) Linda Hurcombe. London: Routledge:104-24.
Woodhead, Linda (1993), 'Post-Christian Spiritualities'. In *Religion* 23 (1993):167-81.
Woodhead, Linda (1997), 'Spiritualising the Sacred: a Critique of Feminist Theology'. In *Modern Theology* 13 2 (1997):191-212.
World Council of Churches (1975), *Sexism in the 1970s: Discrimination against Women*. A Report of a 1974 World Council of Churches Consultation, West Berlin. Geneva: WCC.
Young, Alison (1993), 'Body/Politics: our Bodies Triumphed'. In *Women's Studies: a Reader*. London: Harvester Wheatsheaf: 354-9.

# Bibliography (CWIRES)

*A Chance to Change* (1981), Study Guide. Sheffield: South Yorkshire Council of Churches.

Association for Inclusive Language (1987,1988b,1989) Newsletter and Bulletins. 1987/1988a/1989.

Association for Inclusive Language (1988a), *Women, Language and the Church.* 50 x A4 sheet pack of discussion materials. London: AIL.

'Bad Language in Church' (1983), In *ONE* 4 (1983).

Baker, John Austin (1981), *The Right Time.* Paper to first MOW Annual Conference. London: MOW.

Baptist Union of Great Britain and Ireland (1983), *"Free Indeed"?.* Discussion Material on the Role of Women and Men in the Church. London: Baptist Union of GB and Ireland.

Bishops' Conference of England and Wales Department for Christian Citizenship (1984), 'Women in Church and Society'. Agenda for an informal meeting. London: Unpublished.

Borrowdale, Ann (1988), 'The Church as an Equal Opportunites Employer'. In *Crucible* (Apr-Jun 1988): 62-9.

Braithwaite, Marjorie (1981), 'Some Points Drawn from Reports on Study of the Community of Women and Men in the Church'. London: Unpublished.

Bridge, Hugh (1977), *Feminist Theology and Women Priests.* Introduction and Annotated Bibliography. Dublin: SCM Publications.

Briggs, Sheila (1976), 'Feminist Critique of Natural Law'. In *For the Banished Children of Eve: an Introduction to Feminist Theology. Movement* Pamphlet 24. Bristol: SCM Publications: 2-5.

British Council of Churches (1984), The Community of Women and Men in the Church. Report of BCC Working Group, 1982-1984, to BCC 20th Assembly. London: Unpublished.

Campbell, Helen (1981), 'Are Women Human?'. Sermon for International Women's Day. Banbury: North Oxfordshire Unitarians.

Campbell, Liz (1984), 'Women's Spirituality'. In Lighten Our Darkness. Radio 4 Programme (7 Jan 1984). Reprint in 'Christian Believing 2'. In *ONE* 3 (1984).

Catholic Women's Network (1984b), Called to Full Humanity: Women's Responsibilities as Members of the Church Today. Conference publicity and booking form. London: Unpublished.

Catholic Women's Network (1987), Position Paper Discussion paper. London: Unpublished.

Champion, Freda and Una Kroll (eds) (1978), 'Churchwomanship in a Man's World'. Supplement. *Christian Action Journal* (Spring 1978).

Christian Parity Group (1979), 'A Celebration of Life and Ministry'. Liturgy. London: CPG.

Church of Scotland General Assembly (1980), 'The Role of Men and Women in Church and Society'. Deliverance of the General Assembly of the Church of Scotland on the Report of the Committee on the Role of Men and Women in Church and Society, incorporating the text of the report. Edinburgh: Pr. Blackwood.

Coghill, Mary and Sheila Redmond (1984), Review of *A Map of the New Country* by Sara Maitland (1983), and *Walking on the Water* (eds) Jo Garcia and Sara Maitland (1983). In *Feminist Library Newsletter* (Mar/Apr 1984): 6-8.

Collins, Diana (1978), 'The Rehabilitation of Eve'. In 'Churchwomanship in a Man's World'. Supplement. *Christian Action Journal* (Spring 1978): 4-5.

Community of Women and Men in the Church (1977), Report of Meeting. Ammerdown: Unpublished.

Community of Women and Men in the Church (1978), *Study on the Community of Women and Men in the Church*. Geneva: WCC.

*Community of Women and Men in the Church News* (1980), Geneva: WCC CWMC.

Community of Women and Men in the Church (1981), British Preparatory Meeting Participants List. Sheffield: Unpublished.

Condren, Mary (1972), 'The Celibacy Syndrome'. In *Theology and Sexual Politics*. London: SCM Publications: 20-3.

Condren, Mary (1976a), 'For the Banished Children of Eve'. In *For the Banished Children of Eve: an Introduction to Feminist Theology. Movement* Pamphlet 24. Bristol: SCM Publications: 21-23.

Condren, Mary (ed) (1976b), *For the Banished Children of Eve: an Introduction to Feminist Theology. Movement* Pamphlet 24. Bristol: SCM Publications.

Condren, Mary (1978a), 'Churchwomanship in a Man's World'. Editorial article. 'Churchwomanship in a Man's World'. Supplement. *Christian Action Journal* (Spring 1978): 1+.

Condren, Mary (1978b), Introduction. *Why Men Priests?: Effects of Male Domination in the Church. Movement* Pamphlet 34. Bristol: SCM Publications: 2-3.

Condren, Mary (ed) (1978c), *Why Men Priests? Effects of Male Domination in the Church. Movement* Pamphlet 34. Bristol: SCM Publications.

Court, Gillian (1979), 'Women and Ordination'. London: Unpublished.

Craighead, Meinrad (N.d.), 'Immanent Mother'. Typescript. Unpublished.

Davis, Rex (N.d.), *The Virgin Mary: a Model for Priesthood? An Anglican Catholic View on the Ordination of Women to the Priesthood*. London: MOW.

Duncan, Jen (1982a), 'New, Brave and Colourful: the Peace Camps at Greenham Common and Molesworth'. In *COSPEC Stories*. Birmingham: SCM: 16-17.

Duncan, Jen (1982b), 'New Ways of Working Together'. In *COSPEC Stories*. Birmingham: SCM: 7+.

Duncker, Patricia (1984), 'John Milton's Reading of Genesis'. Paper to Oxford Women's Theology Seminar. Oxford: Unpublished.

Ecumenical Forum of European Christian Women (N.d.), Publicity Brochure. Geneva: EFECW.

Ecumenical Forum of European Christian Women's Organisations and the Women's Inter-Church Council (1987), Memorandum. Plan for a Conference. London: Unpublished.

Edwards, David (N.d.), *Are Women Priests Right?* London: MOW.

Fageol, Suzanne (1989), 'The St Hilda Community'. In *ONE* 3 (1989/1990).

Fedouloff, Kathleen (ed) (1988), *The Wisdom of Christian Feminism: Papers on Wisdom and Human Sexuality*. London: Fedouloff.

Fedouloff, Kathleen (ed) (1989), *The Wisdom of Christian Feminism: Papers on Violence and Peace and Women We Learn From*. London: Fedouloff.

Feminist Theology Project (N.d.), *Our Stories: Feminist Theology Project 1980-1982*. Coventry: FTP.

Flessati, Valerie and Clare Prangley (1987), 'Women's Perspective on War and Peace'. Typescript of chapter in *Peace Together: a Vision of Christian Pacifism*. (Ed) Clive Barrett. London: Clarke.

Flessati, Valerie and Clare Prangley (1988), 'Wisdom as Wholeness'. In *The Wisdom of Christian Feminism: Papers on Wisdom and Human Sexuality*. London: Fedouloff: 5-10.

Frost, Penny (1980), 'Women and Men in the Church'. Paper to the Church of England Board of Education. London: Unpublished.

The Grail (1985), The Feminine in Ourselves and Society. Conference Flyer. Pinner: Unpublished.

Greenham Peace Vigil (1985, 1986, 1987, 1988, 1989), Newsletter. Seven issues. Summer 1985-Epiphany 1989.

Hampson, Daphne M. (1978), 'The Theological Case for the Ordination of Women'. A letter distributed by AGOW to members of the November 1978 General Synod. St Andrews: Unpublished.

Hampson, Daphne M. (1984), 'Women, Religion and Social Change'. In *MC* N.S. xxvi 4 (1984): 19-22.

Hampson, Daphne M. (1985), 'The Challenge of Feminism to Christianity'. In *Theology* 88 725 (1985): 341-50.

Hampson, Daphne M. (1986a), 'Women, Ordination and the Christian Church'. In *Speaking of Faith: Cross-cultural Perspectives on Women, Religion and Social Change*. (Eds) Diana Eck and Devaki Jain. London: Women's Press: 129-38.

Hampson, Daphne M. (1986b), 'Reinhold Niebuhr on Sin: a Critique'. In *Reinhold Niebuhr and the Jesus of Our Time*. (Ed) Richard Harries. London: Mowbray: 46-60.

Hampson, Daphne M. (1989), 'The Theological Implications of a Feminist Ethic'. In *MC* N.S. xxxi, 1 (1989): 36-9.

Hampson, Daphne M. and Rosemary Radford Ruether (1987), *Is There a Place for Feminists in a Christian Church?* Oxford: New Blackfriars.

Harvey, Susan Ashbrook (1981), 'Eve and Mary: Images of Women'. Paper to 1981 Modern Churchman's Union Conference. Birmingham: Unpublished.

Hebblethwaite, Margaret (1983), 'The Motherhood of God'. In *The Tablet* (26 Nov 1983): 1149-50.

Hebblethwaite, Margaret (1984a), 'Giving Birth'. In *The Way* (Jan 1984): 17-24.

Hoad, Ann (1983), Women's Training for Ordination Project. Statement of aims, guidelines and process of proposed women's ordination training. London: Unpublished.

Holdsworth, Philip and Alexina Murphy (N.d.), *Hoping for Women Priests: letters from two Roman Catholics*. London: MOW.

Jenner, Judith (1978a), 'An Introduction to Feminist Theology'. In 'Sisters to Susannah'. Special issue. *ARM Reporter* 11 (Summer 1978): 8.

Jenner, Judith (1978b), 'Women Challenge the Church'. In 'Sisters to Susannah'. Special Issue. *ARM Reporter* 11 (Summer 1978): 6.

Jenner, Judith (1979), 'Liberation Theology: a Feminist Perspective'. In 'ONE Information'. In *ONE* (Aut 1979): 3-4.

Jenner, Judith (1980a), 'Male-Female Issues'. In *Community* 26 (1980): 19.

Jenner, Judith (1981), 'One Woman's Conflict'. In *COSPEC Stories*. Birmingham: SCM Publications: 3-4.

King, Ursula (1981a), 'Mysticism and Feminism: why look at women mystics?'. In *Teresa de Jesus and Her World*. Papers of a conference in commemoration of Teresa of Avila. (Ed) Margaret A. Rees. Leeds: Trinity and All Saints College: 7-17.

King, Ursula (1981b), 'Towards an Integral Spirituality: Sexual Differences and the Christian Doctrine of Man'. In *Vidyajyoti: Journal of Theological Reflection*, (Sep 1981): 358-71.

King, Ursula (1982), 'Current Perspectives in the Study of Women and Religion'. *Women Speaking*, (Oct-Dec 1982): 4-9.

King, Ursula (1989), 'Woman and Spirit'. In *Everywoman* (Mar 1989): 17-18.

Kroll, Una (1976), 'God According to a Woman'. In *For the Banished Children of Eve: an Introduction to Feminist Theology. Movement* Pamphlet 24. Bristol: SCM Publications: 19-20.

Kroll, Una (1984), 'Veils, Mantles and Girdles'. WIT Inaugural Address. London: WIT.

Laity Commission (1982), *Why Can't a Woman be More Like a Man?* London: Catholic Information Services.

Long, Pauline [Asphodel ] (1981), 'Woman Magic'. In *Spare Rib* 110 (Sep 1981): 50-3.

Maitland, Sara (1984), 'The Radical Rosary'. Paper to Oxford Women's Theology Seminar. Oxford: Unpublished.

Maizel, Judith (1980), Open Letter concerning Revision of Methodist/URC Hymnbook. Birmingham: Unpublished.

Marsh, Trish (1979), C.W.I.R.S. Christian Women's Information and Resource Service (incorporating the Ecumenical Feminist Trust). Publicity Leaflet. London: unlisted.

Marsh, Trish and Caroline Smith (eds) (1981), *Women and the Christian Future: Issues in Christian Feminism*. Second Women's Study Pack. Second edition. Birmingham: SCM Publications (Women's Project).

McEwan, Dorothea (1989), 'Attitudes to and of Violence within Society from a Christian Perspective'. *In The Wisdom of Christian Feminism: Papers on Violence and Peace and Women We Learn From*. (Ed) Kathleen Fedouloff. London: Fedouloff: 5-10.

Mertes, Kate (1982), 'On Being Children of God'. Paper given at St Albert the Great Parish, Edinburgh and Scottish Justice and Peace Commission. Unpublished.

Mertes, Kate (1984a), 'The Mask of Eve'. Oxford: Unpublished paper.

Mertes, Kate (1984b), 'Women and Salvation'. Paper given at Oscott Theological College. Oxford: Unpublished.

Mertes, Kate (1984c), 'Tensions between Theologians and the Women's Movement'. Paper to St James Piccadilly. Oxford: Unpublished.

Mertes, Kate (1984d), 'Ecumenism and Christian Feminism'. Paper to Westminster Cathedral Conference Centre. Women's Voices in Christian Thought Series. Oxford: Unpublished.

Mertes, Kate (1986), 'Women and Canon Law'. Oxford: Unpublished.

Morley, Janet (1978), 'Women's Oppression'. In 'Sisters to Susannah'. Special issue. *ARM Reporter* 11 (Summer 1978): 2.

Morley, Janet (1980), 'A Christian Feminist Group'. In 'ONE Stories'. In *ONE* 4 (1980): 2.

Morley, Janet (1982), 'Sermon Preached at Women's Mass, Blackfriars'. Sermon for Women's Mass. Oxford. Published in *Walking on the Water*. (Eds) Jo Garcia and Sara Maitland. London: Virago: 20-8.

Morley, Janet (1983a), 'The Church and the Women's Movement – a Basis for Dialogue'. Paper to ecumenical audience of theological students. Oxford: Unpublished.

Morley, Janet (1984b), 'There are Going to be Some Red Faces when our Lord Returns – or Bad Language in Church: the response'. In *ONE* 1 (1984).

Morley, Janet (1985a), Open letter re the BCC Working Group CWMC. London: BCC study mailing.

Morley, Janet (1985b), 'Leadership Models of a No-longer Patriarchal Church, and What Do These Imply for Patterns of Training?'. Paper to Cuddesdon consultation, Now We Are Ten. Unpublished.

Morley, Janet and Hannah Ward (eds) (1986), *Celebrating Women*. London: WIT and MOW.

Morris, Joan (1976), 'The Lady Was a Bishop'. In *For the Banished Children of Eve: an Introduction to Feminist Theology. Movement* Pamphlet 24. Bristol: SCM Publications: 9-11.

Morris, Joan (1980), 'A Return to the Older Tradition of Women in the Church'. Text of 1980 Siena Lecture. London: Unpublished.

Movement for the Ordination of Women (1981a), Festival of Women. Event Flyer. London: Unpublished.

Movement for the Ordination of Women (1982), Festival of Women. Programme and covering letter. London: Unpublished.

Movement for the Ordination of Women (1983a), Honouring Julian. Event flyer. London: Unpublished.

Movement for the Ordination of Women (1983b), Honouring Julian. Report on Celebration. London: Unpublished.

Movement for the Ordination of Women (1984b), 'A Wilderness Liturgy'. London: Unpublished.

Nash, Daphne, A. Birchall, J. Garcia, J. Shay and A. West (1978), 'On Breaking the Rules – a Feminist Reply to J.M. Cameron'. In *New Blackfriars* (Dec 1978): 555-64.

Nielson, Martha Lynne, (1972), 'Eve Got the First Bite!'. In *Theology and Sexual Politics*. London: SCM Publications: 23.

Norris, Richard (1981), *The Ordination of Women and the "Maleness" of Christ*. MOW Occasional Paper 2. London, Oxford: MOW.

Oxford Christian Women's Group(s) (1981a), Network Addresses. Information sheet. Oxford: Unpublished.

Oxford Christian Women's Group(s) (c1981b), 'Mass Service'. Liturgy. Oxford: Unpublished.

Oxford Christian Women's Group(s) (1981c), 'Women's Mass'. Liturgy. Oxford: Unpublished.

Oxford Christian Women's Group(s) (1981d), 'Third Women's Mass'. Liturgy. Oxford: Unpublished.

Oxford Christian Women's Group(s) (c1982e), 'The Women's Mass'. A5 description sheet. Oxford: Unpublished.

Oxford Christian Women's Group(s) c1982d, 'Women's Agape Celebration'. Liturgy. Oxford: Unpublished.

Oxford Women's Theology Group (1980a), 'Women and Justice'. Leaflet submitted to the NPC. Oxford: Unpublished.

Oxford Women's Theology Group (1980b), 'Women's Mission'. Response to 'The Easter People' re the NPC report, 'Justice, Peace and Race'. Oxford: Unpublished.

Oxford Women's Theology Seminar (1983), Artful Theology: a feminist re-creation of Christian tradition. Conference flyer. Oxford: Unpublished.

Parnell, Nancy Stewart (N.d.), *A Venture in Faith*. London: St Joan's Alliance.

Pepper, Mary and Margaret Hebblethwaite (1984), 'Finding God in Motherhood: Release or Trap?'. In *New Blackfriars* (Sep 1984): 372-84.

Pickard, Jan and Ruth Windle (eds) (1978), 'Sisters to Susannah'. Special Issue. *ARM Reporter* 11 (Summer).

Prangley, Clare (1985), *Women Development and Peace: two short talks*. London: Pax Christi.

Pratt, Ianthe (1980), 'Celebration of the Liberation of Men and Women'. Liturgy. London: Unpublished.

Pratt, Ianthe (1987a), 'Liturgies Available from the Christian Women's Resource Centre, CWRC'. In 'One Worship'. In *ONE* 2 (1987): 2.

Pratt, Ianthe (ed) (1987b), *Woman-Created Liturgies*. 26xA4 sheets available from CWRC. London: Unpublished.

Pratt, Ianthe and Oliver Pratt (1978), 'Mass in Thanksgiving of Twenty Years of Marriage'. Liturgy. London: Unpublished.

Quaker Women's Group (1980), Advice and Query: from Quaker Women's Group. A6 leaflet to Yearly Meeting. Unpublished.

Redding, Maggie (1983), 'Catholic and Lesbian'. In the *Tablet* 15 (Jan 1983): 30-1.

Redmond, Sheila and Mary Coghill (1983), 'Feminism and Spirituality'. Paper and contact list. London: Unpublished.

Rees, Bridget (1983), 'Wilderness Liturgy'. Sermon. London: Unpublished.

Rees, Elizabeth (1984), Christian Morals, Feminist Perspectives and the Situation of the Gay Person Today. Flyer for Conference on Ethics. Bristol: Unpublished.

Religion and Society History Workshop (1983a), Conference Programme. London: Unpublished.

Religion and Society History Workshop (1983b), Poster. London: Unpublished.

Robson, Jill (1981), 'God's Women'. Papers re a four-session group exploration. Derby: Unpublished.

Robson, Jill (1982a), 'Reflecting on Pregnant Images'. Paper to 1st Hartlebury weekend. Derby: Unpublished.

Robson, Jill (1982b), 'Labouring in Hope'. Typescript of article submitted to MOW NL. Derby: Unpublished. Published in MOW NL 8 (Feb/Mar 1982): 6-10.

Robson, Jill (1982c), 'Myself as Daughter and Mother'. Reflections on Hartlebury weekend Ourselves as Daughters and Mothers. Derby: Unpublished.

Robson, Jill (1982d), 'Pregnancy & Childbirth as an Image of the Spiritual Life'. Transcript of unpublished paper by unknown author. Derby: Unpublished.

Robson, Jill (1982e), Preparatory reading for Hartlebury weekend on Spirituality and Sexuality. Derby: Unpublished.

Robson, Jill (1982f), 'The Assumption of Mary'. Typescript of article submitted to *Christian Feminist Newsletter*. Derby: Unpublished. Published in *CF NL* 19 (Aut 1982): 5-6.

Roman Catholic Feminists (1980), 'National Pastoral Congress: Resolutions'. London: Unpublished paper.

Ruether, Rosemary R. (1972a), 'Mother Earth and the Megamachine'. In *Theology and Sexual Politics*. London: SCM publications: 6-11+.

SCM Women's Project (1977), Nun, Witch or Playmate: Women and the Christian Future. Conference Flyer. Bristol: Unpublished.

Slee, Nicola (1983), 'The Gospel Parables and Women's Experience: "She who has ears to hear, let her hear!"'. Paper to Oxford Women's Theology Seminar. Oxford: Unpublished. Published as 'Parables and Women's Experience'. In *MC* N.S. xxvi 2 (1984): 20-31. Reprint of extract in *Feminist Theology: a Reader*. (Ed) Ann Loades. London: SPCK, 1990: 41-47.

Smith, Carol (1985), 'On Eve'. Paper to Oxford Women's Theology Seminar. Oxford: Unpublished.

Speller, Lydia (1980), *Theological Objections?* MOW Occasional Paper 1. London: MOW.

Summer, Naomi (1989), 'Womanspirit in the 1980s: Origins, Beliefs and Practices'. Unpublished dissertation.

Swidler, Arlene (1967), 'An Ecumenical Question: the Status of Women'. In *Journal of Ecumenical Studies* 4 1 (1967): 113-15.

Swidler, Arlene (1976), 'Catholics and the E.R.A'. In *Commonweal* CIII 19 (1976): 585-9.

Swidler, Arlene (1978), 'Women in Ministry: Some Ecumenical Lessons'. In *Spirituality Today* 30 1 (1978): 4-14.
Swidler, Leonard (1971), 'Jesus Was a Feminist'. In *Catholic World* (Jan 1971): 177-83.
*Theology and Sexual Politics* (1972), London: SCM Publications.
Unitarian Working Party on Feminist Theology (1985), *Growing Together: the Report of the Unitarian Working Party on Feminist Theology*. To the Unitarian General Assembly. Unitarian General Assembly.
Wakelin, Rosemary (N.d.), *Call Accepted: Reflections on Women's Ordination in the Free Churches*. London: MOW.
Walsh, Kathleen, Dorothea McEwan and Diane M. Brewster (1987), *Celibacy in Control: Three Papers on Sexuality and Power in the Roman Catholic Church*. London: Fedouloff.
Webb, Pauline (N.d.), Interview. 'The Place of Women'. In *Methodist Recorder*.
Webb, Pauline (N.d.), Research on number of women on WCC committees and associated bodies. Geneva: Unpublished.
Webb, Pauline (1968), Untitled draft article for submission to the *Methodist Recorder*. Unpublished.
Webb, Pauline (1974), 'Personal Reflections on the Sexism Consultation'. Geneva: Unpublished.
Webb, Pauline (1977), Women and Theology. Proposal for Urban Theology Unit study week. Sheffield: Unpublished.
West, Angela (1980a), 'A Feminist Slant on Sin, Evil and Hell-Fire'. Oxford: Unpublished.
West, Angela (1980b), 'The Bishops and the Bourgeois Revolution: a Contribution from the Oxford Christian Feminists'. Oxford: Unpublished.
West, Angela (1981a), 'Genesis and Patriarchy, Part I: What has feminist discourse got in common with the language of biblical theology?'. In *New Blackfriars*, (Jan 1981): 17-32.
West, Angela (1981b), 'Discerning the Body'. Sermon for Women's Mass. Oxford: Unpublished.
West, Angela (1981c), 'Genesis and Patriarchy, Part II: Women and the End of Time'. In *New Blackfriars* (Oct 1981): 420-32.
West, Angela (c1981d), 'Mass and Mission and the Ministry of the Baptised: Commentary on the Easter People Sections 59-69 and Congress Report Sectors A, B and D'.Oxford: Unpublished.
West, Angela (1982a), 'A Faith For Feminists?'. Oxford: Unpublished. Also in *Walking on the Water: Women Talk About Spirituality*. (Eds) Jo Garcia and Sara Maitland (1983). London: Virago: 66-91.
West, Angela (1982b), 'Bodiliness and the Good News: the Story of the Holy Spirit and the Oxford Catholic Women's Group'. Oxford: Unpublished.
West, Angela (1983a), 'The Loaf of Fellowship in I Corinthians'. Oxford: Unpublished.
West, Angela (1983b), 'The Politics of Sex and Food in I Corinthians'. Oxford: Unpublished.
West, Angela (1984a), 'Sex and Salvation: a Christian Feminist Bible Study on I Corinthians 6:12-7:39'. Oxford: Unpublished. In *MC* 29 3 (1987): 17-24. Reprinted in *Feminist Theology: a Reader*. (Ed) Ann Loades. London: SPCK, 1990: 72-80.
West, Angela (1986), *The Widow's Mite – Good News for Women?: A Bible study/ reflection on Mark 12:38-44*. London: CWN and Pax Christi.
West, Angela (1988), 'Wisdom in the Faith of our First Century Sisters'. In *The Wisdom of Christian Feminism: Papers on Wisdom and Human Sexuality*. London: Fedouloff.

West, Angela (N.d.), 'The Relevance of Feminist Theology for Feminist Theory'. Oxford: Unpublished.

West, Angela and Roger Ruston (1981), 'A Theology For Britain in the '80s?'. In *New Blackfriars* (Nov 1981): 455-64.

Wilks, Eileen (ed) (1973), The Place of Women in the Church. Oxford Conference Papers. Oxford: Unpublished.

Willis, Elaine (1982a), 'Breaking the Silence – Visibly'. Typescript of article submitted to *Gay Christian Movement NL*. Unpublished.

Wilson, Kenneth (1977), 'The Community of Women and Men in the Church'. Ammerdown: Unpublished.

Windle, Ruth (1978), 'The Feminine in the Pattern of Redemption'. 'Sisters to Susannah'. Special edition. *ARM Reporter* 11 (Summer): 9.

Women in Theology (N.d.), Liturgy Framework. Extract from mailing. London: WIT.

Women in Theology (1988), *Who Are You Looking For? Easter Liturgies to Launch the WCC Ecumenical Decade.* Churches in Solidarity with Women 1988-1998. York: Ecumenical Forum of European Christian Women, and Women's Inter-Church Consultative Committee.

Women, Men and Power (1983), Programme/Flyer for a day conference at Kings College. London: Unpublished.

Woollcombe, K.J. and J.V. Taylor (1975), *No Fundamental Objections to the Ordination of Women to the Priesthood*. Durham: AGOW.

World Student Christian Federation (Europe) (1978), Women's Project *Newsletter* 2.

WSCF (Europe) (1984), *Women and Peace.* Conference papers of Corrymeela conference Sep 1984. (Ed) Carola Towle. Uppsala: WSCF Europe Region Women's Working Group.

# Index